AMONG THE
BEARS

A JOHN MACRAE BOOK

Henry Holt and Company   New York

AMONG THE
BEARS

Raising Orphan Cubs in the Wild

Benjamin Kilham and Ed Gray

Henry Holt and Company, LLC
Publishers since 1866
115 West 18th Street
New York, New York 10011

Henry Holt® is a registered trademark of
Henry Holt and Company, LLC.

Library of Congress Cataloging-in-Publication Data
Kilham, Benjamin.
 Among the bears : raising orphan cubs in the wild /
Benjamin Kilham and Ed Gray—1st ed.
  p. cm.
 ISBN 0-8050-6919-4 (hb)
  1. Black bear—Behavior—Anecdotes.
  2. Kilham, Benjamin. I. Gray, Ed, date. II. Title.

QL 737.C27 K56 2002
599.78'515—dc21   2001051556

Henry Holt books are available for special
promotions and premiums.
For details contact:
Director, Special Markets.

First Edition 2002

Designed by Paula Russell Szafranski

Printed in the United States of America

1 3 5 7 9 10 8 6 4 2

To my wife, Debra, for her love and support
and in memory of my parents,
Lawrence and Jane Kaufholz Kilham,
for my early introduction to the natural world

Contents

Preface

WHEN I WAS in high school—a very difficult time for me—I wrote a story into which I placed what I thought was a vivid depiction of the way a crocodile resembled a floating log. My teacher, thinking I had lifted the description out of a book, suggested that I compose something about which I had personal knowledge. Little did she know that I was writing from experience: a Nile crocodile, brought back with us after my father's sabbatical year in Uganda when I was two, had for a time lived in the downstairs shower of our house. It could have been worse, I suppose; in my story I hadn't mentioned the half-grown leopard that had the run of our house in Entebbe.

From my earliest memories, our household has always included a cast of orphaned and injured wild animals and birds. My father, Lawrence Kilham, was a medical doctor and research virologist with a deep-seated fascination of the natural world, which he shared for fifty years with my mother, Jane Kaufholz Kilham, also a physician. The way most families talked about sports, we talked about nature. We still do. For though both my parents have passed on, that part of their legacy has, if anything, grown stronger. In the house I now share with my wife, Debbie, my sister, Phoebe, and—when they're still little—an irregular parade of orphaned black bear cubs, nature is an unavoidable and continuing topic of conversation.

Until I set out to write this book, however, that's primarily what it was: conversation. I'm dyslexic. Though I've worked hard all my life to adjust, hard enough to have earned a bachelor's degree in wildlife biology from the University of New Hampshire, the defining event in my educational odyssey was more likely in 1957 when I flunked out of kindergarten. Reading words in sequence will always be an obstacle for me.

I have overcome my reading disability by learning to scan, searching for key words. When I find something important, I often have to read it over several times to understand it completely. To remember it, I have to attach it to something I have already stored in my memory. Because this is so difficult, I don't try to remember anything I can look up at a later date. In spite of these self-taught tricks, I still completely fall apart trying to remember stray knowledge. I got through college by reading course material once, the night before the exam with the television on; otherwise I could read for only fifteen minutes before I fell asleep. I managed to get through because I had already acquired a good deal of knowledge about wildlife. My grades for my liberal arts courses were dangerously low.

Over the years I have developed a number of techniques that allow me to remember essential information and to think clearly as well. Being interested in a subject is the first requirement. The second is to be systematic. I like figuring out systems, especially how things work. Any information that sticks to one of my systems sticks like glue. Third and last is simplicity. I am constantly reducing things to their simplest forms, trying to make them easier to remember and easier to think about.

That's the approach I took as I set out to convert my extensive journals into this book, but I also knew that with my dyslexia I'd need help keeping it linear. Fortunately I live across the street from Ed Gray, a friend for more than twelve years, an accomplished editor and outdoorsman, and someone who has not only walked with me and my bears here in the woods around Lyme but who has been listening to my stories about them from the beginning. Ed did a good job of keeping the book structured as I wrote it, and the happy result is what you now hold in your hands. This is my story, the way I've lived it with my bear cubs, and what I've learned from them as their lives unfolded. It's a story that's far from over.

So come on along—let's start following bear tracks.

AMONG THE
BEARS

CHAPTER 1

The First Cubs

SPRINGTIME IN NEW HAMPSHIRE begins in February, with the lengthening days that deliver the first thaws. The bright sun and deep blue skies give way to star-filled nights, when subzero temperatures remind us we're still in winter's grip. These are the wake-up calls that prod my wife, Debbie, and me to get ready for the maple-sugaring season in Lyme, the small town on the Connecticut River where we live. It's a glorious time to be outside after a long cold winter, though the work seems unending: digging out the snowshoes; repairing sap lines, which stay on the trees year round unless they've been downed by fallen limbs and trees or chewed by fox, coyote, bobcat, and squirrel; and finally tapping the trees themselves. All of this before the elusive first sap run.

Until 1993, the year the bears came to stay with us, life in the Kilham household had taken on a comfortable rhythm during the early spring. From that first promising sap run, usually early in March, to the last one at the beginning of April, my time was always split between our sugaring operation and my mainstay of gunmaking, an exhausting work schedule entirely dependent on the sap runs. On a typical morning at our house on the village green back then, I would see Debbie off to her office job at seven and within the hour be out the door myself. The mud and snow would crunch beneath my feet in our driveway as I walked by the empty raven cage on the way to my shop.

The ten-foot-high cage—one side of which covered the south side of my shop and the other attached to the house—had only recently gone empty, a quiet testament to the aging of my father that I tried not to think about. The cage had once been a vibrant and life-restoring place, holding a number of recuperating ravens and crows as my father patiently observed their behavior while we nursed them back to health. But now he was in his late eighties, and though his mind was still sharp and would stay that way for several more years, the frailties of his advancing age had finally come between him and the handling of his beloved birds. A way of life for our family now seemed to have passed, and there was little I could do about it. The cage, I thought, was likely to stay empty for some time to come.

Meanwhile, I had work to do, and lots of it. At the door of the shop, I'd grab the lock in my hands to warm it a bit before dialing the numbers of the combination. The door would then open and close behind me with a loud, extended creak. (Old friends and even new customers still tell me I should fix the door. It's not much of an advertisement for your mechanical skills, they say, usually with a smile but not always. I don't mind. I learned a long time ago to live with the friendly jibes and open criticism of people who don't understand my methods. So I don't bother to explain that I leave the door that way on purpose; the loud creaking serves me well by announcing anyone entering the shop, even when I'm operating high-speed machine tools. That's another thing I learned a long time ago, even before I learned I had dyslexia: to accept a good solution when it presents itself, even if others would never have done things that way and still can't see that it is a solution.)

As always, a blast of warm air would hit my face with the smells of a gun shop—a mixture of machine oil, solvents, and cutting oil which permeates the room. Then, as now, the shop was cluttered with too many tools, too many guns, and too many papers. As I walked past my desk and the oak-and-glass counter, I reached out to poke on the radio to a country western station; I like to listen to songs with lyrics I can understand. Passing the bluing tanks (which I use to put the black finish on guns), my old 1940s Cincinnati horizontal milling machine, my new heat-treating furnace, the Buffalo drill press, and finally the most important machine in the shop—the Bridgeport vertical milling machine—I would reach my bench. Behind the bench is a large South Bend lathe, surface grinder, welder, and assorted polishers and sanders. Along with the machine tools, on a given day I might work with a multitude of hand tools, including micrometers, calipers, screwdrivers, punches, chisels, rasps, and files.

I have been in the gunsmithing business for twenty-four years. Most of the time, I'm juggling five or six projects at once. Short-term projects, such as adjusting trigger pulls, I can complete in one sitting; longer projects, such as building a custom rifle, require a lot of planning and a variety of skills. I don't think I would have found this career without the understanding and encouragement of my high school principal, who gave me the chance to pursue it when barely anyone had even heard of dyslexia, let alone knew how to handle someone afflicted with it. Today, even with so many programs and required funding for special education, it's hard to imagine a high school principal encouraging one of his or her students to pursue gunmaking as an independent study project—even when it is exactly the right thing to do.

During sugaring season, I'd generally work in the shop until noon, when the sun was high enough to make the maple sap run; then I'd drive the five miles out to our sugar house. Our eighty-acre, 1,200-tap sugar bush is situated on a series of wooded ledges with plastic-tube sap lines that flow into a central holding tank. The holding tank is partway up the hill behind the sugar house; when the tank is full, we run the sap into another tank by the sugar house and then directly into the evaporator.

As I approached the sugar bush on a day in early April 1993—the day before my life changed forever—the sun was bright and the water glistened off the mud on the town road, a good sign that the sap would be running already. In New Hampshire during this time of year, you can count on both frost heaves and mud, and the driveway leading to our sugar house was muddy that day. But I knew where the soft spots were, and I drove up to the sugar house without getting my old pickup stuck or unnecessarily adding to already-deep ruts in the path. I could hear the sap splashing against the side of the holding tank as I got out of my truck. The day looked promising.

After transferring the sap into the tank by the sugar house and filling the five-by-fifteen-foot evaporator with wood, I lit the fire. The evaporator's firebox can handle firewood four feet long; it provides enough energy to remove 250 gallons of water an hour, which produces five gallons of pure maple syrup. The heat built up, and soon steam billowed out of the cupola and from both ends of the building. There was so much sap that I ended up boiling it through the night and into the next morning. I got home just in time to hear my telephone ringing. It was Forrest Hammond, calling from neighboring Vermont.

"Ben," he said. "Would you consider raising a couple of orphaned bear cubs?"

"Frosty" Hammond was the Vermont Fish and Wildlife biologist in charge of the ongoing Stratton Mountain Bear Project. Of course I'd heard of it. And the question itself hadn't come completely out of the blue; I was a licensed wildlife rehabilitator with both state and federal permits, and there aren't that many of us around. I even had some experience with a bear; a yearling, which was thought to have been struck by a car that past December, was then in one of our rehab cages. Because the little bear seemed to have lost her coordination, Debbie and I had named her Wobbly Bear. Like all the other creatures we had helped, Wobbly Bear was a rehab project; our hope was to get her on her feet and back in the woods as quickly as we could, even though her neurological condition might make that impossible. But cubs? Even with my limited knowledge of bears, I knew this much: cubs were a long-term project.

Frosty explained his problem: In seven years, forty-nine wild black bears had been closely studied, primarily by being monitored with telemetry, a process by which bears are fitted with special collars that transmit radio signals on individual frequencies so the bears can be tracked separately. In a normal year, Frosty continued, sows with cubs can usually have their collars changed without disrupting the family, but 1992 had not been a normal year. The beechnut crop failed in the fall, and six of the seven sows in the study had no cubs. The seventh sow, the mother of twins, was underweight and abandoned her cubs after having her malfunctioning collar changed. Frosty monitored her activities over the next five days with telemetry until he was sure she had taken another den and would not return. Concerned about the cubs' health after at least two days alone in the den, he asked Alcott Smith, a local veterinarian, to help him remove the cubs from the den. Then he called me.

Although I had the required state and federal permits, Frosty would still have to handle the red tape. The permit to raise black bear cubs could only be given at the discretion of the executive director of the New Hampshire Fish and Game Department, Donald Normandeau. Since the cubs came from Vermont, Frosty would have to obtain permission from the commissioner of Fish and Wildlife in Vermont as well. Both departments were aware that I had Wobbly Bear in my care at the time, so Frosty thought he could go through channels and obtain permission rather quickly. The cubs, he said, could be ready for me by April 13; if I decided to take them, that would give me just a few days to make preparations.

My feelings about taking the cubs were, to say the least, mixed. On the one hand, I knew that in many cases black bear cub rehabilitation has been unsuccessful, usually because the cubs become too habituated to people to be returned to the wild. Two years down the road, Debbie and I could end up with a couple of unreleasable bears for which we'd have to find a "home." But there wouldn't be any homes. Not for meat-eating animals that weigh hundreds of pounds, with appetite and strength to match.

On the other hand, I already had my own unconventional theory on how the cubs could be raised successfully. Instead of keeping them in a cage, my idea was to walk with and handle them without restraint, and to do so in an unfenced, big-woods setting. But for this scheme to work, I would have to establish a relationship with the cubs, to become one with them. At the same time, I would have to turn a deaf ear to the "known fact" that tame cubs would become troublesome bears. While this might be true with pen-raised bears, I guessed that the exposure of the cubs to their natural habitat and to the wild bears living there would override their dependence on me. After all, if cubs naturally leave their mothers at eighteen months, surely they should be able to leave me, a surrogate who isn't even a bear. If I was right, these cubs, when given the choice, would choose the company of wild bears over the company of humans.

My plan, radical to others but not to me, was to raise the cubs in as natural a set of circumstances as possible, so that their instincts and ability to learn would enable them to develop normally. In the process, I hoped, I would be given an unprecedented look into the intimate lives of wild bears as they were growing up. But I also knew my limitations. Could I teach the cubs what natural foods to eat? Could I respond quickly enough to danger to send them up a tree and out of harm's way? If bear cubs learn by following and imitating their mother, which was the currently accepted theory, how would it affect them to follow and imitate me? Was it ethical for me even to try? And then, even if I was able to get them back in the woods, there was a three-month bear-hunting season to deal with.

Despite these reservations, I figured that their chances for survival were as good with me as with anyone else—short of living in captivity. And as for ethics, there was no dilemma at all. Since the animals that come to rehabilitators are incapable of surviving on their own, they're already dead as far as nature is concerned. Our charge as rehabilitators is to try to return those we can to the wild. I decided to take the cubs.

And thus, not quite on a whim—but close enough—and without a hint of what was to come, began a fifteen-month adventure that would teach me more about black bears, and about myself, than I could ever have imagined. For the next seven seasons—two springs, two summers, two falls, and a winter—I would live with the cubs, visiting and nurturing them nearly every day of their lives except during the denning period. I would walk with them unrestrained through miles of New Hampshire woodlands and spend more than two thousand hours at the task, observing and caring for them as they were growing up. In essence, I would become a mother bear.

While the cubs were getting a routine medical checkup at the veterinarian's office, I spent time converting an empty room in the basement of our house into a den so the cubs would be handy to feed while they were still nursing. The den room is fourteen feet by fourteen feet, with a concrete floor and eight-foot stone-and-mortar walls. There are a half dozen wooden upright posts in the room. Some of these posts had served to support woodpiles, and two support the house; for the time being, they would make do as trees for climbing. I took some of the three-foot firewood for our furnace and built a crib in the middle of the room, about sixteen inches high and hollow in the center. I filled it with bedding material and covered the top with logs and a shag carpet. For toys, I provided four dried deer legs, sticks, bark, and some store-bought dog toys. The floor of the room was covered with newspapers.

On the evening of April 13, Frosty, his wife, Cheryl, and their two daughters, Christine and Kate, arrived with the cubs, a female and a male. The female was suckling on Cheryl's neck when she came through the door, and judging from the number of red welts, or hickeys, in evidence, this had been a routine activity for the little cub. She had also, Frosty said, made an attempt to suckle the veterinarian's neck when he removed her from the den.

The male cub weighed 4.8 pounds and the female 4.2 pounds. Unknown to me at the time, these cubs were severely malnourished for April bears; I subsequently received cubs that already weighed that much by mid-February. But their build was solid, and they had large feet and claws like needles, twenty of them on each cub. With the bear's propensity to climb, I was to learn quickly that I'd have to wear two layers of clothing to prevent these tiny needles from making my legs look like claw-marked beech trees.

The cubs were almost entirely black, with brown muzzles, brown eyebrows, and brown tufts in their ears. The female had more distinct brown patterns, especially over her eyebrows; the little male wore a bold V-shaped white blaze on his chest. Their eyes were small, showing expression only when they moved them, exposing the whites. The tip of each nose was a light brown, and the inside of their mouths and their tongues were a soft pink. Their incisors, or front teeth, were still cupped for nursing, with an oval gap between the upper and lower incisors to accommodate their mother's nipples. In spite of their small size, they already had the lumbering walk of mature bears.

After the Hammonds left, I settled quickly into the routine I had planned for my little charges, which involved minimal interaction with people, myself included. I wanted to make an effort not to "train" them, not to give them undue human affection, not to allow them to socialize with dogs or other elements of human life. I thought this effort would simplify my observations of their natural activities and aid in the cubs' eventual survival in the wild. In short, I wanted to be on the receiving end of their behavior, not the other way around. I restricted people from seeing the cubs, spent only the time needed for feeding with them, and tried to speak very little around them. These restrictions seemed a good idea at the time but later proved impractical.

And finally, because I didn't want to humanize these small creatures any more than necessary, I named them LB (Little Boy) and LG (Little Girl).

I began with four feeding sessions a day. Every three hours, I put the cubs on my lap and gave each one a bottle containing four to eight ounces of Esbilac, a synthetic dog's milk substitute. Because of the cubs' sharp claws and unbridled enthusiasm, it was necessary for me to wear heavy work gloves. LB would usually come out ready to eat, but his sister would always go for my neck to suckle and she would have a tantrum when I intercepted her to stick a bottle in her mouth. With clenched teeth, she would fight me all the way until I got the nipple in her mouth. LG's misbehavior ensured that the sessions would be interactive and spirited.

If one cub finished first and wanted what was left in the other one's bottle, a snarling and roaring knock-down-drag-out fight would erupt. A typical scenario: LB usually began and finished first, burping several times to relieve himself of the air he inhaled while nursing. At this point he would climb down onto the newspaper and further relieve himself with two bowel movements, backing up as if to aim the droppings out of the den, arching his back, yawning, extending his tongue, and lifting the little protective flap he had for a tail. Then he would climb back on my lap, only to find that LG had not yet finished with her bottle, at which point he would decide he was hungry again. As he moved to displace his sister from the bottle, her ears would go back, and with her lips extended and somewhat squared off she would then produce the most horrifying roar. The warning stage was short lived, and she would then strike out with a rapid bite to the base of LB's skull. That's all it took: an intense bear fight would erupt on my lap. My best option at this point was to stand up and dump the little monsters on the floor.

In spite of the ferocity of the food fights between the siblings, the cubs' fervor was extremely well focused. I could reach in barehanded to break them up, and they never bore a grudge; when the fight was over, it was over. Similarly, if I were to reach down while either of the cubs was feeding and remove food, I could do so without eliciting any response. When the feeding sessions were finished, LG would suckle gently on my neck, and LB would often fall asleep on my lap or shoulders.

Neck suckling on humans was already routine for LG before I got her, and she had arrived with one of her ears ragged; it looked as though LB had been suckling on it. Whenever either of them suckled, they would emit a nursing sound, a low chuckle reminiscent of a vacuum pump. I learned to call this the "sound of contentment," because it would be used in a number of other moments of pleasure, and although this activity was cute, it was sometimes painful. If LG got to my neck before she had her bottle—and she always tried to—she would suck hard enough to cause a hemorrhage under the skin. On one occasion she sucked so hard that the pain was excruciating; I had to pry my finger between her jaws to break the suction. When I would try to remove her prematurely from my neck, her temper would flare and she would strike out with a rapid bite, causing more bruising of my already tender skin. LB, on the other hand, was the perfect gentleman.

These young bears did not respond positively to the affectionate physical gestures that people are used to bestowing on cats and dogs, like patting, scratching, or stroking of the fur. If they did respond, it was likely to be with a nip, or an irritated moan indicating displeasure, or by reaching with their paws to remove one's hands from their head, neck, or back. By the same token, I did not observe any mutual licking or grooming between them. (This behavior—called allopreening—is usually seen in social birds or mammals and is a means of strengthening the bond between two individuals. House cats, for example, will commonly lick not only each other but also their human housemates.) The only time I saw one cub lick the other was when his or her sibling was covered with milk or formula. Instead the cubs maintained the bond between them by ear suckling, or pseudonursing, and play.

Strong bonds between mother and cubs, and between siblings, are necessary for the youngsters' survival. While they are with their mother, cubs receive protection and security, are exposed to their environment, and have time to develop physically and socially. A strong relationship between cubs ensures that they don't separate or wander off in their mother's absence. LG's obsession with suckling may well have been a symptom of separation anxiety or an excessive need to belong. LB, on the other hand, maintained an independent air. Such a difference, I thought, might have been related to gender or to individual character, but with only two cubs it was impossible for me to tell.

By the time ten days had passed, the bears were eating well and beginning to put on weight. After each meal, they would wrestle with each other, climb on me, and take delight in untying my shoes before settling down to sleep on my shoulders or cuddling in my lap. The evidence of scattered toys indicated that they were playing in my absence, too. It was time, I thought, for our first outing.

CHAPTER 2

The First Walks

LYME, NEW HAMPSHIRE, is a quiet town by the Vermont border. The town's fifty-five square miles rise rapidly from the lowest point along the Connecticut River to the summit of Smarts Mountain, 3,240 feet above sea level. Of its 1,500 residents, about 90 percent live on the west side of town, in an agricultural zone along the river. The eastern, more mountainous, side of town is almost entirely forested, and that's where our two woodlots, the Turnpike Lot and the Lambert Lot, are located.

The Turnpike Lot is our eighty-acre sugar bush, and on it Debbie and I have built a small but well-appointed cabin near the sugar house. We call it the Turnpike Lot because it lies on the westerly side of the Grafton Turnpike, a winding, narrow dirt road that was part of the original 1800s thoroughfare that connected Woodsville, the Grafton County seat, and Concord, the state capital; what's left of it today runs for eight miles through unbroken forest from the Dartmouth Skiway in Lyme to the neighboring town of Canaan. Our lot rises for about six hundred feet through a series of four levels, or "tiers" as they were called in the old deeds. Each level has moist rich soils supporting sugar maple, red oak, and white ash and is separated from the next by one of the sheer granite ledges rimmed with stunted red spruce and rockfalls.

Our other lot, the Lambert Lot, consists of nearly 130 acres running from an old homestead clearing at 1,300 feet almost to the top of Lambert Ridge, which tops out at 2,200 feet; with a forest type of mostly northern hardwoods, Lambert is the southern ridge of Smarts Mountain. For more than twenty years, I have worked to save the orchard surrounding the cellar hole of the homestead, which was abandoned sometime before 1850. The clearing had last been open during the late 1930s when it was used as a landing for a pulpwood operation. At that time, three small shanties were built to house the woodcutters' families. When I bought the property in 1976, there was a thirty-inch-diameter pine growing out of the cellar hole, and most of the apple trees were overgrown; today the wild apples and hawthorn trees are thriving. The orchard now has nearly fifty apple trees of various ages; many of the young ones got their start in bear droppings or regurgitated apples. Moose, white-tailed deer, bobcat, coyote, and fisher are also frequent inhabitants of this woodlot.

Between these two lots, each surrounded by thousands of acres of unbroken forest, I knew that opportunities for the cubs' education would be abundant and diverse. At the end of April I loaded them in a pet carrier in the front seat of my pickup truck for their first outing, at the Turnpike Lot.

It was a warm sunny day; the hepatica were nearly done blooming, and yellow violets and red trillium were just starting. But I didn't really notice because I was preoccupied. Even though they had been with me for only ten days, I had assumed that the cubs would follow me as they would their natural mother, but I also knew there can be a big gap between an assumption and reality. Here I was about to turn my cubs loose in an unfenced expanse of woods that stretched for miles in every direction, a forest that they were born to live in. What would they do with this, their first whiff of the wild? Cling to me in fright? Disappear over the first hill, never to be seen again? I suspected they would stay near me, but I had no way of knowing.

I shouldn't have worried. The cubs loved the woods from their first steps. They climbed on stumps and logs, chased each other and wrestled in the dry leaves, and stayed near me the whole time. I allowed myself to relax and watch them while they played, and it didn't take long for me to notice that they weren't interested in sniffing anything. This was a big surprise; I had thought that this first trip to the woods would trigger individual responses to all kinds of strange and interesting smells. Instead they stayed close to each other and responded to my movements in the same way, keying in on the sound of crunching dry leaves and brush as I walked. Where I went, they went. With their instinct to survive and only a few days of my nurturing them, it really did appear that a bond was beginning to form between us.

The walk went without a hitch, and soon we were back in the truck, riding home. While I drove and they rested in the pet carrier beside me on the front seat, my mind pored over the day's events. It was important to remember that these cubs had come directly to me from the den and had no experience of the world outside it, thus simplifying my analysis of their behavior. It seemed to me the decisions I had watched them make today could only have originated from four possible sources: from their instincts; from something they had learned from their mother; from something they had learned from me; or from something they had learned only today through independent experimenting. But their mother could hardly have taught them anything in such a short period of time, all of it confined to the natal den. I certainly had nothing to teach them since I had no experience in raising black bear cubs, and had even refrained from reading the literature in an effort to remain an unbiased observer; plus I had carefully avoided directing them in any way on this walk. And since this was their first outing, they had no experience yet. So their instinct had to be the source of virtually all of their behavior so far.

The next day we went out again. The woods were showing the first signs of spring: tree buds were beginning to swell, water flowed from the melted winter snows, and the mats of brown leaves lay relatively undisturbed by new growth. We moved slowly through the woods because the cubs had to climb on and explore everything. When we came to a wet area, they cautiously approached it as this was new to them, but they were soon drinking from it. This was a welcome sign to me, that the weaning process might be beginning. At their first brook crossing, I tried to get the cubs to imitate me and follow me across a log. But, taking nothing at face value and needing to find out everything for themselves, they ran right through the water. Wet but undeterred, the cubs made their way toward the wild apple orchard located on my second woodlot. They scampered behind me and made a practice of running from tree to tree, hiding behind or hugging the base of each just long enough to assess the situation and plan their move to the next.

Several large white pines proved irresistible to the cubs. Only a week out of the den, their tiny bodies were dwarfed by the size of these immense trees, but with their innate ability to climb, they had little trouble with even the largest of them. Their method was to hang on and reposition themselves with their arms and walk up the tree with their legs, which are short for their body size but ideal for climbing. Their hind feet appear, from a human standpoint, to have been put on backward, yet they are ideally suited to the round contour of the trees. Their front paws toe inward when they walk, a further adaptation to their arboreal lives.

We drank from the spring, and I settled down by a large basswood log to give the cubs a rest. But rest wasn't what they had in mind; they scrambled and climbed on the log and chased each other up, down, and around a six-inch-diameter white ash tree, which was ideal to climb because of its size and its tight, deeply cut bark.

On the south end of the ridge we came to a large stump that had been excavated by a wild bear the previous night. This was the first time I noticed them actively interested in scent. They sniffed the site carefully, and LG found a spot on the ground that she was particularly interested in, probably a urine scent mark. As she lingered, LB and I kept walking, thinking she could catch up. We had gone over a hundred yards when LG finally noticed that she was alone and started running in our direction, loudly bleating her distress call: "BaaWoww, BaaWoOoww." LB climbed to the safety of my shoulders in the commotion. LG was about twenty-five feet off course when she went tearing by us. LB scrambled off my shoulders, ran in her direction and intercepted her before she disappeared from sight, then returned with her. This was strikingly new behavior on his part; during times of stress, he would typically climb up on my shoulders or take cover on the ground right behind me. But his actions on this day appeared to be directed toward LG's safety, not his own. Could it be that bears are capable of this sort of altruistic behavior?

All the way home and into the night I let the events of the day play themselves out in my mind. It was only our second walk, and already I was faced with trying to make sense of three very interesting observations.

13

First, if I was right and LB had felt obligated to prevent his sister from getting lost, here was a good indication of the strength of the bond between the two and, more intriguing, evidence of an altruistic nature. Altruism—that is, having concern for others and the willingness to act on that concern with a degree of risk to oneself—is thought by many to be solely a human trait. While LB's risk might not seem to have been that great, he did leave a situation of complete safety on my shoulders to run a distance of more than forty yards to prevent his sister from becoming lost. Or had he?

Second, and more certainly, the cubs appeared to follow me by sight and sound, not by smell. When LG had run past, I was standing still, wearing clothes of mixed colors that blended with the surroundings. LG, coming from a distance of over three hundred feet, had missed me by only ten yards, but had missed me completely; it was obvious that she hadn't seen me or hadn't recognized me. It dawned on me that bear cubs probably key in on the solid dark color of their mother well before their olfactory abilities are fully developed. Later, armed with this insight, I had Debbie buy me a pair of solid navy blue coveralls that seemed to remedy this problem.

Third, although the cubs had not reacted to any other smells, they did react to the scent of the wild bear, which I suspected was a female, since it had occurred to me that bear cubs probably imprint on their natural mother's scent while they're still all together in the den. If so, it would help explain why the cubs were not following me by scent at this point in their lives.

Answers to these questions would come slowly, and only after thousands of hours with these two and the many other bears still in my future, but already, after only two walks with the cubs, I was beginning to get a sense of what remarkable animals I was dealing with. LB's rescue of LG by itself put the cubs in a category above and beyond any animal I've had the privilege to work with, including the much loved and well-trained bird dogs that have always been part of our household.

CHAPTER 3

The Beginnings
of an Education

ARLY IN MAY, I developed a schedule that would accommodate my
gunsmithing business as well as my interactions with the bears. As a
result, my time with the cubs in their basement den became limited to
four twenty-minute feeding sessions a day, and our number of walks in
the woods decreased from three to one a week.

So the cubs were eager for a walk whenever they got the chance. In
the middle of the month I took them from the High Walls pasture to
Lambert Clearing and out the lower woods road. When we arrived, the
cubs weren't interested in following me; they just wanted to play and
climb. Soon they went up a large dead pasture pine and were afraid to
come back down because every time they reached with their hind feet
for a good footing, the tree's loose bark would crumble and break away.
I rescued them by reaching up and holding my hands beneath them as
they lowered themselves into the safety of my arms. Once on the
ground, the cubs were ready to follow me up the path to my clearing,
known locally as Moore's Orchard.

In the clearing, the cubs ran and played wildly. Standing on their
hind legs for the first time, they knocked over poplar saplings while

sniffing the leaves. The cubs were really beginning to develop their sense of smell now, and every day they used it more; while scenting spots on logs and on the ground, their sniffing was audible and easily differentiated from their nearly silent breathing.

On this outing they did something else I hadn't seen before: after sniffing some poplar leaves, they began mouthing them. Mouthing the leaves? What was this? I watched more closely and noticed that they were holding leaves and flowers in their mouths for several seconds before releasing them unchewed. What was the significance of such behavior? Did they have some ability to identify foods this way? It occurred to me that they might be tasting the leaves, but if that were the case, I would expect them to chew the leaves to maximize the flavor. But they didn't; the cubs just held the vegetation gently—barely closing their mouths—for a few seconds and then let go. Was there something inside their mouths sensitive enough to determine the safety or delicacy of a new food item? Here was something to watch for. From now on, I would carefully record every instance of mouthing behavior, noting what the vegetation was and how they reacted to it.

Later on the walk, both LB and LG, after a lot of mouthing, chewed on their first wild meal of apple blossoms. LB climbed out on the slender limbs at the top of a small apple tree and foraged for about fifteen minutes. LG didn't join him; she wasn't crazy about limb walking and stayed mostly on the straight trunks of trees large enough to support her.

I was thirsty and left the clearing to go to the spring. LB stayed up in the apple tree, and LG came with me, lapping up water as she lay in it to cool off. Meanwhile, although we were less than forty yards away, LB suddenly noticed our absence and let loose with a series of desperate bleats. LG and I ran back to the tree to rescue him. The thought of being alone was clearly frightening to these five-month-old cubs, each of which weighed only about ten pounds. They were not yet on a diet of natural foods and, like their wild counterparts, would have been quite defenseless if they became separated from their mother, a comparison that came so naturally to my mind that it almost slipped by without my taking note of it: LB and LG weren't orphans anymore. They'd been adopted, and, for better or worse, they now had a replacement mother to watch over them. Whether I liked it or not.

Or, more important, whether I was going to be any good at it. Or not.

On our next trip to Moore's Orchard, during the second week in May, we approached the clearing from the lower side, and both cubs became alarmed by a scent they picked up in the air. They stood on their hind legs to assess the smell and then ran to me for safety. There was a gentle moist breeze at their level, so I knelt down to sniff an odor that was strong enough even for me to detect but which I couldn't positively identify. I suspected a porcupine, as there was a brush-and-stump pile nearby that could have been used by one for shelter.

In the clearing near the apple trees, there was a fresh wild bear dropping in the grass. I took a sample of the bear scat so I could try to identify what it had been eating. LB looked on, and when his turn came he sniffed and "slow-licked" the scat: he literally stuck the tip of his tongue on the scat and held it there for several seconds before returning it to his mouth. Clearly, the scat was a source of information to him. But was he actually tasting it or doing something else? Like putting leaves in his mouth without chewing them, this minimal touching with his tongue didn't seem very flavor-oriented to me. Time would pass before I eventually figured it out, but I initially thought that while sniffing enabled the cubs to locate the source of a smell, "slow-licking" enabled them to make whatever identification of it they needed.

The next time out, our destination was the southwest corner of the Turnpike Lot on the third level of the ledges, a spot that I knew would interest the cubs. In that corner was a small sphagnum moss pond that wild bears had been using for a wallow. Dense spruce surrounded the wallow, and a small knoll rose to its eastern side. The eastern boundary of the knoll was a precipitous drop. To the west of the wallow, there were about fifty yards of reasonably level ground and another granite ledge rising vertically a hundred feet or more. On the knoll was a large red pine that I considered to be a "bear tree."

I had read about bear trees in my ever-growing library of bear books, most of which said the trees are used primarily by male bears in the breeding season. To keep the rest of us confused, some authors have suggested that females may also be involved, but give no further explanation. All I knew at this point was what I could see: this tree bore old scars—tooth marks at a level about six feet off the ground and claw marks in the bark—as well as a few strands of black hair. The age of the scars told me that this tree had been used by wild bears for many years. But how often or at what time of year they came here I had no idea. Perhaps the cubs could enlighten me.

We made our way up the steep survey-line trail to the pass carved by a small runoff brook in the second set of ledges. LG had to try her own route up through the rocks but found her passage blocked by steep ledges. Her pitiful screams for help forced us to backtrack and rescue her. We then followed the stream up to the wallow pond and the bear tree. As we approached the big red pine, the cubs started sniffing the lower limbs of nearby small spruces, then moved to the bear tree itself. Very curious to me, but not noticed by the cubs as they paid all their attention to the tree, was a trail of large, deeply embedded bear tracks—leading from the wallow to a small red pine, then up to the bear tree itself, and then ending rather abruptly about twenty yards beyond it.

My questions were accumulating. What were the cubs sniffing? Bear scent? If so, how old was it? How often and why do the wild bears come to this tree? Were the sunken bear tracks made by a very large bear in the early spring when the ground was soft? If so, why hadn't I seen them anywhere else? If not, how were they made? Was the fact that I was visiting this apparently well-used haunt of the local wild bear community with two strange cubs going to affect the wild bears' behavior? Was there something to be feared? Would they track us down and eat us now that we had come here? I didn't know the answer to any of these questions. What I did know for sure was that if I didn't have the cubs with me, I wouldn't even have the questions.

As I stood there, in a place obviously frequented by wild bears, some of them big enough to leave bite marks six feet up a large tree trunk, my heart was racing and my senses were all on full alert. But it really wasn't fear that ran through my veins. Our chances of actually running into a bear were quite low. Having the cubs with me might have slightly increased the odds, though. Should I have feared for the cubs' safety or even my own? I didn't think so. I've tramped the New Hampshire forests since I was a boy and have seen maybe a dozen wild bears; none of them have ever shown any interest in me beyond a desire to get away from me as quickly as possible. Black bears are reasonable animals; I could see that in my cubs. Their reputation for being unpredictable, I suspected, came from a general lack of knowledge about bear behavior. In fact, the more time that I spent with my cubs, the more predictable I found them to be. A wild bear that we might encounter would need a reason to attack us that was compelling enough for it to risk its own security. I didn't think that would happen, but there was, of course, another possibility. I could be wrong!

We left the bear tree and the sunken tracks, and at the lookout on the rim of the second set of ledges, LB spent a lot of time biting and mouthing the blueberry bushes. I knew that blueberries were a preferred bear delicacy, but these early-spring bushes didn't have any berries yet; in fact, they were just showing the first sprouts of green leaves. After assessing the blueberry futures, both cubs moved to the edge of the ledge and hung on with their hind feet while they explored the lichens near the precipice itself. Unlike the sightseer's dog that had jumped off nearby Holt's Ledge—a two-hundred-foot drop—in 1992 and amazingly survived, these cubs had a built-in sense of caution about heights.

In a small wet area near the central pass between the ledges, I noticed some small evidence of digging that might have been done by a bear. Just beyond that we found a fresh bear scat, then another one in an opening between the ledges. There was a well-defined bear path crossing to the other ledge, and along this trail another very fresh bear scat, the outside not yet dry. Coming down through the upper middle section of the sugar bush, I saw lots of bear-feeding sign. Clearly, there were plenty of wild bears around. How long would it be until we had an encounter with one?

The cubs never trailed more than forty yards behind me, nor ventured more than five yards ahead, staying in close, safe contact until they recognized the last downhill stretch to the truck and ran playfully in wider, happier circles, making leaf-scattering passes as they raced past me and attacking my legs from behind as we ended the day's walk.

Near the end of May, I transported the cubs in the truck for a walk that wasn't on my property. Our destination was a series of beaver ponds affectionately called Moose Bog. These ponds range from mudflats to highly productive aquatic centers supporting a diversity of life. Moose especially frequent the bog to eat aquatic plants, which are an important source of minerals for them. (Moose Bog is actually a fen, but most people around here, including the settlers who named it, don't make that fine distinction. In New England they're pretty much all bogs. Except, of course, for that ballpark in Boston.)

Right after I released them from the truck, the cubs found some silty soil in a moist area on the logging road, and both of them ate soil from this spot at the beginning and again at the end of our walk. I had seen this behavior on previous occasions, but now I started wondering what purpose it served. Was the soil a source of minerals or intestinal organisms? Why did the cubs restrict themselves to only one spot? How did they know what specific dirt to eat? Another mystery for me to try to understand.

I proceeded as usual with the cubs running from tree to tree, and along fallen logs, while staying within thirty yards to the rear of me and fifteen yards to either side. Eventually, we picked up the game trail that led to the beaver ponds at Moose Bog. Heavily imprinted with fresh deer and moose tracks, it wound downhill through boulders and ledge outcroppings and a thicket of striped maple saplings and blackberry brambles that was the result of a logging operation ten years before. At the bottom of the hill was an area of recently logged hemlock and spruce. The sun shone upon the first large beaver pond, and the cubs went down to the shore to drink, careful not to go in too deep. When I approached the second pond, I noticed a young moose feeding in the water of the third pond about 150 yards away. The moose heard us and looked our way, ears alert. I wanted to get closer, but keeping quiet with the cubs proved impossible. I was doing my best, by stepping on rocks and logs to avoid getting wet or snapping a stick that might spook the moose, but the cubs were climbing into the brambles of fallen dead spruce tops and seemingly snapping twigs with glee while they ran through the mud and up logs, covering as much ground—and making as much noise—as possible. I looked back at the moose and noticed that its attention was focused on their sounds and movements. Fortunately, the wind was right for us to advance, even though the moose knew something was up.

With the cubs thus running a diversion, I was able to approach as far as the dam of the third pond, where the moose was in full view about forty yards across the pond. Sensing no threat, the young bull—I could now see the nubs of his newly growing antlers—began moving slowly toward us while feeding off the bottom of the pond. While I was busy taking pictures, hordes of black flies were busy taking blood samples from my face and neck. I took great care to swat at them only when the moose had his head in the water, but it was hard. When the moose was about twenty yards away from me, he stopped moving and stared in my direction. Normally, I can stand motionless in a situation like this for as long as required, but I don't usually have a hungry cloud of blackflies swarming around—and feeding on—my head. When I couldn't take it any longer and swatted, the moose spooked, turned, and splashed loudly off through the water.

The cubs reacted by making a mad dash to the nearest tree, a tall sugar maple. They got partway up and hesitated for a moment, so I snorted twice (as I thought a bear would), and they responded by climbing to the very top branches of the ninety-foot tree. Up in those thin branches, the cubs were safe even from climbing adversaries like other adult bears. The treeing of the cubs was textbook behavior, and I was delighted to see it, but I was a half mile from the truck and the cubs were scared. Would they come back down?

I tried some grunts and moans—I had read that mother bears do this when they want their cubs to come down—but the cubs didn't seem to respond. They disregarded all of my efforts to coax them down. So I sat down and waited until I could no longer hear the moose snapping branches in the distance, then waited some more. Eventually, I became discouraged and in exasperation called out, "Hey, guys! Come *on!* Come *on!*"

The cubs slid right down out of that tree and followed me back to the truck. It was as simple as that. Apparently, my tone of voice was more important than what it was I actually said. For lack of anything better to say, I've used "Come on! Come on!" ever since.

One evening while Debbie and I were in the kitchen talking, she was distracted by a strange sound in another room. Investigating, she found that the copper heating pipes leading from the basement to the second floor were shaking and rattling up and down.

"Ben, look at these pipes!" she exclaimed. "Something is wrong. You'd better go down and check *your* bears!"

Calling them my bears was a little out of character, but she had every right to be annoyed. Debbie truly supported the bear project; still, she knew it substantially reduced our time together and made it unlikely that we would go on vacation for some time to come, because finding a suitable baby-sitter would prove to be difficult. But beyond her support of the project and her willingness to give up time together, Debbie made a more concrete contribution: her more-than-full-time employment (as the manager of a pension administration and consulting group at a local accounting firm) freed me from the economic shackle of my own business and allowed me to spend the time I needed to work with the bears. So when the house itself began to come apart, she had plenty of good reason to snap out at "my" bears.

Down in the basement I found both of the cubs up in the ceiling insulation supported by the pipes. LB was peering out at me with a very satisfied look on his face; LG was hidden away in their new insulated ceiling den. They were clearly having a good time, but the basement was a disaster area: they had pulled the insulation not only from the pipes but also from between the joists. By this time, the cubs were completely weaned and required feeding only twice a day. So at that moment, as I mentally calculated the number of hours it would take me to undo their remodeling efforts, it was abundantly clear that "my" bears were ready to go to their new outdoor home.

I had been working hard out past our sugar house on the Turnpike Lot to complete a remote cage for them. Ten feet high, twelve feet wide, and thirty-two feet long, the enclosure included an eight-by-twelve-foot lean-to with a dry den area. The cage's wire—plastic-coated, two-by-four-inch mesh, and welded—was surplus inventory donated by the Vermont Fish and Wildlife Department for the project. The cage itself was situated between two hundred-foot-tall white pines surrounded by mixed hardwoods, and inside it I had built a climbing structure out of ash logs and brought in numerous rotten logs the cubs could tear apart. The floor of the cage was crushed stone, which would keep it dry and prevent digging, while the interior of the den was bedded with dry hay. Finally, I was careful in placing the structure in an isolated area of the lot so that none of my other buildings could be seen by the cubs.

The next day, I drove the cubs out to the Turnpike Lot, and we started the walk to the cage, which required going through the cleared ground around the small man-made pond to the east of camp. The cubs did not seem to like being out in the open. While we walked across the dam on the freshly mowed grass, they clustered at my feet and repeated a nervous "gulp" vocalization before finally breaking and running for the trees. I moved down to the edge of the woods to catch up so we could continue our journey.

At the base of the berm surrounding the pond, there was a large block of wood upon which a pileated woodpecker had recently fed. Suspecting ants, I knelt by it to attract the cubs. To the cubs, kneeling meant either that I'd found something for them or that I would submit to suckling. Wild mother bears nurse their cubs in an upright sitting position, so I suspected that the cubs' response to me when I knelt or sat was instinctive, because they always reacted to these positions. Obviously, I didn't spend much time sitting around while I was out with them!

Lifting the bark on the block, I saw an ant colony with eggs. LB arrived first; he sniffed and started ripping at the bark with his claws, licking up the ants. It appeared that the eggs and larvae did not smell because he targeted only the ants. LG joined the melee and became very excited, smelling and tearing at the bark until she found another colony of smaller ants, which she rapidly licked up. Attracted by the commotion, the larger carpenter ants began to come to the surface. LG licked up a couple of them but shook her head as though she was surprised by their size and feel. I doubted that anyone had ever made observations of this sort of behavior at this level of detail—I was only a foot away, and the cubs paid me no attention at all.

When we approached the cage, the cubs were noticeably apprehensive, but they followed me anyway, another sign that our bond was getting closer every day. Once inside, they cautiously explored every inch of the enclosure. LG climbed on me and suckled on my neck more than normal; I guessed that the stress of change stimulated this desire to bond. I left the cubs alone to explore and get used to the cage. Debbie and I returned that evening with their supper, a collection of their favorite toys, and familiar-smelling bedding from their basement den.

It didn't take the cubs long to settle comfortably into the new cage, and when I came out for one of my twice-daily feeding visits near the end of the month, they were almost as eager to go for a hike as to eat. This was surprising, as food had until now been the central part of their lives. I took them out to the snowmobile trail, which passed through the lot about a hundred yards from their cage. In the area between the cage and trail, I had made a winter sugar-wood cut of poplar, creating a small clearing the year before. I had planned the cut to regenerate poplar and enhance wildlife habitat and have been rewarded by seeing evidence of increased use by deer, bear, grouse, and woodcock.

In the clearing I dug a corm of a jack-in-the-pulpit, one of the plants I knew to be a black bear staple. I thought that if I bit into the corm with my front teeth I could introduce the cubs to one of their most important foods, but I also knew that the corms were poisonous to humans, so I didn't plan on swallowing any. The flavor was quite nice at first, but then the delayed burn kicked in with a vengeance. Cayenne pepper and horseradish pale by comparison! I spat and tried to ride out the waves of pain until I could think straight again. Then I offered the corm to the cubs. They sniffed it but did not lick it and in fact flatly refused it. My experiment to teach them by imitation had been a failure. For me, anyway. For the cubs, it had been a smashing success; even at their young age, the bear cubs were smart enough not to follow my example. I, on the other hand, suffered the indignity of burning lips for the next three days.

I really should have known better. Jack-in-the-pulpit corms are also known as Indian turnips and have been used as food not only by bears but by Native Americans, who prepared them in various ways: by boiling, by slicing thinly and drying, or by grinding into a powder and drying, all good methods for neutralizing the nasty calcium oxalate crystals that had stung me so viciously. The fact that both the black bears and the earliest human inhabitants of these woods had developed separate but functional ways to avoid getting burned by one of its most common plants may not have been a scientifically valid illustration of parallel evolution at work, but for the moment it had plenty of authority with me. Meanwhile enough was enough; I figured it was time to end the day's adventures.

Back at the cage a problem had arisen, one that I had foreseen but which was vexing nonetheless: getting the bears to go willingly back into the cage. The first few times had been easy, but now the cubs were beginning to find excuses, avoiding me and climbing trees in their efforts to escape confinement. I had tricked them a few times by allowing LG to suckle me and then carrying both cubs into the cage. Tricks work, but they don't work very long with intelligent animals, as I had learned long before this.

I used to fly a raven without restraint. My father had been studying ravens for his book, *The American Crow and Common Raven*, published in 1989. In 1986, while watching a raven nest on Holt's Ledge, he saw one of the young birds fall eighty feet out of the nest to the rocks below. When he got to the base of the ledge below the nest, he found the young raven with a dislocated leg and a broken tail, lying with another nestling that hadn't survived the fall. There had not been enough room on the branches around the nest for older fledglings to get out and exercise their wings, and as a result, they had pushed their younger siblings out of the nest. My father then rescued the surviving bird, named it Raveny, and proceeded to rehabilitate it.

After the raven recovered, I would lure him into the truck with goodies and drive him out to the Turnpike Lot. (He used the back of the passenger seat for a perch.) It turned into a hit-or-miss affair every time I wanted to get him into the truck or back into his cage. If I could think up a new trick, things would go quickly, but once he caught on to a ploy, there would be prolonged negotiations that usually ended with his roosting in the sugar house. I mention all of this because bears and ravens have something in common with respect to being fooled. I could fool them once; I might fool them a second time; but the third time I would invariably be the fool.

So now I needed a better solution to the problem of getting the cubs to reenter the cage. Behind the sheltered portion of the cage is a large white pine tree that represented security to the cubs. When scared, they would often retreat to the pine or hide behind the shelter. This suggested a solution to my problem: I would build a small cub door through the back wall of their lean-to, right near the pine tree.

I returned in the morning with the tools needed to complete that door. The cubs treed with every strange noise: the hammering, the sawing, the operation of the screw gun and especially the chainsaw, whose noise sent them eighty feet up their large white pine. When I was finished with each tool, I would call them down, and they would respond immediately. I spent the whole morning with them loose near the cage. They began by climbing trees and working out among the branches of an old dead top of a fallen spruce. That activity lasted an hour or so, then they moved on to a high-speed chase, ambush, and tussle. I was included in this game and suffered repeated attacks; the cubs would either make a running jump two feet up my leg or give me a bear hug and bite my back. At one point, LG, now able to support her full body weight with her neck muscles alone, leaped up, grabbed my glove with her teeth, and hung there, a sensation not unlike somebody looping a twenty-pound bag of fertilizer over your wrist when you weren't looking. While I worked on the cage, the cubs stayed within twenty-five yards of me, and amazingly, in spite of the commotion, the cub door got finished. Testing it, however, would have to wait for the next walk.

CHAPTER 4

Delicacies, van Gogh,
and a Dark Cloud

A S I QUIETLY approached their cage for a walk in early June, I could see the cubs were both asleep in the hay on top of the den box. I was able to get all the way to the cage door before being noticed. LB quickly jumped down and disappeared into the den, and LG jumped to the floor and looked at me cautiously. With every move I made to elicit a response, she made a responding retreat toward the den entrance, and then she turned and stared intently at me, trying to figure out what kind of danger I was. Due to the direction of the wind, she couldn't catch my scent, and it was obvious that even at this close range she didn't know who—or what—I was. I prolonged the moment to fully observe the situation before I uttered my usual greeting: "Hi, guys!"

Both cubs responded with a mad dash to greet me at the door. It was clear to me that these cubs were not nearly as visually oriented as humans are. I had approached the cage about the same time as normal, wore the same dark blue coveralls as always, came from the same direction, and still a second signal was required for recognition.

Bears are often thought to have poor eyesight, an assumption probably based on this kind of behavior. People assume that bears will react to visual clues in the same way humans do. But they don't. The primary

27

means of recognition for a human may be visual, but for a bear it's olfactory. Bears will respond immediately to an odor, but a visual clue requires a second piece of evidence, such as movement, sound, or smell.

A few days later, Alcott Smith, the veterinarian who had originally examined the cubs when Frosty Hammond's team had found them, came with me to the bears' cage. I had invited him because I was curious to see if the cubs could differentiate between me and other humans—an important question for their later survival. I sent Alcott to the cage first. They treated him with the same caution they exhibited toward me initially, except that when he greeted them verbally, they turned and ran up the nearest tree. This was good and bad: good because they clearly differentiated my verbal greeting, and bad because they hung around until they received a greeting. Now almost six months old, the cubs were responding extremely well to their wild environment, but dark clouds were beginning to loom on the horizon. I worried about their ultimate contact with the supposedly civilized community of humans, whose first response to the unexpected sighting of a bear generally is fear, and whose second response all too often is gunfire. How was I to prepare them for something I knew so well, but over which I—and certainly they—had so little control?

The walk we took with Alcott that day was one of the better ones. Heading up through the three tiers of ledges on the Turnpike Lot, we made our way eventually to a brook that runs directly under the sheer face of Holt's Ledge. The Great Ledge, as it is referred to in my deeds, has an almost four-hundred-foot vertical drop and is the nesting ledge for both a pair of ravens and a pair of peregrine falcons.

Once we passed the band of spruce, the cubs did their usual running around, climbing on fallen spruce trees, and occasionally pouncing on one another. LG found a fallen hornbeam, locally known as leverwood because its tough wood was once used to make good levers. What attracted her to it I'm not sure, but she tore, sniffed, and bit at the fibrous rotting bark while emitting what I've previously described as the "sound of contentment"—that low, vacuum pump–like chuckle. After several attempts to dislodge her from her find but showing no interest in it himself, LB lay down and started eating something he had found on the ground. When LG came over to try to disrupt him, he fought her off; then, as if to show her what he had, he reached over to the back of her head and pushed her nose in it. Finally, they lay down side by side and quietly enjoyed this delicacy.

I was excited because, until now, the only things that they had eaten in any quantity on these walks had been ants and soil. Now they were actively seeking out new treats. Stooping down for a closer look, I found this latest food item to be fresh, still-moist white-tailed deer droppings. This really was something new. In all my recent reading of the literature, I had found no references to bears eating deer scats, nor did I find any later, when the day's events sent me back for a specific search. What was going on here? Was deer scat a source of nutrition, or were the cubs benefiting from the organisms that help dissolve cellulose in a deer's digestive tract, or both?

Bears have a simple digestive system, not unlike our own, and are inefficient at digesting cellulose, a cell covering in most plants that protects the cell nucleus. We humans make cellulose digestible by boiling our vegetables, and since a large portion of a bear's diet is herbaceous, it shouldn't be surprising to find that they too have developed techniques to aid in their digestion of plants, even though it has been reported that black bears have no specialized means for accomplishing this, unlike some other animals. Ungulates—deer, moose, sheep, cows, and other animals with four-chambered stomachs—rechew their food in a cud, utilizing enzymes and microbes to break down the protective cellulose in the cell walls. Mammals such as beaver and horses have specialized gut compartments, or ceacums, where these same types of organisms break down cellulose. Bears, I had read, have stomachs that are too acidic for any of these organisms to survive, thus preventing them from digesting cellulose, but that argument didn't hold up for me because I know that we humans have highly acidic stomachs and yet we're still highly susceptible to diseases caused by intestinal microorganisms. If these microorganisms died in our stomach acid, we wouldn't get sick from them, would we? On this walk the cubs fed heavily on fresh deer scats two more times and once on moist woods dirt. Did they know something that the experts didn't?

It was almost dark by the time we got back to the sugar house. Alcott split from the group to put his camera in his car, and I continued toward the cage with the cubs. We had just gotten to the edge of the woods when, down by the cabin, Alcott's car door slammed, instantly sending the cubs scrambling up separate trees. From her perch, LG made a rapid series of huffs, then barked, and finally roared; she was as upset as I had ever seen her. What I didn't know at first was that it wasn't just the door slam and Alcott's movements that set her off; she had also gotten a strong blast of the very pungent fermented scent of some freshly split poplar logs. The combination of sound, sight, and smell must have created quite a monster in her mind. (LB apparently had not caught the scent and did not react in the same way.) It took a lot of coaxing to get LG down from the safety of her tree. I had to wait patiently for her to calm down, and even then I had to get LB to follow me to the cage before she was willing to come down and join us.

In the following weeks we began to have a number of visitations by wild bears near the cage. I never saw any of the bears themselves, but I found tracks of different sizes in various places, all within fifty yards of the cage. I couldn't prove it, but it seemed almost certain that during the night the cubs were getting visitors right at the cage. The wild bears had evidently been feeding on jack-in-the-pulpit corms in the adjacent wet areas.

The sizes of the tracks hinted at who the nocturnal visitors might be. With LB's two-and-a-quarter-inch-wide pad on his front foot giving me a frame of reference, I could gauge the maturity of the other bears. In one spot I found a three-and-a-quarter-inch sow track along with that of her cub of the year. In another spot there was a noticeably larger, three-and-three-quarter-inch sow track and a two-inch cub track; this mother and her cub were apparently traveling with a much bigger bear, probably a male, that left a full four-and-a-half-inch track. That was a lot of wild bear activity quite close to the cage. Were these bears curious about the cubs and attracted to them, or was it just a coincidence and the cubs just happened to be in their feeding area? I guessed that both scenarios were plausible.

I also knew it was the height of black bear breeding season, perhaps explaining the track of the normally solitary boar with the smaller-tracked sow and her cub. The fact that these three were traveling together was interesting, however, since cubs stay with their mothers for a year and a half and the sows only breed every other year. It occurred to me that males might investigate all females at this time of year and not necessarily with the best of intentions. Infanticide by male black bears is well documented, with three suspected reasons: to reduce competition for territory, to provide food, or to create a breeding opportunity, as the death of her cubs allows the female to come back into estrus. It isn't Disneyland out there.

Meanwhile, and perhaps not coincidentally, LB was beginning to exhibit dominance over LG. I didn't know whether it had anything to do with the emergence of his testicles in the previous week or not. (The late emergence of LB's testicles was unusual. None of the other male cubs I've raised have had this problem.) Until recently, their food conflicts had been continuing, with bowl swapping and a horrifying roaring, biting fight over the last bit of food. Back when they had first been weaned, the cubs had become very concerned that one might be getting more food than the other. As a result, they switched bowls until there was food left in only one; then they would erupt in the same knock-down-drag-out fight as when they were fighting over their bottles. By the time they were finished, their porridge of lamb's milk replacer, dry baby cereal, and a vitamins and calcium additive was spilled from their knocked-over bowls and they were covered with it. Seeking a remedy to the problem, I called Joan Perkins, who had raised cubs in Maine for a number of years and was generous with advice. When her cubs had the same difficulties, her solution was to fasten the bowls to heavy beams, bolting them down ten feet apart. That worked like a charm. My cubs continued to circle and fight, but they no longer spilled their food.

But now I had another problem. With his newly established dominance, LB could bump LG off her bowl without a fight. If LG made a move toward his bowl and he did not give it to her, she would just back off. Although LB was in his first year, perhaps it was no coincidence that he was dominant at the peak of the breeding season. LG was in danger of not getting enough to eat, but, like so many of the worrisome, unforeseen aspects of their development, this problem took care of itself.

Our hike up to the ledges in the middle of June was a turning point. For the first time the cubs began to forage on natural vegetation in earnest. Until now they had eaten primarily ants, organic soil, fresh deer scats, and flower blossoms. On this walk alone they ate moose droppings, deer droppings, ants, raw blueberries, and other raw fruit, shad bush leaves, blackberry flowers, and raspberry flowers. Free to forage on her own, LG would from now on have much less trouble getting all the food she needed.

Back at the cage, I weighed both bears by holding them one at a time while standing on a scale, then subtracting my weight. LB tipped the scales at thirty pounds and LG at twenty-three. Both cubs were getting too fat for their frame size, mainly because the volume of food they demanded kept increasing. Their growth rate had reached five pounds a week, which wasn't acceptable: At that rate they would be grotesquely overweight at denning time, when wild New Hampshire cubs should weigh between forty-five and sixty pounds. Cubs in prime southeastern bear habitat such as in Virginia or other areas in the southern Appalachian Mountains may weigh as much as one hundred pounds. My goal was to have them weigh seventy-five to eighty pounds before going to den, so I cut back on the amount of lamb's milk replacer I was using and kept the volume of solid food the same.

With the food problem stabilized, I turned my attention to other aspects of their development. The cubs were still dragging their toys, deer legs, cut sticks, a terry washcloth, the bathroom scales I used to weigh them, the apple feed bowl, and bedding material into their den box, a sign that they were happily at play when I wasn't there, but I did begin to notice that LB seemed less contented than he had been. In fact, he was getting downright moody by the time I arrived to take them for a walk at the end of June.

When I got to the cage, LB was a little growly, and LG was trying to suckle on my neck. Suckling is an important behavior that maintains the bonds between the mother and cubs. I wondered if wild cubs ear suckled on each other, as my cubs did, or if this behavior was unique to orphans. LB's irritated moan was louder than usual, giving me cause to stay away from him. I had learned that as the intensity of his moans increased, so did the likelihood that he would play rough enough to bite me in the process. While these bites sent a message and were not intended to do great harm, without a bear's thick fur and loose skin, I would always end up with painful bruises where he nipped me. The solution was always to move quickly away from the cage to divert the cub's attention by finding things for him to play with or eat; soon his mood would change back to normal. But on this day, when LB stayed dark and glum, another solution came to me. LB's foul mood had started almost a week before, when I had noticed LG's ear was dry. She was refusing to let him suckle on her ear. While listening to LB's irritated moan, it dawned on me: when LG had shut him off, he felt he was no longer part of the group. She was still suckling on me, but he had no one. Despite his growly mood, and the thoughts of van Gogh that were flashing through my head, I leaned down and offered him my ear. He began suckling on it immediately, and, of course, LG joined in. This worked beautifully, as I should have known that it would. The basis of the bond between the cubs and me was trust; how better to display my trust and commitment to LB than by offering him a piece of my body that he could remove in a nanosecond?

I was beginning to learn that if I took the time to listen, these cubs were perfectly capable of communicating with me. By making an effort from the beginning of this project not to inflict my ways on them, I now found that they were being quite successful at inflicting their ways on me. I was discovering, as any first-time human mom knows, that the young possess powerful abilities to ensure that they are cared for properly.

CHAPTER 5

Impossible Lessons
and the Fabric of Learning

WITH LB REASSURED and back to normal now that I had let him suckle on my ear, we took another walk to the bear tree. Each time we visited the tree, there would be a progressive increase in their interest and range of behaviors. On this visit—our third—there was a quantum leap—literally. LG began sniffing audibly and then suddenly leaped onto the trunk of the tree and took bites at the bark, just below the healing wound made by the wild bear earlier in the spring. After hanging that way for a minute or two, she slid down the trunk and vigorously rubbed her head and body against the bark. LB also sniffed loudly and reacted to the scent by standing with his back to the tree and his head pushed back, rubbing and trying to get as much contact with the tree as possible. When he was finished, he sat quietly down with his back to the tree and, for lack of a better way to describe it, started musing, something he also did at other trees of importance like the large pines by the cage and his favorite oak trees nearby.

After I had put the cubs back in the cage, I drove home and tried to sort out the events at the bear tree. Both cubs had certainly reacted strongly, but was there any significance in the way they had each reacted differently to whatever scent was on the tree when we arrived? Why such strong reactions? Was the scent fresh? Was it from a male or female bear? An adult or juvenile? Or for that matter, even a bear? New clues and more questions were increasing the intrigue. It was too soon for me to draw conclusions from their actions, but it was clear that raising these cubs was definitely going to be more than just one big baby-sitting session. I was beginning to realize that locked inside these cubs were many of the secrets of black bear behavior, and now they were beginning to reveal them to me. The mysteries, I knew, wouldn't be revealed all at once, and some of them almost certainly never would be, but already I was getting tantalizing clues not just to their feeding habits, which I had expected to learn, but to something much more intriguing: the cubs were beginning to show me how they communicated with other bears. They were getting messages. And they were posting their own.

When I arrived back at the cage that afternoon, I found LG pacing. Like her excessive need to suckle, her pacing was, I believe, a manifestation of the anxieties that stemmed from her early separation from her natural mother. While pacing is typical of large carnivores when they are penned up, and probably reflects their need to travel over large expanses, these cubs had a daily outing, and it was only LG who paced. I worried constantly about her future; life would be challenging enough for a cub without any afflictions.

Sitting with the cubs after they had eaten, I noticed that guard hairs were just emerging through what I called their "lamb's wool" coat. In the past two weeks, they had finished shedding their baby hair, leaving this soft dense layer of wool, which, when coated with their natural body oils, would keep them warm and dry through their winter's sleep. As I ran my hands over LB's back, I thought momentarily of what a nice sweater this wool would make, a speculation that quickly faded with the image of trying to shear him. An angry bear is a handful at any size.

Across the road from the Turnpike Lot is a small fen, about two acres in size, and in it is a bear wallow. Wallow Bog, as I decided to call it, was dug over a period of years in the thick mat of sphagnum and peat that carpeted the floor of the bog. Growing in the bog are thickets of black spruce, mountain holly, and leather leaf, and in the few openings can be found cinnamon fern, pitcher plant, and a few bog orchids. These thickets are crisscrossed with well-worn game trails, used frequently by deer, moose, and bear. The bog itself is set in a valley of thick red spruces broken up with steep rock outcroppings and a ledge on three sides. It's a beautiful, quiet place, and one I knew would interest the cubs.

We left the cage, but before we got to the road crossing, LG found a small stump she seemed greatly interested in, although her brother was not. After first sniffing and slow-licking, she began rolling her head, neck, shoulders, and back on it. I inspected the stump and found no sign of anything visible that could have gotten her so excited, but her behavior was consistent with what she had done at the bear tree. By now I could guess that she was responding to bear scent, probably a urine mark because of its location, but was the mark made by a male or female bear? Why was one of the cubs interested and not the other? And why had this mark been made in the first place? Again I had too little information to draw any conclusions, but I was confident that the answers would come in time.

We crossed the road without any mishaps, but I was always anxious whenever there was an encounter with moving automobiles. Although the cubs had climbed on and ridden in my truck, they were unaware of the dangers that vehicles presented. I tried to express to them the urgency of the moment, but I could never get them to perceive a threat that they were not experiencing for themselves. Had I the foresight and financing in this venture, I would have tried electronic dog-training equipment as a means of conditioning to back up a command like "Watch out!"

On the way to the bog, the cubs ate wood sorrel flowers, buds, and finally leaves. This interested me because just three weeks ago I had tried to get them to eat the leaves without success. Evidently the cubs seemed to know not only what to eat but when. My earlier efforts to teach them failed, not because what I was offering them wasn't bear food, but perhaps because their systems could not yet handle the calcium oxalate in the leaves.

At the wallow, the cubs expressed interest in a scent on the low spruce boughs, again consistent with their response to bear scent. Although the air temperature was in the eighties, the cubs showed no interest in entering the wallow. So, in a mischievous moment, I got them interested by shoving them in one at a time. Aside from their surprise, the cubs showed me no animosity. In fact, when they bobbed to the surface and scrambled to shore, their coats covered with a thick layer of peat, they ran over to me to share their wealth. There was plenty of the wet, foul-smelling muck to go around, and once they had recovered from my mean trick and sorted out the visiting bear smells around the wallow, the cubs ran wild, scampering up and down the game trails, chasing and ambushing each other, and climbing scattered trees.

On our return trip, as we approached the road, a truck went by, and each cub scrambled up a suitable tree and made barklike alarm calls as the truck passed. Once the dust had settled, I called them down, and, upset and nervous, they followed me closely. Thereafter we stopped to listen for cars before crossing any road.

When I weighed the cubs at the end of month, LG weighed eighteen pounds and LB twenty-five; the diet I had put them on had been perhaps a little too successful, so I increased the lamb's milk replacer. At this time I was preparing three meals at a time with a mix of four quarts of chopped white clover, three cups of lamb's milk replacer, three multi-vitamins, a tablespoon of cooked bone meal, and enough oatmeal to bind the mixture so it wasn't runny. Each cub got two quarts of this, plus six apples, twice a day. Regardless of what I fed them, they were always hungry and would eat anything edible they encountered on our journeys.

Typically, when feeding was over, I would leave the cage and start out on a walk. One of the cubs would usually come right along, while the other would make sure no food was left to spoil. One day, I caught a half-grown wood frog and offered it to the cubs. As I held it by the legs, LG sniffed it, then took its torso into her mouth, holding it in the same manner the cubs had been using when mouthing vegetation, directly exposing it to the sensory portion of the roof of her mouth. She immediately rejected the frog as food and spat it out completely unharmed. I then gave LB a shot at it, and he too sniffed it and rejected it. I was not surprised by the lack of interest in the frog, as we encounter them routinely on our walks and I've never seen the cubs respond to the movement or smell of any reptile or amphibian.

Another postfeeding activity was play. With LB chasing LG, they would go on a wild run from tree to tree. At the trees LG would either climb partway up before dropping out and taking off again or take a stand behind the tree and reach around to fight LB off. These melees of running, biting, and wrestling would usually come full circle with the cubs making running passes by or through my legs. When they became bored with each other, I would become a victim of their onslaughts. Running tackles of my ankles were always accompanied by biting my boot tops and leaping at me while trying to grab on to my clothing with their teeth, though they usually got a little more than clothing. LG's game was to bite onto my gloves and be swung by me, hanging on by her teeth. I admired the cubs in these situations because things would never get out of hand; they always maintained a high degree of composure.

Alcott joined us on our last walk in June to do some filming. At the log landing on Cole's property he became distracted by something and stopped walking while the cubs and I continued on our way. When he ran forward to catch up, LG let out a yelp and made a few huffs as she beelined to the nearest tree. She was so shaken up, it took both LB and me to get her down, and once on the ground, she stayed in the thicket near the tree. Just when I thought she was ready to move with us, she went right back up the same tree. Again, she made some woofing noises and her distress bleat: "BaaWoOow." Finally, LB and I got her down and moving. It was clear that although she had accepted Alcott into the group at the beginning of the walk, when he left and then tried to reenter, he was a stranger.

Toward the end of the walk, the cubs found a three-foot-long piece of birch bark stripped from a log by woodcutters. Thinking it would make a good toy at the cage, I started dragging it back. All of the way to the cage, the cubs jumped on, tore at, and playfully attacked the large moving object.

It's appropriate, I think, to end the month of June here, with the six-month-old cubs at play. Play was so commonplace in their lives that I failed to give it enough attention in my daily notes. Yet it was the fabric underlying the cubs' development.

CHAPTER 6

Summertime,
and the Living Is Easy

IN EARLY JULY the daytime temperatures ranged from the upper eighties to low nineties, and the cubs' two water tubs in the cage required filling twice a day. Every time I arrived at the cage, the water would be nearly gone, and what was left was extremely dirty—clear evidence of repeated trips through the water and lots of playful activity. LB would sit in the empty tub as soon as I dumped the dirty water, waiting for a refill. Since there was no running water near the cage, I used my tractor to transport water from the pond in sixty-gallon plastic barrels, then pumped it into three other plastic storage barrels that I had set on an elevated platform just outside the cage. This arrangement allowed me to fill their water baths for several days by siphoning water from the storage barrels.

These long summer days accommodated bears and work quite nicely, however. Typically, I would feed and water them in the morning, then return around five in the afternoon to give the cubs their evening feeding and take them for an extended walk.

The hot sunny days of June had left us with a drought, leaving the wallow by the bear tree on the third level dry. On one of our walks there, a mass of several thousand wood frog tadpoles were beginning to bake in the sun. Attracted by the smell, the cubs investigated, but after close scrutiny and some audible sniffing, they walked off. Their pronouncement that such a large amount of protein just lying there for the taking was not bear food amazed me. It also pleased the local raccoons, who subsequently ate the whole mass.

Reversing the trend, the cubs' behavior at the bear tree was considerably more subdued than it had been on previous visits. LG did a neck rub on the base of the tree and LB did a back rub, but they did not show much excitement, leaving me to suspect that any scent they were responding to was several days old.

Caught up in all this activity, I failed to notice the time; it would be dark in less than a half hour. The survey line on the southern boundary of the lot was the fastest route back to the cage, but it was also very steep and edged with a low, dense cover of hardwood saplings on the Coles' side of the line that was sure to distract the cubs. On an ant hill on top of the first set of ledges, I found a fresh four-inch track, from a large male bear, which had not been there on our last walk up the hill. The lingering bear smells weren't going to make this trip any faster, and, sure enough, when I got to the bottom of the hill I was alone. Within a minute, however, LG came right along, but LB was nowhere to be seen. When twigs began snapping seventy yards up the hill in the thick cover, I assumed that LB was snapping them, but LG made no such assumption; she let out a series of grunts and huffs and scampered up a sugar maple. As far as she was concerned, LB had evidently exceeded the bounds of our group and as a result was now being treated as an intruder. Or—another possibility—she was right; the twig snaps weren't LB.

We waited until it was almost dark, and still LB had not appeared, although I continued to hear what I thought was him. LG was getting nervous and anxious while I called LB repeatedly with no response. I had no flashlight, which would have been handy. Fortunately, I was used to roaming around in the woods at night without one, or I might have joined LG in her emotional state. Still, I worried. The cubs hadn't yet spent a night out of the cage, and at twenty-one and twenty-five pounds they weren't large enough to defend themselves. I knew they were perfectly able to take refuge in the trees, but knowing there was a large male bear in the vicinity, I wanted the cubs safely in the cage for the night. Determined, I backtracked to where I had last heard LB. When I found him, he was at the base of a good-sized oak tree that was surrounded with brush, settled into a comfortable bed for the night. He looked at me as if he was wondering why we weren't doing the same.

Now, if I were a really good mother bear, we would have all just curled up under that oak tree, but I knew Debbie was probably already calling the neighbors to see where I was last sighted. My wife and I have had a long-standing disagreement over what constitutes darkness.

Reaching into my bag of tricks, I allowed LG to suckle on my neck while I lifted her up and carried her more than halfway back to the cage. This worked only until it dawned on her that LB wasn't with us. She broke out of my arms and scrambled up the nearest oak tree. I continued toward the cage and hoped she would follow, but she didn't. When I returned to her tree, I could hear LB moving seventy-five yards away; at least I thought it was him, as it was now pitch-black outside. Well, it was him, and when we connected he allowed me to pick him up and carry him back to the cage. Progress. But this set LG off, and her "BaaWoOow! Baa-WoOow!" bleats shortened to barks: "WOW! WOW!" LB and I had abandoned her, and she was letting the whole forest know. It occurred to me that there were other large wild creatures, whose night-visiting signs I had been seeing near the cage, that might also respond to these distress calls, so I left LB in the cage and returned to LG in order to quiet her and coax her down out of her tree. But no sooner had I gotten back to her than LB let loose back in the cage with his own ursine aria of low, guttural, and somewhat piglike sounds. As I said, until this point, I had not left the cubs out for the night, but that was rapidly turning from an option to a plan.

I walked back to the cage to release LB, and we went back to LG's tree to see if she would come down if we were both there for her. No such luck. She stopped yowling, but she wouldn't come down. By now I'd had it. With the full intention of leaving them out and going home, I gave up and returned to the cage to get my camera before going to the truck. While I was still in the cage, LB came to the door while LG was barking loudly again from her tree. Regaining my composure, I decided to stay and sit this one out. I took my usual seat on the den box next to the cub door, and LB came over and lay across my lap, whimpering and chewing on my glove. For thirty minutes I answered LG's "WOW!"s with "Come on!"s. Finally, at a quarter past ten, an hour and a half after dark, she finally gave up and returned to the cage.

The fact that the cubs lacked the energy to go on long walks in this heat gave me time to work on projects around the cage. I also continued to experiment with their diet. If I gave them just the milk supplement, they gained weight but remained hungry and got "the runs." The trick was to develop a food that had the right amount of nutrition but also the right amounts of fiber and bulk to satisfy their hunger and firm up their stools. Bears do not digest lactose, which was partly responsible for their loose stools, but on my budget special zoo formulas weren't an option; besides, the cubs were flourishing. My latest mixture had been milk supplement and beet pulp, which is used for roughage for cows on dairy farms. That seemed to work well; the cubs liked it and were producing well-formed scats. Dry dog food was supposed to be a good supplemental food for bears, but I had tried it for more than three weeks with no luck; maybe it was an acquired taste. I checked the cubs' weights and found them to be in good shape, with LG at twenty-five pounds and LB at thirty. Their build was solid, but not too fat, their hair was now shiny black, and their fur was already thickening for winter.

I brought a little surprise for the cubs and placed it on the path on my way to the cage one day later in July. It was a piece of wood that had been urinated on by Wobbly Bear, the ataxic yearling that I still had in a cage at the house down in the village. Her condition had not improved; in fact, it had worsened, but she did continue to eat and grow. The cubs followed me from the cage and found the piece of wood right away. They were very interested, sniffed and slow-licked, but didn't show any real excitement by rolling on it or marking it the way LG had the wild sow's urine.

The next day, as the cubs and I walked down the snowmobile trail toward the Cole's Lot, I looked back to see LG break-dancing—on her back and spinning, literally grinding herself into the ground. She had to be responding to a urine mark of a wild bear, one I had just walked over and had no means of noticing, but her response to this mark was more aggressive and animated than anything she had ever done before. She was so involved with rubbing and rolling on the spot that when I approached her she spooked wildly, letting out a loud huff as she ran and jumped five feet up a medium-sized oak tree next to the trail, her hair all bristled up and her eyes staring back at me with a wild-eyed, disoriented look. This was a beast I had not seen before.

When she finally did recognize me, LG dropped off the tree and went right back at it—rubbing all sides of her head in the scent while intermittently scratching the ground in a very excited manner, as if to release more of the scent from the soil. LB responded to all this commotion by sniffing the area, then doing a chin-first rub. But his response was still minimal compared with hers. What was this powerful potion? If it was a urine mark, it certainly was different from what we got from Wobbly Bear. I'm no bear, but I couldn't resist getting down on my hands and knees to smell for myself what all the excitement was about. Wow! A pungent, musky, urinelike odor dominated the area, similar to the doe-in-heat buck lure sold to deer hunters. Since this was the breeding season for bears, I concluded that the mark was probably made by a sow in estrus. Thirty yards down the trail in the wet mud was a fresh series of four-inch bear tracks, possibly made by the bear I had just imagined. If so, she was fully mature, 150 pounds or more; tracks over four inches wide are usually made by males, which grow to twice that size. The largest black bear on record in New Hampshire weighed about five hundred pounds in the fall.

This was fascinating: Why wasn't Wobbly Bear's scent mark worth overmarking by the cubs? Was a bear's status, or perhaps its age and sex, reflected in its mark? Maybe the resident wild sows' urine carried hormones such as estrogen that might be lacking in that of a yearling female like Wobbly Bear. LG's sensory reaction to the different female's urine marks convinced me, but comparative chemical analysis of the sows' and Wobbly Bear's urine would have to be done to be conclusive.

A nagging question came to mind each time I witnessed the cubs rolling in some kind of scent: were they rubbing on a foreign scent to mark it with their own, or were they rolling in it to alter their own scent? In pursuit of answers, I returned with the cubs the following day to the urine mark. LG rubbed and rolled in the spot again, but without the enthusiasm she had shown earlier. This time, however, she marked the urine spot with ten drops or so of her own. LB was basically not interested, and as we started up the last rise before the height of the land, LG located bear scent and marked it with a few drops of urine. Another fifty yards up the road, she found some more bear scent, but this time, instead of marking with urine, she wiped the ground with the scent of the wild sow from the sides of her face. Had this mixture of her own scent and the wild female's urine empowered her? Or was this an act of submission? Was she trying to be accepted by the resident bears? In my quest for answers, all I was getting were more questions.

Not that LG didn't try to help clear things up for me. Back at the cage, she solicited suckling, which I still submitted to at least once a day. On this

occasion, however, she had a very special treat for me. Twice while suckling she wiped my head and neck with the sides of her face, depositing
on me the cherished perfume she had obtained from the scent mark of the
wild bear. Going home would prove interesting—one long-standing disagreement Debbie and I do *not* have is what constitutes a pleasant odor.

That evening, I returned to feed the cubs and take them for a short
walk on the Loop Trail afterward. Only thirty-five yards south of the
cage, the cubs hit a scent, bear scent, I assumed, as this was the only
scent they had shown a real interest in. But I wasn't completely comfortable with this assumption, so I looked for a confirming bear sign. It
wasn't hard to find: fresh digging for ants and the typical bear trail of
trampled vegetation.

As darkness fell upon us, the cubs didn't want to return to the cage. I
didn't have a problem with them staying out, but I had another life, and
since I couldn't leave without them following me, the cage was the only
solution. I carried LB into the cage and waited for LG to come by herself. I must have failed to consult with LB on this plan for he went to the
cub door and tried to get out, emitting an irritated moan as he clawed at
the latch. Deciding to test his resolve, I pulled him away from the door,
but each time I did, his moans grew louder. I then tried the mother-bear
swat of discipline across his muzzle, only to have him bite my gloved
hand, hard. It hurt, but still I admired his self-control for he easily could
have chomped right through the glove. As I continued to try to pull him
away from the door, his moans became a deafening roar—truly the
sound of an angry bear. At thirty pounds, standing about three feet tall,
and with a roar that made a man out of him, LB finally convinced me. I
opened the cub door and let him out.

But within ten minutes of our altercation, both cubs were in the cage
and LB was suckling on my ear while LG suckled on my neck. LB evidently harbored no more of a grudge with me than he did with LG after
their food fights. Offering him my ear after this quarrel had been a
strong statement of trust, and his eager response suggested he was as
anxious for my approval as I was for his.

By the middle of July, the cubs' primary wild foods were ants, moist
organic soil, poplar leaves, wild sarsaparilla fruits, raw and ripe red raspberries, raw and ripe blueberries, raw blackberries, and wild lettuce
leaves. The order in which the cubs showed interest in these natural
foods supported my idea that they were using their sensory organs to

identify what to eat: first they mouthed budded twigs, then the leaves, then the flowers and raw fruit, and finally they ate the ripe fruit. By this point, I was feeding each cub a cup and half dry measure of lamb's milk substitute and five sliced apples twice a day, and yes, by this time they were eating three and a half cups of dry dog food. LG weighed in at twenty-seven pounds and LB at thirty-five.

One of my projects in July was to make improvements to the cub door on the cage. When I had built the door, I had secured it with a hook and an eye on the inside. Within two weeks the cubs had figured how to undo the latch but failed to get out because they kept trying to push the door when it opened inward. But even undoing the hook and eye was impressive, since it was no simple task for the cubs. Unlike our own wrists, the cubs' wrists are quite rigid for tree climbing, so they couldn't simply rotate a paw and unhook the latch. On top of that, the cubs' natural motion was to reach out and pull toward them with their paws, which would only result in the hook staying firmly latched in the eye. Their solution, which required some real thinking, was to climb up on the bench next to the door and reach down to pull the latch toward them from above, thus lifting the hook out of the eye. Now I needed a more secure latch on the door, so in addition to the hook and eye I installed a hasp, which I fastened but didn't lock. I also attached a pull handle and wondered how long it would take for them to figure out the new system.

Not long at all. When I returned the next morning, I found the cage empty. The cubs had managed to undo both latches and pull the door inward, three coordinated movements that facilitated their escape. I was impressed. The cubs were exhibiting not only mechanical abilities but also a thought process by which they sorted out a relatively complex sequence of events.

Meanwhile, wild bear activity near the cage continued. On July 20, the cubs reacted to a scent right on the stones at the front door of the cage. LG sniffed the nearby low branches and saplings, and LB sniffed and slow-licked a spot on the leaves behind the cage, then followed with a chin-first rub. At the yellow birch "mark tree" on the way to the snowmobile trail, the cubs found more fresh scent. LG sniffed, licked, and rubbed the sides of her head and neck on the base of the tree. LB sniffed the ground, slow-licked, and did a chin-first rub. The cubs were totally absorbed in identifying the scent and equally deliberate in the ways they responded to it; I had to wonder in what other ways an animal this intelligent might be using these methods that were obviously so important to them. Were they communicating intentionally?

Several times now, I had seen the cubs' reaction whenever Alcott or I had left the group and then tried to rejoin it: they would treat us like strangers and tree until they were sure everything was all right. Finally, I got a chance to see what would happen when one of the cubs left. While working near the cage one day, I spooked LG eighty feet up one of the pine trees by the cage with the noise I made raking crushed stones. LB had also treed a short distance away but then he came down and followed me when I walked away from the cage. Feeling abandoned, LG started making her distress call, while LB sat quietly at the base of an oak tree without responding. I kept going to see if I could get him to move with me and her to follow. It worked, and she came down out of the tree and headed toward us. When they were about fifty feet apart, the two cubs suddenly saw and heard each other and "short-treed"—each cub running a few feet up separate trees. They stared at each other for a moment, then backed down onto the ground. With their ears back, they made a cautious approach, but even at a distance of just three feet they were still not confident enough to make a positive ID. Finally, stretching toward one another, they touched noses and then stuck out their tongues and touched them as well. Bingo. Full recognition. They embraced and tumbled into a joyful routine of play.

At the end of July, I had scheduled a day of filming of the cubs with John Charpentier, film producer for the New Hampshire Fish and Game Department. John and his young female assistant joined me for the morning feeding, leaving their equipment outside the cage. The cubs started their day off in the usual vigorous manner with a bear fight over food; apparently their idea of makeup before filming was an equal splattering of milk and cereal. Fortunately, the vegetation was wet from a heavy dew, and most of the mess would wash off before we got going. John was ready to start when I brought the cubs out of the cage, but the cubs had another idea: they wanted to play with the equipment. LG grabbed the pouched still camera in her mouth and headed off in one direction, while LB picked up the leather bottom to one of the knapsacks and headed into the woods in another.

Even after we got that sorted out, the day looked like it might be a bust. When the cubs weren't trying to run the video camera on its tripod, they were clinging too close to me. Three people and all that equipment seemed to be all they could handle. We finally got a break when LG found something on the ground, dug at it, then ran away shaking her head hard enough so we could hear her ears slapping the sides of her head. But after about twenty-five yards she stopped, hesitated for a moment, then ran right back to where she was digging. She repeated this performance three times. She had found a ground nest of bumblebees.

Here was a perfect opportunity to film, so we approached the nest cautiously and John set up the camera about six feet away. Fortunately for us, the bumblebees were relatively docile and seemed to be targeting only the bears, though I was a little concerned for John's assistant, who was wearing black—a bear color.

Inside the ten-inch hole that LG had dug were a bunch of angry bees, and by the time the camera was ready to roll LG had lost interest, but LB was just approaching with a high head, sniffing to see what all the fuss was about. At a distance of fifteen feet he got wind of the bees, rushed in, and jammed his head into the hole full of bees, then he began digging vigorously with his forepaws, wiggling his furry little butt as he moved his hind feet back and forth to get a better angle. The yellow-and-black bodies of the bumblebees adorned his ears like jewelry, but if the stings distracted him, it was only long enough to use his paw to clear the bees from his ears from time to time. LG came back, was immediately set upon by an angry bee, and, to lose her pursuer, made a quick pass through John's legs; busy with the camera, John didn't even notice. But the nest was well protected; despite all the digging, the cubs never did get to it. Instead both cubs gave up and relaxed near the hole they had dug, casually pulling and eating the defending bees that still clung to their fur.

Later, after the camera crew had gone, I tried to return the cubs to the cage for the night, but they stopped following me about forty yards from it. I went ahead and cleaned the cage and then called them; there was no response. Going back out, I found them in the wooded wetland area adjacent to the cage. This thicket of low, closely packed hardwood saplings and an understory of ostrich ferns provided exactly the dense cover the cubs required to feel secure. Scattered nearby were a few mature oak and pine escape trees, making this a nearly ideal wireless cage for the cubs. Their message to me was clear: we're staying out for the night. My answer to them was equally clear: I'll see you two in the morning.

As I said, I had another life.

CHAPTER 7

Nature's Bounty
and a Long Walk Home

AUGUST IS THE harbinger of the fall harvest for the black bear. The blueberries ripen in early August, the blackberries by midmonth, and before the first of September the bears will be feeding in the tree-tops for beechnuts and acorns, with apples, elderberry, and mountain ash ripening shortly thereafter. It's usually a time of feasting, but some-times late spring frosts will literally nip all this in the bud, or heavy rains will hamper pollination, or a summer drought will wither fruits or cause premature dropping of nuts. All of these problems can be local or wide-spread. But bears are flexible; their staples in a lean year are hardy species like jack-in-the-pulpit, jewelweed, wild lettuce, and bees and ants that are usually abundant and available no matter how limited the growing season.

Luckily, this was to be a year of plenty, with all signs pointing toward a bumper acorn crop and a reasonable number of beechnuts. The sarsa-parilla berries, once plentiful, were now waning, but blackberries were set on their stems, showing the first signs of ripening. The cubs and I made our way through the sugar bush to the oak stand on the south boundary of the Turnpike Lot, where LG found a tree with a lot of early acorn drops and lay down to feed. When she was done, she marked the site with several drops of urine, something that until now she had only done on another bear's scent. But neither cub's actions had indicated the presence of bear scent nearby. Was LG preparing to defend a particular food supply? Was she claiming this area as her exclusive feeding territory?

On the way back, the cubs followed me down a difficult path through the ledges on the north side of the lot. At one point, where there was a six-foot drop, I needed to get a toehold in order to let myself down. When the cubs were smaller, I would lift them over this spot, but they were big enough now to do it on their own. After a little hesitation, LB came down front first. LG tried next, but partway down she couldn't get a good foothold. Attempting another way down, she ended up on a blind ledge. Stranded, she started in with her distress call as LB and I walked away. LB immediately turned back and tried twice to get her to come along before finally going back up and showing her how to follow him, step-by-step, off the ledge. Was this another display of altruism on LB's part? It sure looked like it. He could have, as I did, stayed safely at the bottom watching to see how his sister was going to get out of the predicament. Instead, he risked his own safety by climbing back up on the steep ledge to help her.

While LG eventually would have solved this problem on her own, there certainly were other times when the danger to one or both of the cubs was very real indeed, and one of the problems I hadn't yet solved was how to communicate to them a potential danger they had not directly perceived for themselves. When my dogs would go with me on a wood-cutting trip, they were so trusting they would stay right beside me even when I fired up the chainsaw. To train them to keep a safe distance, I would have to cut a sapling big enough to scare but not to hurt them, and fell it in their direction while yelling, "Watch out! Watch out!" It would only take one demonstration for the dogs to learn this lesson, but I did have to go through the drill. The bears were different: in the same situation, they would tree at the first sound of the chainsaw. Since they so acutely perceived all tangible signs of danger, it was very difficult to convince them that a hazard existed if they hadn't detected it themselves.

On our way back to the Turnpike Lot, we passed through a newly cut clearing full of logging equipment and human smells. Here was a chance to relate the potential danger of humans in general, so I tried mimicking the "gulp" vocalization I had heard the cubs make whenever they perceived danger and were nervous. My imitation was flawed, but I made a short hard note at about the same frequency as they did and took off through the clearing at a fast walk. It worked like a charm; the cubs came with me, clinging to my heels all the way.

Later, I suspected that the openness of the logging area had helped in conveying the danger, for I used the same technique under other less stressful situations without getting anything like the same response. I think that the cubs responded not just to the vocalization but to their sense of my mood as well. My feelings of urgency had to be honest.

The next evening, I took them back to forage from the oak tops of some recently cut timber on the woodlot just south of mine. Although acorns were the main attraction, the cubs ate, as usual, a variety of foods including poplar, tall white lettuce leaves, and ants, though they also sniffed but did not eat a sulfur shelf mushroom, the much-prized "chicken of the woods" delicacy so avidly sought by human mushroom fanciers. Lately, a half hour before dark the cubs would no longer follow me, preferring to spend the night outdoors. On this night, they selected a spot in some dense spruce cover. Knowing it was time to let go but worrying nonetheless, I decided to respect their decision. I left them there and went home.

I returned for the cubs in the morning and found them about a hundred yards up the hill from where I had left them. Although it was clear that the cubs were not going to run off, and that they would be easy to find in the morning, it took me a while to get used to the idea of leaving them out. They responded to my call and eagerly followed me back to the cage to be fed.

LB was so excited about the prospect of receiving his milk supplement, he followed me from the door of the cage to the feed bowls while walking on his hind legs. With tremendous anticipation, he held his arms outstretched and spun in tight circles waiting for me to remove the cover from the bottle to feed him. He had developed a habit of putting his nose in the milk and sucking it down very quickly, whereas LG lapped hers up with her tongue. Finishing first, LB would then challenge LG for the balance of her milk, and a fight would ensue. LB would always end up with most of the milk, while his sister would get most of the dog food.

As the days passed, LB's sex drive began to develop, and the cubs' innocent game of chase now culminated with LB trying to get LG into the mating grasp: he would hug her around the thorax from behind, bite at the back of her neck, and vocalize the "sound of contentment." LG's reaction to these advances was always simply to roll away, bite at his face, or resist in some other way; in other words, she just said no. Always a gentleman, LB would back off. LB was also taking an interest in the bodily smells of my armpits and groin, which he checked on a daily basis, but LG showed no such inclination. I had to ask myself: was LB becoming sexually mature at such a young age? I knew that most wild males don't reach this point until they are three or four years old. I began to wonder what did cause sexual maturity in wild males. Size and strength? Pressure from other males? Both? Other factors?

Little did I know as I loaded the cubs into their individual transport carriers a few days later that this would be our last excursion of this kind. I drove them halfway up Finn Casperson's new haul road, a truck road built by timber companies to get better access to properties being logged. We walked from there on a twitch trail to Lyme Holdings's haul road, which had been put in seven or eight years earlier and promised to have a good blackberry crop for the cubs. It did, and they ate lots of them, picking the berries rapidly off the bushes with the prehensile front parts of their upper and lower lips. As long as there were plenty of berries, the cubs ate peacefully side by side, but when we came upon only a single bush, LG's ears would go back and she would drive LB off, snarling and biting at him. She was being territorial over her food supply. Do female bears do this only at a certain time of the year? Why was LB backing off?

Around the next bend in the trail was a large open area where fill had been excavated for road building; a vernal pool about fifteen feet in diameter had been unwittingly created here by the equipment operator. Ever since I was a kid, I've been attracted to these pools as a source of frogs, toads, and salamanders. Now as a woodlot owner I watch with vigilance as each new crop of these forest predators go forth to protect my trees from insect pests. Of all the vernal pools I've found, over the years, 50 percent were inadvertently created by humans.

This one was a welcome sight to the cubs, for they were thirsty and ready for a swim after a long walk in the hot sun. The pool was about a foot deep, and both cubs waded out into the center and sat down. Using their arms, they propelled themselves around in the sitting position. Then, as they left the water, they shook themselves to dry off, reminding me of a dog's behavior.

In order to make a loop that wouldn't retrace our tracks, the cubs and I followed a twitch trail down to the flatlands along Tinkhamtown Brook. The brook meandered through a large wet woodlands, then into several acres of dead standing timber, killed when the whole area was flooded by beaver in the early 1980s. Now there was a pristine carpet of sphagnum moss with blueberries growing on the hummocks. In this idyllic setting, the cubs lay down, both in the same bush, and individually picked off the ripe berries.

The edges of the swamp had been logged a number of years earlier and had been kept open by the heavy browsing of deer and moose. We followed a well-worn moose path, easily cutting our way through the thickets. Just off the path, the cubs found a moose bed, still hot with scent. LG very intently checked it out, taking some leaf matter into her mouth to identify the scent and sniffing the entire bed. After inspecting the area to her satisfaction, she lost interest completely.

When we got back to the truck, oblivious to what was about to happen, I put away my cameras and waited for the cubs to show some interest in getting back into their carriers. LG loaded easily, but LB gave no indication that he was going to cooperate. His avoidance was obvious as he walked in a wide circle around the truck, paying little attention to my efforts to coax him into the box. LG was getting upset and beginning to fuss because we weren't all in the truck and on our way. I needed to get moving, so when LB stuck his nose in his carrier I tried to stuff him the rest of the way in—not a good idea. His temper immediately flared into a rage. He stood up on his hind feet, then spun around with his arms raised above his head, and let out a deafening roar as he lunged at me and began to bite. But even then, enraged as he was and quite capable of seriously hurting me, his bites—though substantially harder than normal and coming so fast that I had no time to back off before his teeth were upon me again—were still restrained. I was painfully bruised but not actually injured.

Well, this was quite a learning experience. I had learned how to provoke a bear to anger and how it then behaves. But there was just one problem: even though he had quite adequately made his point, the angry bear was still roaring and not backing down. LB wanted no part of his carrier, and—weighing forty-seven pounds and standing nearly four feet tall—he certainly was going to get his way. Quickly I thought of how the cubs would settle this; in their wrestling matches, the winner was always the one who knocked the other over to establish dominance. So I leaned back and pushed LB over with my foot, firmly, but not hard enough to hurt him. If he could show restraint, so could I. And that was it; the dispute was over. LB calmed down quickly, I let LG out of her cage, and we set out on the two-hour unplanned journey on foot back to the cage.

As we walked along, LB stayed close to me, making a light moaning sound; perhaps he was uncomfortable with our altercation and was sensing my anger. LG, with her newfound and insatiable appetite, lagged behind all the way, cleaning up as many blackberries as possible. From our cottage at sugar camp, I phoned Debbie to get her to pick me up so we could retrieve my truck. As we drove home, I told her every detail of the scuffle, but still I hadn't put together the extent of the remarkable event that was taking place. Because it wasn't over yet.

When I returned the next morning, the cubs were very eager to eat and allowed me to slip out quickly and return to work after I gave them their food. At the evening feeding, after slurping down his milk replacer, LB, still moaning, grabbed my pants pocket and let me know what he needed in no uncertain terms. I leaned over, and he proceeded to suckle on my ear for about thirty seconds before returning to his meal, and then he came back for a second dose of bonding. It was unusual that he, and not she, had initiated this kind of forceful touching to reinforce our relationship. LG had been insecure and demanding of bonding ever since she came to me in April, but LB had always been independent and self-assured. Something fundamental had changed.

It really did seem to me that LB had a conscience, that he was sorry and sought reassurance after our altercation the previous day. Was it possible that an animal could have these kinds of feelings? I've always had a pretty quick red flag for anthropomorphic conjecture, but then again not many people have ever had as full a relationship with an animal as I was now developing with LB and LG. Did that make me simply more susceptible to unwarranted anthropomorphism, or did it make it possible for me to begin to see something that might actually be there?

Logic and optimism both told me that someday the ratio of questions to answers would shift in favor of the latter, but that day was nowhere near any horizon I could see from here, in the fifth month of my time with the cubs.

One overcast and drizzly morning in mid-August, I had a little time and took the cubs on a short walk. We did the loop trail to the New

Pond site and back, after which the cubs loitered outside the cage, show-ing no indication of wanting to reenter. Their message to me was clear, so I let them stay out for the day, the first time I had done this. By now I was comfortable with the fact the cubs could plan to thwart my inten-tions, but what I couldn't understand was how they communicated to each other to do so in unison.

A little concerned about them, I returned in the afternoon, called out to the cubs from the empty cage, but got no reply. I walked down to the swamp where they liked to hang out and still got no reply. Fifty yards east on the trail I called again, and finally LB appeared from behind me, very irritated, nervous, and excited. LG soon came running in from behind the boundary stone wall, agitated as well. They both hastened back to the cage ahead of me to eat. While they did, I took my usual place on the den box, expecting they would want to suckle when they were finished. LG looked up, made eye contact with me, and bounded up beside me on the bench. Bears leap with their forepaws outstretched in front of them, and LG in her excitement misjudged the distance, coming in too high and raking my neck with her claws, leaving three nasty wounds that took weeks to heal. Her sucking, like her mood, was hard and bitey; when I was sure she had none of my skin in her teeth, I put my hand on her chest and removed her with a shove. I'd sustained enough damage for one day, so I left them for the night to calm down by themselves while I sought out some topical antibiotics. I'm not positive what had stirred them up, but it was likely to have been another bear.

On our next walk to Wallow Bog, we had a guest: Eric Orff, a senior wildlife official with the New Hampshire Fish and Game Department and a veteran bear biologist. Traveling with two cubs is slow, and it took us nearly an hour to reach the bog. At the entrance, along the game trail, the cubs located a bear tree: a six-inch-diameter black spruce that had all of the limbs facing the trail broken off, with bear hair imbedded in its bark to a height of about five and a half feet. According to the cubs, the bear scent was still hot. Besides the scent on the tree, they followed scent on vegetation at about the two-foot level and on the spruce limbs over-hanging the trail, as they rambled ahead of us.

The water in the wallow was clear, and there was a partial bear track in the mud at its edge. Within six feet of it, the cubs found another mark tree. This one was a small black spruce that also had all of its branches on the trailside broken and its top bitten off at about six feet several years earlier; a new top had regenerated. Bear hairs were stuck in the bark, and it too, according to the cubs, was covered with fresh scent.

Our next destination was the Marshall Brook haul road, to pick blackberries. LG was the most persistent forager, but Eric, who had forgotten his lunch, came in a close second. I had told Eric that the cubs wouldn't eat amphibians or reptiles or any insects but the social ones, and how I thought that the cubs identified what to eat. He had already noticed that they didn't respond to the movements of insects and frogs as they walked and had tested them with a red eft (the land stage of the red-spotted newt), a bark beetle larvae, and a large earthworm; all of his offerings were refused. Instead the menu for the cubs on this outing included blackberries, hobble bush fruits, all three types of lettuce, jewelweed, purple aster, and fresh deer and moose droppings. Eric stuck with the blackberries.

At the end of six hours, the cubs ran willingly back into their cage. I asked Eric what he thought of the bear project. "I learned more about bears in the last six hours than I have in the past twenty years," he said. That was more of an answer than I could have hoped for!

Other than gunsmithing, one of my summer projects had been to sort out the property lines on my back boundary. There were three small lots back there, composed almost entirely of vertical ledge, which had been in and out of my deeds so many times I wasn't sure of their status. But I had found a description of the line that separated my lot from the three, and I wanted to check it with a compass. It was a Sunday and I had plenty of time, so I stopped by the cage to get my two helpers.

Where my upper sugar bush trail meets the boundary trail, there is a couple-of-acres patch of low dense spruce and hardwood whips that never failed to get the cubs to run wild. Whether they were following me cautiously through the open hardwood or shifting into high gear and running way out ahead in a reckless game of chase in this spruce thicket, clearly it was cover density and height that governed the cubs' sense of security. Wherever we traveled, the cubs behavior was controlled by the density of the vegetation.

The cubs' next point of interest was the bear tree on the corner of the lot. On our approach, the cubs ran wild in the low spruce thicket that surrounded this mark tree. LB ran up and leaped, hanging momentarily on the tree before losing interest, dropping off, and running down to the small wallow pond for a drink and a bath. Now LG came to the mark tree, sniffed audibly, rubbed her neck and head at the base of the tree, and then, turning her neck, she bit and scratched at the bark before climbing to the old scars and biting at the hardened sap. The whole display lasted several minutes, and when she was done she dropped down from the tree and marked the spot immediately in front of it with a dribble of urine. Both cubs were detecting plenty of bear scent on the vegetation. They followed the bear path along the bog to a smaller mark tree, which they both quickly climbed.

My surveying duties started at this corner. I had a bearing and would tie bits of yellow surveyor's ribbon on selected trees to mark my course. The cubs figured out quickly how to help: they removed the ribbons behind me as I progressed. In fact they had such a fondness for surveyor's ribbon, they made the "sound of contentment" while they chewed on it. Fortunately, my assistants found the hobble bush berries equally inter-esting, so a few of my ribbon markers did survive. I might note that plas-tic ribbon passes very nicely through a bear's system.

Just above the pass through the ledges on the north side of the lot, the cubs hit fresh bear scent on the vegetation. A slight breeze came up the ridge toward us, and both cubs took off with high heads following the scent into the wind. When I caught up with them, I found LG sniffing a large bear scat in a dense thicket of red spruce; nearby I found five other scats, all vegetative with a scattering of hobble bush berries. I broke up some of the droppings with my fingers to see if I could figure out what kind of green food the bear had been eating. Things were pretty well digested so I didn't have a clue, but the scat did have a distinctive smell like tobacco. There were three recently used beds, suggesting that a large male had spent at least three days here feeding on the mystery plants.

The next day on our way back to the Waterbury Lot, LG discovered a bear-marked spot on the sugaring road. She went through her usual antics with head and neck rolls, thoroughly covering the top of her head, sides and back of her neck with the scent, while LB stood by with no apparent interest. I got down on my knees and sniffed. Along with some very earthy smells, I detected a strong odor of urine. Once we reached the Waterbury Lot, the cubs found no new bear scent, so I decided we would head up to the fourth level to see if we could figure out what type of vegetation was in the bear scats we had found at the bed site on that level.

We made our way to the base of Holt's Ledge to look for what the big bear might have been feeding on. I watched as LB worked a scent trail up a fallen log to the base of a wet ledge outcropping where he located a large scat. After checking it out myself, I looked up and saw the cubs on the wet stream bank eating the remains of a jewelweed patch that had been ravaged by a wild bear. There were large bear tracks scarring the moss, and a path had formed at the base of the ledge; there the jewel-weed was mangled and stripped of leaves, with only a foot of bare stem remaining. The mystery of the tobacco-smelling scats had been solved.

But now there was a larger concern, at least in my mind if not in the cubs'. Where had that big bear been hiding while we were stomping around in his larder, the one he had been using nonstop for the last four days? Was he close? Had we been watched?

It seemed almost a certainty.

CHAPTER 8

Mysteries, Gunfire, and the Escape Artist

E ARLY IN SEPTEMBER, Frosty Hammond came back for another walk with the cubs and me. Staying in the softwood strip on the crest of the great granite ledge that leads up the pass onto the fourth level, we followed a freshly worn bear trail that still had large, new tracks in the leaves. Reminded of the deep, clearly defined, permanent bear tracks that had been so evident at the bear tree on the corner that spring, I asked Frosty if he had ever seen anything like them.

"Oh, sure," he replied. "I've seen them at bait sites, but I don't know what to make of them."

I nodded. Ben Hudson, a local forester, had just the week before told me about finding a bear wallow in a cedar swamp that had well-defined footsteps cut into the moss. "Neither do I," I replied to Frosty. "But I'd really like to know how they're made."

While we had been talking, the cubs had disappeared, and we had to backtrack to find them. They were moving along, sniffing scent in the brush, and soon they led us to a new red pine bear tree, leading to and from which was an unmistakable set of sunken bear tracks. Frosty and I looked at each other and shook our heads. Had the cubs been listening to us? Bear trees, wallows, bait sites. I wondered: Are sunken tracks a bear's way of marking places of interest? Do they mean something? Or do they just reflect a lot of bear traffic?

Leaving the great ledge, we passed through a stand of hardwoods that had no understory. The cubs started to play—or so I thought—as they faced off on the ground with their mouths open, then stood up with their mouths still open, their arms outstretched, and, in a very sumolike contest, pushed and twisted each other back and forth until LG was tipped over and pinned. The wrestling match was repeated four times in ten minutes, with LB the winner every time. Was this just play, or was it a test of dominance? If the latter, was this test developed over time so that two strange bears—possessing more than enough ability to do per-manent harm to each other—could establish dominance without injury? Were the cubs practicing this behavior in play to prepare themselves for the real thing later on? Or was LB simply trying to maintain rank over LG?

Questions, questions, questions.

A week later, Alcott Smith came back for another walk, and we took the deer trail that crosses the upper end of the old beaver meadow. The half-acre meadow, created when the beaver moved out three or four years before, was aglow with purple aster and goldenrod already begin-ning to show their autumn color. The three-foot height of the riotous vegetation provided just enough cover for the cubs to run ahead, play, and forage on jewelweed, blackberries, and cattail. The small stream that meanders through the area was crisscrossed with fallen logs and proved a delight to the cubs as they chased each other, wallowed in the water, and walked on the logs, a habit seemingly irresistible to them.

On the upper edge of the clearing I found a path with more of the mysterious sunken bear tracks. The cubs joined me and took the lead in tracking fresh bear scent on the bushes, following an invisible path that led directly to another new bear tree, this one a large red spruce. LB sniffed and slow-licked, LG sniffed, rubbed her neck on the bark, and climbed six feet up the trunk to check out scents, then dropped down and marked the area in front of the tree with urine. The sunken tracks, both coming and going from the tree, were unmistakable but disap-peared within thirty feet. There was spruce pitch oozing from an old natural wound on the tree, but none of the scarring that we had seen on the red pine bear trees.

From the beaver meadow we climbed a steep slope covered with hemlock, spruce, and intermittent hardwoods, then traversed a stand of yellow birch and beech before arriving at Wallow Bog. Immediately the cubs detected fresh bear scent. Completely absorbed in the smell, they thoroughly worked out the details of the last visitor to the bog. This bear, perhaps a male, had them worried, for after marking the black spruce by the wallow they came to me emitting a persistent "irritated moan" while standing on their hind legs and pulling on my clothing. I knew what they wanted, and after they had reassured themselves with a few minutes of suckling on my ears their behavior returned to normal for the rest of the journey.

On the way back, we found mountain ash covered with large clusters of orange berries growing near the ledge outcroppings. LG defended them fiercely by roaring loudly, flattening her ears, and running at LB; if he didn't move quickly enough, she would then bite him to make sure he got the message. With the consistency of her defense of any food supply and her corresponding weight gain, I wondered if all female bears behaved this way in the fall. And why not? Shouldn't females take priority when high-quality food is available to ensure the weight gain they would need in order to carry, bear, and nurse their cubs through the long winter of hibernation? And didn't it make equal sense for male bears, even though they were bigger and stronger and had already established physical domination the way LB had over LG, to stand aside and let that happen? Exactly the way LB was now doing? To me it did. The more time I spent with these two as they developed, the less random their actions seemed.

On the other hand, LB hadn't moved all the way into the backseat when it came to food. Far from it; if there was one thing that LB really cherished, it was his daily share of milk supplement. Whenever I came into the cage carrying the milk bottle, he would stand upright and run along in front of me in hopes of getting it all. Driven by this anticipation and impatience, LB would do pirouettes with his arms held high and back over his head, all the time uttering his "hungry moan," as I unscrewed the bottle top. Then he would bully the bottle all the way to the bowl, trying to get an early taste, and if I turned or tried to step away, he would reach out with his clawed paws to grab my leg, an act that had progressed from cute to annoying to difficult as he had grown. By now, he weighed almost sixty pounds and stood nearly four feet tall.

The cubs were usually loose when I arrived to feed them and would come to greet me when I called out, then run ahead of me and into the cage through the cub door and wait for me while I unlatched and came through the main door. Eventually, LB devised a scheme in his endless attempts to get it all: He would let LG head toward the cub door as usual, then he would scoot through the main door, charge back to the cub door, and barricade it with his body trying to prevent me from unlatching it to let LG in. While she then attempted to tear the door off its hinges, I'd have to muscle LB out of the way in order to open the latch. On one occasion he actually started lunging at me after I let LG in, not only to get at his food but also apparently to punish me for spoiling his plan. I had to use my foot to push him over—a tactic I had learned in our earlier transport cage bout—and he calmed down immediately. Again, as with all of their almost daily bear fights, once the fight was over, it was over. There was neither retribution nor any hint of lingering animosity.

Nevertheless, this was getting a bit out of hand. LB was growing dangerously larger every day, and it was only a matter of time before I got hurt in one of these fracases. So I decided it was time to wean LB from the milk supplement. The next morning, I arrived without it. First he thoroughly checked out the pail full of apples and then turned, standing on his hind legs and emitting the "hungry moan," to mug me for the formula. I was body-searched with his nose, and when he was convinced that I had nothing hidden, he simply turned away to eat his apples and dog food.

LB followed me as I started out on a walk a couple of days later, while LG remained a few more minutes in the cage to clean up every scrap of food. As we walked up the rather steep road that switches back up through the sugar bush, the cubs fed on acorns, spikenard berries, and purple flowering raspberries growing in the disturbed soil at the edges of the trail. All the while, LB continued his low irritated moan and at one point came up behind me on his hind legs and bit my fanny pack hard while vigorously shaking his head. For the last two walks he had behaved in this same unhappy way, and I began to suspect that it had something to do with weaning him from the milk. He now came back with a deliberate "slow-bite" to my belly, the second time he had done this in two days. It hurt, so I pushed him away with my hand and then over onto his back with my foot. Then, feeling sorry for him and thinking he might need some reassurance, I let him suckle my ear. He didn't try to bite me anymore, but his irritated moan persisted. Self-preservation being the mother of wisdom, I decided that I would bring back his milk formula in the morning.

LB's mood meter immediately swung back to normal, and our daily walks were once again a pleasant affair. It didn't take long for the cubs to teach me their next lesson: it was time, apparently, for me to learn where all those sunken bear tracks came from.

While walking on Calvin Waterbury's land in the middle of September, the cubs found some fresh bear scent and began following it onto a high granite knoll and down the adjoining ridge. LG tracked it to a scraggly red pine with low dead limbs and no obvious bear signs, then sniffed and slow-licked it, climbed up one body length, bit the bark, and dropped off. She then did something she had never shown me before: locking her legs into full extension as she moved forward, she did a slow, deliberate, "stiff-legged" walk as she ground her paws into the duff with each step. She did this so hard that her body shook with each impression she made on the forest floor. Later, at a second red pine farther along the ridge, she repeated her performance. LB did none of this, nor did he respond to either tree, even though he did spend ten minutes following the scent up and down the ledge. At one point, he lay down on a small patch of thick moss and did a genital drag, a recurring action since the emergence of his testicles.

At the weigh-in a few days later, both cubs were at a full sixty pounds. After eating, LB climbed onto my lap and went to sleep; he used to do this a lot when he was small, but now he was quite a lapful. When he woke up, we took a short walk in Cole's swamp. LG responded to something about sixty yards from the cage with heavy sniffing, followed by the stiff-legged walk and then marking with urine. I took a look to see why she was acting this way and found a wild bear scat. It was two days old, judging by its light coat of mold, lack of maggots, and consistency with two-day-old cub scats I'd seen at the cage. Suddenly, all the marking LG had been doing at the cage over the last three days made sense; a wild bear had been visiting in the night.

We then left the area of the cage and continued our walk to the bear tree on the corner. The cubs were behind me when we arrived. The sunken footprints that led up to it caught my eye, and upon inspection I noticed there were very fresh scuffmarks within them, made by a bear with about a four-inch pad! I knew the scent was going to be hot, so I positioned myself where I could watch and take pictures of the cubs as they approached the tree. Both were sniffing the lower limbs of the small spruces with great scrutiny, and LB rose on his hind legs to mark some of the limbs that overhung the trail. At the tree he sniffed and rubbed a little before losing interest and coming over to lie down at my side. LG, on the other hand, showed tremendous interest in the tree: heavy sniffing, slow-licking, and rubbing with her neck, head, and back. When she was done rubbing on the tree, she aligned herself with the sunken footprints and began to display her stiff-legged walk. With each step her straightened legs forced her front feet forward and hard into the ground, leaving scuffmarks as she walked. At the same time, she dripped, dribbled, and gushed urine to mark the occasion. Twenty feet from the tree, she turned and marched past the tree and down the sunken trail thirty feet in the other direction. Then she repeated the performance, passing the bear tree a total of six times.

Here was the answer. Although LG's stride couldn't yet match the sunken tracks, which were made by mature bears, she clearly showed how those tracks were made. Walking normally, a bear will leave no sign on the forest floor. The stiff-legged walk was something else; now I could see it was designed to leave tracks. Or to match ones that were already there. Based on LB's lack of interest and LG's reaction to the estrous urine mark—a known female mark—on an earlier walk, I further deduced that the fresh scuffmarks had been made by a female bear.

But what was the significance of this display? Was it done only by females? Were the sunken tracks visual clues to important bear places: bear trees, wallows, food areas, and the like? Was the function of the stiff-legged walk just to make sunken tracks at important bear places, or was this display done in other places as well?

Early in October, Donald Normandeau joined me for a walk with the cubs. As the director of the New Hampshire Fish and Game Department, he was the one who had made this whole experience possible. LB greeted him with a quick sniff and a full back rub, making him part of our group. This greeting wasn't as peremptory and accepting as might seem to us. With the sniff LB noted that this was a stranger, and with the back rub LB put his own scent signature on him so he would be of no further concern.

The cubs started out from the cage a little too frisky, running, grabbing onto me and biting, settling down only when they started foraging on acorn drops. Our destination was the corner bear tree, where I knew the cubs would put on a good performance. Plus it was important to me to return with the cubs to this tree as often as possible to document the constantly changing intensity and variety of displays by each of the cubs.

The conditions for our hike were near perfect, with blue skies, a cool temperature, and the foliage nearly at its peak. My guest and I felt privileged to have two black bears as escorts into a portion of their lives.

Watching the cubs, I could tell that the bear tree was hot with scent, as both cubs sniffed, slow-licked, and rubbed their necks on the bark and the surrounding vegetation. LB did his first stiff-legged walk—answering one of my lingering questions about this whole process—and LG did as well, but neither walk came close to the exaggerated display put on by LG during our previous trip to this tree. In fact it was LB who showed the stronger reaction to today's new scent and finished off with a full-scale back rub. On our return to the cage, we hit more scent in the sugar bush; both cubs sniffed and did the stiff-legged walk, and LG marked the spot with urine. There was also a fresh scat with blackberry seeds in it, left during the rain the night before.

Our walk ended at two in the afternoon, and I returned at half past six for the evening feeding. While I was gone, a bear with a four-and-a-quarter-inch pad, probably a young male, had made tracks in the loose soil on the path to the cage. The cubs spooked and huffed on my arrival but calmed down with the sound of my voice. After they were fed, I left them in the cage for the night.

When I returned the next morning, again the cubs spooked and huffed on my approach, and again calmed down with my greeting. Exiting through the door when I opened it, both cubs went into a stiff-legged walk when they hit scent just thirty feet from the door of the cage. LB defecated in the center of the trail, and LG urinated, both in response to the scent, which they detected throughout the area around the cage. An acorn and vegetative scat—just hours old judging by the oxidation of the acorns—less than seventy yards from the cage let me know I had again just missed the visiting bear. I found his tracks in the mud on the snowmobile trail and in the sand on the beach of the pond, where the bear had also rolled over my canoe and finished the corn in my wood-duck trap.

A few days later, the cubs were eager to leave the cage after eating only a small amount of their morning meal. Once out of the cage, they started to play, running, chasing, wrestling, and climbing and leaping on me. Soon they were on top of the cage chasing each other around on the two-by-fours that held up the wire. At one point, LG turned to fight off LB, and both cubs lost their balance, slipping off onto the wire, which gave way. LG started to drop through but just caught on with her claws. I ran in and helped her down, but now there was a gaping hole in the top of the cage. Always on the lookout for an experiment, I decided to leave this opening to see how long it would take them to make their escape through it. After going on a short walk with the cubs so they could forage for acorns, I locked them in and left them for the day.

Returning at five o'clock, I found the cubs gone. Evidently, they had escaped shortly after I left in the morning, as their food was unfinished and there were no scats in the cage. I called them from the cage and, when they didn't immediately respond, returned to my truck down by the sugar house to get a hammer and some staples to fix the hole. I met the cubs coming from the ledges beyond the snowmobile trail, and they followed me to the truck. LB climbed in the back and found a plastic bag coated with tomato sauce that I had left there after putting table scraps out for the wild ravens. Before I could stop him, he had licked up the tomato sauce and swallowed the plastic bag. I returned the cubs to the cage, where they ate only a little supper; their stomachs were apparently full from eating acorns all day.

I didn't get a chance to staple the wire until the next morning, but apparently the cubs had eaten too much to make a second escape overnight. I started but couldn't finish the repair, as I needed to go back to town to get some wire ties to secure the open seam between the two pieces of welded wire. When I returned in the evening, LB had escaped by reaching up from the interior climbing structure and squeezing through the seam, leaving LG in the cage. On top of that, I had forgotten the wire ties. After one more escape I finally remembered to bring along the wire ties but, wanting to see what he would do next, I decided to wire up just the widened hole LB had been using for his exit. LB arrived back to the cage after I had finished doing this, and when he entered the cage, he stood upright and slowly walked around in a circle with his eyes fixed on the new repair, apparently inspecting my handiwork. The next night he simply escaped farther down the seam.

This time, I needed the stepladder to make the repair, and LB was on hand to supervise. When I climbed one side of the ladder, he climbed the other, taking a great deal of interest in what I was doing. I was equally interested in what he was thinking, so again I repaired only the hole he had just used, leaving him one more opportunity for escape. LB, only a few feet away must have thought, "Boy, this guy's not too smart. I can still get out."

That night he took advantage of the last unwired seam, and the next morning he observed its repair as well, by climbing up the back side of the ladder for the second time. Once I was done, he went outside the cage and climbed on top, carefully walking on only the two-by-four rafters with a lowered head as if he really were inspecting the remaining seams. Was he?

Was it possible, with all the interest he had taken in the repairs over the last couple of days, that his actions were motivated by some sort of directed thought process? Why was he so interested from one day to the next? Just because I was doing it, or also because he was curious about the repairs themselves? Could he know in advance he had something to gain? Had LB observed, planned, and executed his escapes from the cage over a period of days?

CHAPTER 9

Bear Hunters and
Late-Night Dining

As I was leaving to feed the cubs one day in early October, I was surprised by somebody walking up our back driveway. It was Robert Perkins, a wilderness adventurer-filmmaker and an old friend of ours whom I hadn't seen in several years. I asked him if his car had broken down. He said no, but he had left his canoe down by the river and had walked up to see us. It turned out he was making a solo television documentary, which he called "Home Waters," about paddling alone from the headwaters of the Connecticut River, 180 river miles north of Lyme, all the way to the sea, another 230 miles. He was very excited to hear about my bear project and readily accepted an invitation to go out with me to feed and walk with them.

Pulling out his small video camera, Rob started interviewing me as soon as we got into the truck. The cubs and I were on our way, it seemed, to a featured role in the production.

But Rob also wanted to get something off his chest, something that had been bothering him for the last few days. Eighty or so miles upriver, in Lancaster, he had met a bear hunter who had just shot a large bear in a cornfield "just to shoot it" and had no plans either to eat it or use its head or hide. The experience had clearly upset Rob, and for most of the ride out to the cubs' cage that's all he wanted to talk about. I listened without saying much.

The cubs were in the cage as we arrived, and when I opened the door they rushed to greet the stranger, or so it appeared to him. Of course, in reality, with the aid of their noses and other chemically sensitive organs in their mouths, they were just giving him a good going over. Once their assessment was made, LB marked Rob with his now customary back rub.

With the cubs walking at my side, Rob asked me if I didn't agree that bear hunters were a pretty horrible lot. I surprised him by saying no, because, as I went on to say, I understood the critical role that hunters as a group play in the management of wildlife populations. As repugnant as the attitude of a particular hunter may be, the actions of that individual are no more an indictment of hunters as a group than they are of society as a whole; there are good guys and bad guys in every mix. As for hunters as a whole, they further the goals of the wildlife manager, who seeks to protect populations of animals from becoming either so small that they are no longer viable or so large that starvation and disease can threaten the population as a whole. Incidental conflicts between bears and humans, bear damage to crops, and society's fear of bears in general are the social and cultural forces that work hardest to reduce bear populations all across the country. But it's the fee-paying hunters, ironically, who fund the professional wildlife management that work hardest to *increase* bear populations. In my opinion, I told Rob, until we get a better-educated and more bear-tolerant public among the growing suburban populations rapidly advancing on the remaining black bear habitat in the eastern United States, I believe the least of our concerns should be the habits of licensed hunters.

After our brief political discourse Rob and I, like the cubs, calmed down quickly and proceeded to the bear tree on the corner. There was a heavy cloud cover, and we got caught in some brief rain showers. The wet leaves produced brilliant color patterns on the forest floor but made the steep climb through the ledges a bit treacherous for Rob and me. For the cubs, the footing wasn't a problem at all, nor was the rain. Their long guard hairs captured most of the water, which they would then simply shake away; their soft, lightly oiled inner wool prevented even the notion of water from reaching their skin. Impervious to the weather, the cubs foraged leisurely on acorns as we made our ascent.

At the mark tree, both cubs sniffed, licked, rubbed, and bit. LB did a short stiff-legged walk and LG did a stiff-legged display, walking past the tree twice and marking nearby with urine. While the motion of stiff-legged walking is always the same, the energy put into it is highly variable. LG's display in mid-September had been very exaggerated and forceful; today's were far less so, leading me to ask the same continuing questions: Were the cubs reacting to different bears on different days? To different bears on the same day? To the same bear but to older scent? And do they respond differently to male and female scent, young bear and old?

These were questions that I knew I had to answer, so a few days after Rob's visit, I ordered a TrailMaster 1500 active infrared counting device that could be set to count only bear-sized animals. It would also tell me the date and time the infrared beam was tripped, and it could be rigged to trigger a camera as well. After setting up just the TrailMaster on the bear tree and testing it without the camera for a week to be sure that it was working consistently, I decided it was time to install the camera. I called Alcott Smith and asked him to come along as a distraction.

At the tree LG began with a full stiff-legged display, parading by it three times, and both cubs marked a dead spruce by arching their backs to rub against it. After all that, LB did a full back rub on the mark tree. This was pretty hot activity, which the trail timer explained: a wild bear had been there only thirty minutes before we arrived. Alcott moved ahead with the cubs, while I set up the camera. Now I really wanted to find out which bear was using this tree.

In mid-October, Conservation Officer Fred Oleson dropped off a road-killed deer that I had requested so I could plant it in the woods to see how the cubs would respond to it. They followed me from the cage and became very cautious as soon as they encountered the strange smell in the air. LG moved toward the carcass rather quickly, sniffing until she got only a foot away. Evidently that was enough; she turned and ran as fast as she could to the safety of a large oak a hundred feet away. LB took a more cautious approach, circling downwind, standing upright to catch the scent in the breeze, then moving forward with curiosity before retreating completely to the base of a large red maple. All this time, LG kept the trunk of the oak between her and the dead deer, peering out with only her head exposed, vocalizing a nervous "wwoOoww," until joining LB in the final retreat.

I brought the cubs back by the carcass in the evening, watching as they approached the rotting venison from downwind. This time, they both stood up to pick the smell out of the air, then took refuge behind a large red maple while only peeking out at the danger. When I got them back to the cage, some of the scent drifted in on the wind, sending both cubs up a tree, responding to this unknown but potent smell much as they had earlier with fermenting poplar, moose, and—when they were very young—a porcupine. A prudent approach that only time and experience, it seemed, would teach them to adjust.

On the morning of October 20, I heard severe chipmunk scolding coming from the second level as I arrived at the cage. The forest was so alive with the sound, it was hard to believe that a chorus of small mammals could put on such a commanding performance. I've heard chipmunks scold hawks, owls, deer, and even me, but this was of a much greater intensity. My first impulse was to follow the sound and see what it was, but I knew that never worked; the animal they railed at would always be gone when I got there. Besides, the chipmunks would only start scolding me, and I'd end up chasing my own ghost.

Instead, I continued to the cage to find the cubs nowhere in sight. I called for more than ten minutes until LB appeared from the direction of the second level, where I had heard the scolding. He was definitely the culprit, but why the excitement? Not only was he a regular around here, but I'd never seen the cubs make a serious move toward a small mammal. LG had not yet arrived, so I continued calling. It was noisy that morning, and the sound of chainsaws from the logging operation on the Cole lot was making it difficult for me to hear. Through all the commotion, however, I heard a distant distress call from LG. LB and I set out to find her. As we closed in on her call, we heard LG's distinct "rrOOOww, rrOOOww!" She was stationed at the base of an oak tree, unwilling to move until I got to her. She greeted me with the sound of contentment and wanted immediately to do a bit of suckling on my neck. It was nice to be needed.

When we ventured up to the ravine below the bear tree on the corner, the cubs encountered more fresh bear scent. LG ran and hid, while LB tracked the scent trail up through the ledges. This was our first trip here since the leaves had dropped, and looking up the ravine, I could see two more red pines, each with crooked tops. Damaged tops seem to be another trait common to bear trees, both large and small. All four bear trees on this level of ledge are damaged this way, and most of the small red spruce mark trees I've found have had their tops bitten out. Near these trees I noticed a disruption of the leaves that appeared to have been made by a stiff-legged walk, and a drag mark in the leaves that was two feet wide, six to eight feet long, and very fresh. It looked like a genital drag, so I called LB and LG over so I could see how they reacted to the sign and the scent. LG got there first, sniffed the tracks and the surrounding brush, then froze in her tracks. When LB arrived on the scene, he took an immediate interest in the tracks, following them back to the bear tree. I could tell by the tracks in the leaves that a fair-sized bear had spent a considerable amount of time at this tree.

I left the cubs foraging for acorns while I walked off to check my camera setup at the main bear tree on the corner. There had been only one triggering since I had checked the camera on October 17; when I got the film processed, I found that a bear had set the camera off at a quarter past eleven on the night of October 19, and from his photograph I could tell he was a large male. This confirmed my assumption about the drag mark. It made sense that LB would be much more interested in male scent at this time of year than female scent. Now that I had determined the sex of the bear involved, I had some extremely valuable information. While I was still unclear as to all the ramifications of olfactory communication in bears, clearly pieces of the puzzle were beginning to fit together.

It was raining when I arrived at the cage on the evening of October 21. After feeding the cubs and cleaning the cage, I took them out on a short walk to forage for acorns. Both were quietly picking up one acorn at a time, when LB started digging, unearthing a stash of fifty-one acorns, a chipmunk's food supply for the oncoming winter. The harsh scolding LB received from the chipmunk chorus the other day now made sense; he had been competing with them for food. But LB didn't eat the acorns that he dug up; he left them there and ate only the cleaner ones lying on top of the leaves.

As night approached, the cubs followed me back to the cage. I had every intention of locking them up for the night, but LB had another idea. He made a break for it, and LG followed suit; the two of them then ran off into the woods for a night out in the rain. The next morning, I came back and locked them in for the day. They didn't like it, and neither did I. But we were in the middle of the three-month-long bear-hunting season.

The morning of October 23 was bright and clear with high thin clouds, a perfect day for photography and an even better one for a walk to Wallow Bog. We left late in the morning because it was bear-hunting season. If we made an earlier start and crossed the road before the bear hunters and their dogs came down it, the latter might catch our scent, follow our trail, and even chase us. LB and I made the crossing easily, but LG stopped at the base of a tree on the edge of the road and was not about to move. I called repeatedly and finally persuaded her to cross. She made it across the road, only to stop at the base of the first tree she came to. LB and I continued on, hoping that she would follow, but no such luck. Clinging to her tree, she repeatedly uttered her distress call. Two cars went by on the road; she hid behind the tree for the first but was in plain view for the second. Fortunately, the people were looking straight ahead and driving too fast to notice her. LB and I returned to rescue her and found the cause of the problem: a hog's hide that had been dumped at the end of the turnout. A wild bear had hauled it into a low spruce thicket and had eaten a portion of it the previous night. LG followed us closely as we moved away from the tree.

The wallow had relatively fresh bear tracks in the mud at its edge, and the water was free of debris, indicating recent use. While LG checked out the current odors on the small marked spruce tree near the pool, LB floated the front half of his body in the wallow. He reached down to determine the depth, and finding it was deeper than he expected, he backed out. As he stood up, with the small spruce tree that hung over the game trail covering his head and shoulders, he grabbed the green branches with his paws and used them to scrub his neck, shoulders, and upper back, making sure they got a liberal dose of his scent.

When the serious business of sniffing and marking was over, the cubs ran wild, running down the bear paths under the bog's low vegetation, chasing and wrestling with each other, and climbing trees. The dense thicket of black spruce, mountain holly, and black huckleberry with its carpet of sphagnum moss was an ideal setting for cub relaxation.

We left the bog and made our way up through the ledges, across the abandoned log road that was growing up with hardwood saplings and blackberries, to the twitch trail that would lead us to the stand of oak and beech. The white-tailed buck whose sign I had been following for the past five years had scraped the ground in a number of spots to attract a mate, signifying the beginning of the rut. Many of the acorns had already been eaten at the first small stand of oak, forcing the cubs to work hard for their food.

After a while LB made an irritated moan, but this time it was not because of another bear. He was just tired and wanted to nap. As I stood vigilant, LG continued to forage while LB made a nest next to a fallen log; when he was comfortable, LG sauntered over and joined him. They looked so comfortable, I decided to take a little nap too, even though I knew what would happen when I did. Sure enough, within five minutes LG was suckling on my neck and LB on my left ear. I always took a chance when I allowed suckling away from the cage. For if the cubs were to get spooked, I'd get spiked as they clawed away to the nearest tree. This time, however, I had a different problem. At one point LG put her paw over the ear that LB was suckling, and an immediate fight erupted, with LB roaring and biting LG, and LG responding by roaring and biting right back, then running over my shoulder to chase LB off. I ended up unscathed, but it's never a pleasant experience to be right in the middle of a bear fight.

Over the next week, my trail timer and camera continued recording activity on the corner red pine, the main bear tree, and the time-stamped pictures finally made sense of the mixed messages I had gotten from LB and LG there. At least four bears were coming in to feed in the same stand of oaks. The largest male always arrived between ten at night and two in the morning, the most secure feeding time, while the others worked around his advantage in declining order of stature. By leaving their scent, the bears were sorting things out. They had worked out a way to share this favored acorn supply with a minimum of tooth and fang. With oaks throughout my property, why were the bears sharing this spot? Why weren't they eating acorns near the sugar house or on the second level? Was it the security of the third level that the bears were sharing? Were they cooperating?

Slowing Down

B Y THE BEGINNING of November, a thin blanket of snow had fallen, the first of the season. For the cubs, it was the first snow they had ever seen. Little things, like seeing my footprints for the first time, kept them busy as they had to check each one out for scent. The deer-hunting season was on, and before the cubs discovered them, I saw Karl Wing's footprints in the upper sugar bush, where Karl had told me he might try for a buck. I wondered if the cubs would be able to distinguish his bootprints from mine.

They could and immediately did, with a combination of caution, fear, and curiosity. Both cubs made nervous gulps, huffed, then ran and short-treed. But after seeing and smelling that there was no immediate danger, they came back to investigate by following the trail, sniffing each print and every sapling, branch, and tree that Karl's clothing had touched. After giving the cubs enough time to assess the situation, I made my imitation of the gulp and started away in the other direction. The cubs quickly followed, delighted to be out in the newly fallen snow, ranging widely, and making no effort to forage. LB climbed up the steep bank in the middle section of the sugar bush and slid down, dragging his hind legs and propelling himself with his front legs. This genital drag appeared to be a boy thing, as I hadn't yet seen LG do it.

We made our way through the ledges to visit the main bear tree, but there were no wild bear tracks in the snow and the cubs had only a token interest in the tree and its site, confirming that their main concern was with bear scent, not the site itself. The only acorns that the cubs found to forage on were in areas free of snow at the bases of oak trees.

We were in the ledges just above Tyler Road when, a hundred yards away, a four-wheeler went blasting by, scaring the cubs to short-tree. They refused to move until the noise was gone. We then followed a deer trail down through the ledges until we hit a fresh deer track. I could see where the deer had fidgeted in the snow as the four-wheeler passed, then ran off, probably scared by us. The cubs savored a snack of fresh deer scat.

Under one of their favorite food trees, the cubs searched hard for acorns. They tried to sniff the acorns through an inch of snow but couldn't; they had to paw through the snow before they were able to find them by smell. Despite their efforts, they were only marginally success-ful, and I wondered if success hinged on remembering where the nuts had been before the snow fell. Perhaps they now would have to feed where they could see other animals, like deer, had fed in the snow. Or maybe there was some other means of telling where the food trees were?

By November 7, the snow had melted, and Alcott and I took the cubs into the ledges for a walk. Following the cubs, we found the freshly used bed site of a wild bear hidden in a well-drained depression near the edge of a ledge, with good escape possibilities and surrounded by low spruce cover. There were fresh bite marks a foot and a half up a pair of oak saplings and two fresh scats nearby. Both cubs sniffed and slow-licked, indicating fresh bear scent. LG arched then rubbed her back on one of the oak saplings; she also bit on it. In fact, before she had even entered the bed site, LG had bite-marked and rubbed a small striped maple about fifteen feet away.

Farther down the ridge, large bear scats lined the game trail that goes down the crest of the ridge, and several were filled with deer hair. We followed it until LB's keen nose located a bear trail that led down over the southwest face of the ridge. Leading the way, he moved slowly down this second trail, carefully analyzing scent on all the hardwood saplings and spruce limbs that bordered the path. Halfway down the side of the ridge, the path ended, and LB took a hard left into a spruce thicket. Fighting my way in, I found him checking out another bear bed site, complete with a fresh deer hair and acorn scat at each end. At the edge of the thicket there was a large spruce tree that bore some scent and looked as if it had been climbed.

Alcott and I made a loop around the bed site, thinking we might find a deer carcass, but at some point in our forty-minute excursion we lost the cubs. I called and called, with no response. Taking a little time to think, I remembered how content they had seemed while feeding where the wild bears had fed, back up the ridge by the bear tree. Indeed they were both there, happily foraging. There were plenty of acorns in other places, so I wondered why the cubs returned to the site with bear scent. Was it more secure? Do bears regularly share feeding areas?

We returned and put the cubs in the cage. When we hadn't found a fresh deer carcass up by the bear bed, I had begun to think that the source of all the scat hair might be the roadkill the cubs had refused back in mid-October. Sure enough, when I took Alcott over to the place where I had left it, the carcass was gone. We found it by following a drag mark across the New Pond site for a hundred yards, to a secluded softwood stand just seventy yards from the cub cage. The flesh was nearly all eaten from the rather odiferous carcass, and only the head, some skin, and a few bones with scraps of meat on them remained.

The next day, I brought the cubs to the site, and we circled it to see where the wild bear had come and gone. It had approached the carcass from across the road, probably bedding in the dense stand of softwoods in the gully. Both cubs did a stiff-legged walk around the site, and LG marked it with urine. When they came upon one of the deer legs, they sniffed, slow-licked, fed on it, then rolled on it. While they were busy with the leg, I searched the area for the rest of the carcass, finding that the bear had moved it during the night into the densest softwood cover. In the process the large bear had left a nice set of foot impressions in the soft duff, plus some loose but frozen scat containing meat and acorns. The fact that the scat was frozen told me the bear had come to feed in the evening, not the morning. There were also a number of coyote scats around. The cubs moved cautiously and quietly as they inspected the area. They sniffed the ground where the bear had walked, as well as every branch and twig it had brushed on the way. When LG picked up the scent of the carcass and found the head, neck, and rib cage, she sniffed, slow-licked, chewed, and rolled on it, attracting LB's attention to come over and do the same. The cubs pulled the putrid meat from the bone with their incisors. The age of the carcass had certainly made it tender and easier for the bears to feed on, and its odor, to a bear's enhanced olfactory system, probably improved the taste of the meal. I say probably because my sense of duty to scientific inquiry fell a bit short of the required personal affirmation.

But the fact certainly didn't escape me that the carcass they had been afraid of and had so carefully avoided for the past month was now suitable to eat. The cubs had previously decided to eat acorns in the presence of wild bear scent, and now, also reassured by wild bear scent, they had learned that the deer carcass was food. This was beginning to look like a pattern to me. And if it was, what was its significance? Why, in terms of evolutionary success, would one bear benefit from choosing to feed near the presence of another bear's scent?

To make the day complete, when we returned to the cage, the cubs wanted to suckle as usual. Needless to say, the result was an olfactory experience of my own. We returned again the next day, to find that both the bear and the coyotes had again fed on the carcass during the night.

It was almost mid-November, time for setting up the wooden den box that I had asked Roy Day to make for me. Roy and his brother, Jasper, own land adjoining mine on Lambert Ridge; their father, Will Day, had once owned most of the hill, and in the early 1940s he had run a cordwood operation there. The box was four feet by five feet by three feet high, with a sixteen-inch square doorway, and it was bedded with a bale of hay. When Roy and Jasper delivered the box, the cubs joined us as official den inspectors, climbing all over it, inside and out, sniffing cracks, and chewing on holes. I knew they would be good at this inspection business because I had seen them finding, inspecting, and rejecting several natural dens in the past three weeks. But the likelihood that they would have found a suitable natural site on their own on the forty acres that they usually inhabited was remote; an adult bear would have in excess of five square miles. Besides, adult bears probably seek out den sites throughout the year, whereas the cubs didn't start looking until the time their natural mother would have been taking them to den.

The next day, I found the cubs had remodeled the den. They hadn't just gnawed on the ceiling panel; they had hauled it outside and destroyed it. I left to get materials to improve the situation. When I returned, I replaced the roof panel with one-inch boards, putting some more boards over the roofing paper on the top to keep the cubs from tearing it off. On the following day, I added another bale of hay and nailed down the boards on the roof. LB climbed into the den box to inspect, and after sniffing it all over, he curled up and took a nap—his seal of approval.

For the next couple of weeks, while I waited for the longer nights and deeper cold to arrive and draw them into their new den for the winter, the cubs and I continued to take our almost daily walks together. Because the hunting season was still on until the end of November and I had to keep them locked up during the days, LG and LB were really ready for each walk and always made the most of it. Fresh bear scent continued to appear in the now-familiar places, though with decreasing frequency, and the cubs would react with their usual thorough sniffing about, followed by stiff-legged displays and varying intensities of marking—rolling, back rubbing, and urinating. Whenever the serious duty of scent detection wasn't required, the cubs played hard. After they went through their chase, wrestle, and bite antics, LB might run ahead for a solo performance. He would run and leap to grab overhanging branches in his teeth, then fall to the ground, putting great strain on them. Other branches he would get by standing on his hind legs, reaching up and hooking them with his claws, and pulling them down into his mouth. I thought he was done with one particular striped maple sapling that he had been biting at and rubbing on, when he suddenly climbed on a nearby log and launched himself at the sapling, flattening it to the ground with his body. He then climbed a five-inch-diameter red spruce that had pencil-sized dead limbs protruding from the full length of its stem, taking great delight as he powered his way up, snapping and scattering branches everywhere.

Mating was the other thing on their minds, especially LB's. The simple game of chase had developed into pursuit. While chasing LG, LB would swat at her hind legs with his paw in an attempt to destabilize her so he could catch her. Once he did so, LB would try to assume the mating position: standing behind LG, holding her with his arms, and biting at the back of her neck. When he was almost in place, LG would roll to break his grip and then give LB a quick nip to the snout, backing him off. "No" was still "no."

Upon inspecting the den on November 21, I found the cubs had constructed a nest of hay in the middle of the den box, a concave depression with hay built up around the edges. The hay from the corners of the box had been removed and the empty space used for a bathroom. The cubs always backed into the corners and used these bathrooms; they never soiled their sleeping area. Until now, the new den box had been used only for play and cover. I also noticed LG's ear was all wet, which meant she was allowing LB to suckle on it again now that they were in the new den box.

The night of November 24 was one of the coldest of the fall, with temperatures near zero. I arrived at the cage the next morning to find LG nice and warm and LB shivering, leading me to suspect that LG had rebuffed his attempts to suckle and had driven him from the den. Here was a problem I hadn't foreseen: we had built only one new den box; what if the cubs wouldn't share it? Now I had no idea whether this new lodging arrangement was going to be permanent or not, so I secured the door on the original den box and bedded it with hay. But it turned out to be an unnecessary precaution; LG allowed him back in with her the next night. Just in time, too. For the next three days, temperatures stayed near zero at night and were not much warmer in the daytime.

But a New Hampshire fall is nothing if not changeable, and within a week a moderating front brought the cubs out of their snug den to sleep up in the high perch of the cage even in the downpour that came with it. Upon my arrival in the midst of the cold, dreary rain, they simply shook themselves dry, jumped down, and came over to eat.

LB had recently begun to greet his food with a new vocalization, a droning "num-num-num-num." I first heard this sound from adult bears that were being fed when I had driven over to Clark's Trading Post, a longtime tourist attraction in Lincoln, New Hampshire, to ask Maureen Clark what accommodations she made for winter bear dens, but had never heard it from my cubs until now. I wasn't sure what it meant, but suspected something like "This is my food, and I will defend it." The cubs weighed close to eighty pounds now, and their ferocious daily food fights had become a thing of the past. As awful as they sounded, the cubs' fights now appeared to have been nothing more than a social lesson for their future. Here was a system to be admired: As long as the cubs were unable to do each other serious harm, the fights continued; but when they had their adult canines and could do serious damage to each other, this new warning utterance appeared and the fights stopped. Permanently. Humanity, with all its wisdom, hasn't figured out anything nearly as clever as this.

As far as I was concerned, LG and LB could go to den at any time. They were more than ready. At eighty pounds, they weighed much more than their wild local cousins of the same age, and I was due for a winter vacation. A month or two without frequent bruising, daily doses of bear breath, and close inspection of animal droppings had a certain appeal to it. On the other hand, I knew that the cubs might not go to den until January. For I had tracked two different sets of motherless cubs on snow as late as the middle of that month. Aside from the question of when these cubs would go to den, there was a more intriguing one: What would trigger this behavior?

CHAPTER 11

To Den, Finally

URING THE MONTH of December, I waited for the cubs to take more or less permanently to their den. No longer did I go daily to the cage, but instead tried to stay away during the colder periods to give them a chance to make their hibernation decision naturally, in response to the deepening onset of true winter. But whenever the daytime temperatures—or my developing instincts as a surrogate mother bear—rose enough to trigger the impulse, I would drive out to see how they were doing, and to supplement their diets if they were still out and about, still foraging. Usually we would go for short walks if they were, but the cubs were clearly growing less interested in longer hikes, which had been their preference earlier. They would still follow me, but they'd be lethargic, moving slowly and sitting or lying around diddling with dried lettuce stalks, digging in the ground without intent, and yawning frequently. Sometimes I would find the site where they had spent the previous night, and their tracks in the snow would be indicative of very limited activity; they might have fed under some nearby oaks, but that was usually it.

But I had no real idea when, how, or even if the cubs would finally go to den. I guessed that natural pressures like no food and no water would have something to do with it, but my bigger concern was the possibility that the cubs might run off and find a natural den. So as a backup plan, I got from Frosty a used but still functioning radio-tracking collar to put on one of them. The collar had been worn by an adult female, who had lost it in August, and it still had some of her hair caught in the buckle. When I brought it with me to get the cubs used to it, I got some surprising reactions.

I first set the collar outside the cage to let the cubs find it, which they did without trouble. Both cubs sniffed and slow-licked it. LB lay down and vigorously rubbed his neck on it; then he came over to me and rubbed his back on my leg; finally, he went to a small hardwood tree and marked it with a back rub. Meanwhile, LG did a stiff-legged walk back and forth over the collar, marking it with urine each time she passed. Here was an unexpected demonstration not only of the repeatability of the male and female display response to known bear scent, but of the extraordinarily long life of that same scent when it's been absorbed by something that can hold it. Thus a long-lasting olfactory signature intentionally rubbed onto something absorbent like the bark of a tree would seem to serve a different purpose than an abbreviated, rapidly disappearing version of the same signature that is made as a bear moves about, brushing against leaves and twigs.

Although I didn't end up having to use it, the radio collar did seem a prudent precaution, for over the next couple of weeks the cubs several times tried to make a den for themselves. On December 10, following their tracks in an inch of new snow, I came across an attempt by one of the cubs at den excavation. The hole wasn't very deep, because it ran into tree roots, but it resembled a wild bear den excavation that I had found a few years earlier. The cubs were obviously in the market for a natural den, so I took them up into the fall of rocks below the second set of ledges. Each crawled into all of the caverns, inspecting them for bedding sites and hidden chambers. Partway up the rockfall was a small, shielded area with two dry rock caverns where a large red maple had split and fallen with its top covering a portion of the entrance. The cubs seemed to approve of this spot and climbed under the canopy; LG mouthed and chewed on red maple buds, while LB explored the dens. I crawled into one of the caverns and tried to improve it by shifting the rocks around. There was barely enough room for me, but both cubs insisted on climbing over me to join in what I was doing. It was quite difficult extracting myself from the den with my two helpers on top of me, but now that I knew where they'd probably be the next day, I left them to explore the rocks and returned to my truck.

The following day was quiet and rainy, so I decided to climb up in the ledges to catch the cubs at what they were doing rather than call them to me. I spotted them sleeping together on top of one of the prominent ledge outcroppings. They spotted me and began to flee until I issued my verbal greeting, "Hi, guys!" The cubs responded and met me halfway as I climbed up to inspect their choice of bed sites. What I found was a site very similar to the wild bear bed I had found on the ridge south of the bear tree on the corner. The cubs had slept in a shallow but dry depression at the edge of a ledge and within a few feet of two large oak trees. There were scattered understory spruce trees for low cover and another ledge outcropping thirty yards behind the site. As I looked out from their bed, I could see everything of importance to the cubs: my truck, which I had parked about two hundred yards down through the hardwoods, the snowmobile trail, and several of the paths leading to the cage. Strategically, the location was perfect. They could see the approach of any intruders, and—more important—they could see me arrive with food. They had multiple ways to escape, as well as the option of hiding behind or climbing the two large oaks. The ledge behind them and the precipice in front limited the access by intruders to the narrow width of the shelf from each side. The surrounding area was heavily littered with dead branches and fallen spruce trees. The crowning sign of their preference for this area, however, was an attempted den excavation at the base of a leaning tree.

Time came for me to leave, and the cubs followed me back to the cage. After an extraordinarily long suckling session, I left them with two latches on the cub door, the hasp and the hook. Overnight we received eight inches of new snow, and the temperature plummeted to ten degrees.

The morning temperatures were in the teens, and the snow, still falling, was being driven by gusting winds as I left my truck to feed the cubs. I was sure that they had stayed in for the night, but out of habit I scanned the hillside above me. At the base of a small spruce tree almost at the top of the slope, I spotted a small but very black spot obviously lacking a coating of the freshly fallen snow. I watched for movement but saw none until I called out my greeting and the two cubs appeared from hiding. It was quite a sight as they bounded downhill in explosive showers;

their brown-and-black heads leading the way as their bodies repeatedly disappeared in driven plumes of energized, powdery snow.

At the cage I found they had indeed spent the night there and had left in the morning in search of food. I cleaned their den box and found it was still quite warm inside. When they were finished eating and suckling, they both crawled into the den and made themselves comfortable. LB pulled hay up around himself using his claws as a rake, and LG placed her head at the entrance as if she expected me to join them. I blocked the den entrance with hay to help prevent heat loss, then left. When I looked back, both cubs had come out and were pacing at the wire. A wave of guilt flashed over me: The wild mothers were already denned up with their cubs, and my guys were hinting strongly that I should do the same. But this was one role of motherhood that I couldn't fulfill, although the idea of going to bed fat and waking up strong and lean was appealing.

On December 21, the weather was miserable: a wet heavy snow driven by gusts of high wind that littered the ground with fallen trees and branches. On my way from the truck to the cage, I crossed a fresh bear trail, fresh enough that I knew I would find a bear at the end of it. Returning to the truck, assuming that to be the destination of the bear, I heard a faint cry behind me. It was LG; she had heard me arrive and had come to greet me. LB was nowhere in sight, and only LG's tracks were evident in the snow. But when I entered the cage, LB stuck his head out of the den, then slowly climbed out to greet me and, of course, the food I was carrying.

After they ate, I took the cubs to the brook so they could drink and play on the ice. While I watched them play, I was leaning on a medium-sized white ash tree. LB, inventing a new game, ran up the tree. With his rear legs just above my head, he looked down at me and stuck one leg out, insinuating, I thought, that he wanted to stand on my shoulders. I backed off, but in a few minutes, he did it again. This time, I grabbed his foot and held out my arms. He dropped, and I got an armful—an eighty-five-pound black bear. I carried him for a short distance, which he seemed to enjoy, but when I tried to put him down, he held on; I had to get down on my knees before he would let go. In a few more minutes, he was back up the ash tree, and we played the game again.

For the most part, the cubs played hard the whole time we were out, and it dawned on me that while following the tracks they had made when they were alone, I never saw any sign indicating that they had played on their own. The only evidence I found of their playing was either inside or just outside the cage. Play, it seemed, was an indicator of a high level of security. Just as the cubs would play in low dense cover, they would play in my presence and not by themselves. While they play, their senses are compromised, and their activities may draw attention to themselves that could threaten their survival.

I shortly found my own defenses compromised. While I was videotaping LG, LB came over and bit me on the back of the leg, accidentally hooking a tendon behind my knee. I dropped the camera, grabbed his head to prevent him from twisting it, then carefully negotiated a release.

When we returned to the cage, LG demanded suckling, then both cubs climbed in the den. I watched from the den opening as LB got settled quickly and LG took time to rearrange the bedding. Although LB immediately made subtle moves to suckle LG's ear, she would have no part of it. Instead, she came to the den entrance to visit with me and to pull off one of my gloves. Retiring briefly to her bed to play with it, she soon came back. With my bare wrist held gently in her teeth, she maneuvered backward into the den box. Her plan was a good one, except the opening was too small for my shoulders. When her efforts failed, she removed my hat and settled for that, but her desire to have me join them in the den was very clear.

In the middle of a major snowstorm on January 17, I paid them a visit at dusk. Wading through two feet of white powder, I approached the cage, calling out my greeting in an effort not to scare them. I struggled with the deep snow blocking the cage door, which had evidently caused the cubs to bail out of the den and head for the large pine behind the cage. I called for them again, and they changed direction to come and greet me at the door. Physically slow and lethargic, but mentally alert, LG climbed on my knee to suckle and LB followed suit. Their bodies radiated heat with the sweet fresh smell of bear scent and hay. And, as proof that they had finally gone into a hibernative state, they weren't hungry.

Holding on to the rafters of the lean-to, LB did a major stretch, his spine rolling radically inward, demonstrating a bear's remarkable degree of flexibility. Their motions appeared drugged and deliberate as they crawled back into the den, but LG came down to the entrance to be with me before I left. First she pulled off my glove, I presumed to keep as a memento with my scent on it, then once again she gently took my wrist in her mouth and started to back up. In her mind, surely my proper place was in the den with my cubs! As I walked to the door, she followed me and began to pace, but I did have to leave. Disappearing into the darkness of the night, I could hear her wailing, "wwOww, wwOww."

I let ten days go by before I waded through three feet of snow to get to the cage. LG stuck her head out, but then, even though I had called out my usual greeting, she bolted to the large pine behind the cage. LB saw no threat from me and, with his head stuck out of the den entrance, waited for me to clear the door of snow so I could get it open. Once in, I went over and knelt down to greet him. He moaned softly and suckled on my ear; the pulse of the suckling sound had slowed to half of what it had been previously. Meanwhile, LG was still out at the tree and, confused and wary from her rapid awakening, made repeated attempts to return to the den, only to run back to the tree. It took a while to coax her back into the cage.

The cubs were lethargic, and their moves were slow. But then a snowmobile passed on the trail making a loud rattling noise, and they bolted and treed on the large pine. Once the threat had passed, the cubs slowly backed down out of the tree, staggered back inside the cage and into the den. LB poked his head out to visit with me; first he licked my glove, then my fingers, and then, as LG had done earlier, he took my wrist in his mouth and backed up in an attempt to get me to join them in the den.

I was honored and pulled myself partway into the den box, only to get my head suckled from both sides. While being ravaged by the cubs, I could smell the sweet mixture of bear scent and hay. This pleasant odor was an indicator of healthy cubs, as the by-product of burning fat during hibernation is water, the excess of which is lost in their breath, amply shown by the buildup of frost on the walls of the den box. A smell of urine would have indicated the burning of muscle, a lack of fat, and poor condition, but there wasn't any.

The cubs were obviously hibernating, and doing it well. The motion and direction of their heads were followed by the slow deliberate movements of their limbs, as their bodies made concentrated efforts to keep up. In spite of this, the cubs' ability to flee appeared to be unaffected by this winter condition. Although physiologically slow, they were mentally awake. I finally felt secure enough to leave them alone.

CHAPTER 12

Time to Think

W ITH LG AND LB finally denned up for the winter, I now had time to catch up on two things: the backlog in my gun shop and my reading on black bears. The two cubs would reemerge sometime in March, I guessed, giving me six or eight weeks before I would have to resume my maternal duties. Not nearly enough time to gain an in-depth understanding of the state of published black bear research, but it would have to do.

Because of my dyslexia, I knew the reading, even though I wanted to do it, was going to be a chore. (On the other hand, I knew I would really enjoy doing the research.) To get through the material, I would use a method of rapid key word scanning that works very well for me, and I would read only the crucial parts word for word. Besides, this wasn't a required school assignment, this was my work—no tests, no deadlines. And to aid me as I sought out those key words, I was armed with the detailed notes and fresh personal observations from the 392 hours I had just spent walking with the cubs in their natural world—primary research time that didn't include the 2 hours a day I'd spent caring for the cubs (another 510 hours) or the 96 hours I'd spent writing up my field notes. (It's a good thing there are 16 hours of daylight in a summer's day.) I thought those nearly 1,000 hours should count for something. So I approached my winter ruminations with a fair amount of hope.

It was time to sort out my notes and unanswered questions. The first order of business was to study the black bear literature to see how much work of this kind had already been done and if I was on to anything new. The "anything new" wasn't that important, as I had learned from my father that discovering something for myself could be every bit as satisfying as finding something no one else had discovered. Spending the winter in Baker Library at Dartmouth College should help me sort things out.

My review of the black bear literature revealed something unexpected: Only about a dozen scientific articles had been written on black bear behavior. But I found there was another group of large omnivores, which filled a similar evolutionary niche, about which thousands of research papers on the same topic had been written: the great apes. In addition, hundreds of books were devoted to these creatures. Even though bears don't have the humanlike faces that apes have, they are similar to apes in many ways, I was confident that this great body of knowledge would help me make my own comparative study.

My plan was to absorb as many of the defined behaviors of the apes as I could and then compare them with the bear behaviors I had observed for myself, thus trying to build as strong a bear model in my mind as existed for the apes in all that literature. Then, as time went by and new black bear observations were recorded—either by me or by others—my new model should aid in the future analysis of these observations. My methods in building this model were the same as those that had allowed me to get by in school and to succeed as an inventor. They include visualizing a mechanism as a working whole, understanding systems, and solving problems. To design a complex mechanism, one must first understand the whole system and then have the patience to make it work, one part at a time. Learning the bears' life system was the opposite, but analogous: All I saw at first were the individual parts as the cubs demonstrated them—the seemingly disconnected behaviors that I knew had to fit somehow into a very complex behavioral mechanism. But I knew that for a part to work it had to fit into the system; and for a system to function, it needed all of its working parts. The cubs, it seemed to me, were building their individual systems at the same time that they were fitting themselves into the larger system of the bear community all around them. Their conscious minds may not have held a complete understanding of either of those systems as a whole, but their subconscious instincts surely did, and, armed with that instinctual blueprint, the cubs had been building their survival mechanisms one behavioral part at a time while I watched and carefully recorded the whole process in sequence.

Had my study of these two cubs been a more traditionally scientific one, based on the collection of isolated bits of data, a quantitative approach would have been necessary to make some sense of the results. But I was able, because of the continuity of my observations, to adopt a systematic approach where each conclusion had to be supported by all its predecessors. Watching the development of the cubs in daily context enabled me to constantly check and recheck my analysis. If I was wrong, future developments or contrary observations would be sure to set me back on course.

At the end of my winter of reading, I knew that my model wasn't going to be built this year. No one gets to be an expert in this field quickly, and, at least as far as the advanced academic study of it was concerned, I was just getting started. On the other hand, as far as field research was concerned, I could tell even from this preliminary foray into the literature that I was already well on my way to matching the best of the researchers, if not in quantifiable analyses produced then certainly in time spent in close contact with the animals themselves in their natural habitat.

So I was on a good track. Now I could look forward to the spring—and to all the springs to come after that—with genuine enthusiasm that something of real value could come from the work I had now started. While I might not be the one to bring black bears into the brightly lit front rank of animal-behavior science, I very well might play a part in leading them out of the dark woods of relative ignorance where they were now. Meanwhile I had at least begun to acquaint myself with the attributes of higher-developed animals and the kinds of questions I should be asking myself in looking for these attributes in bears.

I had already begun to document some behaviors that led me to suspect that bears show insight, planning, deception, and intentional communication. But then there were other, more complex questions. Ethics: Do bears have a sense of fair play? Altruism: Do they show it? Systematically? Empathy: Can they relate to the current condition of another?

Cognition: Do they have what we would call a mind? Do they have and use cognitive maps? Are they self-aware? Questions about cognition come under the purview of the field—some would say "minefield"—of cognitive ethology, a currently hot one with new books coming out every year, often with completely differing points of view.

With each of these attributes, one must pose the same questions: If they show it, then why? What's its purpose and value to the survival system as a whole?

Answers wouldn't come soon, that much I discovered in Baker Library. I now had the parameters by which others would measure my work, and I had learned the names of some of the commonsense parts of the whole I had already envisioned, but it would be a while yet before I would have enough information and enough observations to begin making sense out of what was happening with the cubs' lives, not only for myself but to convince others that my conclusions were valid.

But I was optimistic. I knew that everything required to make a full-grown adult bear had come in those little four-pound packages when LB and LG had been delivered into my care. All I had to do was to sort it all out.

CHAPTER 13

A New Year in March

F OR DEBBIE AND ME, the maple-sugaring season marks the transition from winter to spring. So on March 14, 1994, as I spent the day tapping trees, I wasn't surprised to note some early signs of spring: barred owls calling throughout the day; the recently returned peregrine falcon against the blue sky above Holt's Ledge, making a sine-wave attack on a group of three ravens trying to establish a competing nest site; chipmunks scurrying about on top of the snow. At the end of the day, worn out from all this physical labor, I had just eased my body onto the soft seat of my truck when I noted a sign I'd been expecting but hadn't heard yet: the distant and repetitive "wwOww" of LG calling for her mother and announcing her awakening from a long winter's sleep.

Even though the three-foot snowpack would surely keep the wild bears in their dens for several more weeks, until the snow receded or they got flooded out, the fact that the daytime temperatures had been above freezing for more than a week coupled with all our noisy sugaring activities so close to their den may have accelerated my cubs' activity. In any case, they were up and fussing, and like every other bone-tired mother, I had to respond whether I wanted to or not. I got out of the truck, put on my snowshoes, and slogged through the deep snow toward the den.

From their tracks in the snow, I could see they had already been out of the cage and that they had spooked and treed on my approach. I called out to them, and they responded by backing out of the tree and ambling over to see me. LG climbed on my knee and commenced to suckle; LB gave my ear a quick suckle before getting distracted by my snowshoes. The attention I was getting from the cubs was more than usual as they attempted to shore up the bond between us that may have eroded over the winter.

Though they had both lost considerable weight, LB's body was now noticeably longer than LG's—his spine had grown. When I got them on the scale with me, I found that LG had lost a full 40 percent of her body weight but LB only 20 percent; they weighed forty-eight and sixty-five pounds, respectively. For whatever reason, a higher metabolism to care for cubs or perhaps she was more active, LG had lost almost twice as much weight over the winter as LB had. After the weigh-in, I looked around the cage and found both of their recently expelled fecal plugs. Although the name suggests that a bear's digestive system actually gets plugged for the winter, the reality is that when they stop eating, the remains of what they last ate and hair from grooming over the winter accumulate at the end of the dormant tract. The plug is simply the first scat out in the spring.

In any case, premature or not, the cubs were up for the spring. My plan, since the labor-intensive sugaring season had already started, was to keep the cubs locked in the cage except for their daily walks. That was my plan, not the cubs'. When I arrived around noon the next day with my brother Josh, who was helping with the sugaring, we heard my dog Scotty barking and discovered that the cubs were up in the ledges looking down on us. But they didn't come down right away, so Josh and I went to work. Over the next hour, the cubs slowly worked their way down toward us, and when they began to get close, I grabbed a bag of kibble and hurried to get my snowshoes on before they actually got to the sugar house and tried to assist. I called the cubs as I set out, and they ran willingly, emitting hungry groans all the way back to the cage. I gave them their kibble, and despite their obvious hunger it took them twenty minutes to finish what would have only taken five in the fall.

While they ate, I discovered that they had escaped by pushing and pulling on the wire until it fatigued and broke. I made a makeshift repair with bailing twine and went back to work at the sugar house. A half hour later the cubs appeared to remind me that I needed to make a more permanent repair to the cage. For the next few weeks, the cubs broke out at will. Only cold and nasty weather was effective in holding them in the cage.

The daytime temperatures rose into the forties as the snow slowly melted—it was still more than two feet deep in the woods—exposing patches of bare ground where the sun could get to it and creating small ponds of standing water in the wet areas. Seemingly invigorated by their long winter's sleep, the cubs ran, chased, and climbed many trees, mostly white ash and hemlock. LB would pop the bark on the ash trees with his canines while climbing; the spring bark slips easily, leaving a readily seen bite-mark scar. I couldn't tell if his bite marks were for play or practice, but either way, LB was adding another message to his growing repertoire. (Since that time, I have seen where a wild bear marked in a similar fashion in the spring—and only on a maple. I suspect that this type of mark is not only visual but olfactory, since the freshly made scar emits an odor from the evaporating sap.) Sometimes, after his ash-biting performance, LB would chase LG twenty feet up an ash tree, grab one of her feet with his mouth, and then drop, forcing her to come scrabbling down the trunk with him. This would be so much fun that she'd run back up the tree so they could do it again. Other times, LG would run up the tree with LB in hot pursuit, and then, before he could grab her, LG would free fall on top of him, trying to knock him off the tree.

The cubs got particularly excited whenever they found speckled alder. These alders are small trees, rarely taller than twenty-five feet or greater than six inches diameter at the trunk. The cubs would try to harvest the seed catkins, which were always on the smallest exterior limbs of the trees (to catch the sun). In one classic performance, LB went up first, climbing out on limbs less than an inch in diameter, then reaching up and breaking off the even smaller catkin-bearing ends—until the limbs supporting his upper body gave way, leaving him dangling by his feet. Taking a few seconds to assess the situation, he just let go, dropping eight feet and landing on his butt in the snow. He collected his thoughts for a few moments before scrambling back up into the tree to give it another try.

LG tried going after the catkins in the next tree we found. She was more than eight feet up when both the limb she was standing on and the one she was feeding from both broke at the same time, sending her crashing down to land on her back and sinking more than a foot into the snow. She never missed a mouthful as she continued to forage on the limb for more than a minute after she landed.

With the snow still covering the ground, I wanted to continue an experiment I had started in the fall: to see how the cubs react to known bear scent under controlled conditions. To establish these conditions would be easy; all I'd have to do was ensure that there were no wild bear tracks anywhere nearby when I set out the known bear scent. On March 31, Frosty brought the known scent: two used bear collars from his ongoing project in Vermont. The test would be easy enough to control and observe, but as I set it up I found my anticipation running higher than a little experiment like this would normally warrant. I knew that one of the collars had been removed from Bear Number 15 of the Stratton Mountain Bear Project. This bear was a ten-year-old female weighing about 140 pounds. She was also the mother of the cubs.

I laid the collars out, then went to get the cubs. The first collar they scented was their mother's. LG approached it first, cautiously searching. She sniffed to locate it, then slow-licked to identify it, then rolled on it to mark it with her own scent, then walked over it in a stiff-legged display, and ended by marking it with urine. She repeated this routine several times. In the meantime LB exhibited the same set of behaviors, in the same order, but did this just once. On the second collar, which I had planted about two hundred feet away, they both responded with less intensity but in the same sequence. I had now confirmed with a controlled test that the behavior I had been seeing for the last year was indeed in response to wild bear scent, but what about the cubs' reaction to their own mother's collar? Had their stronger response to it indicated any recognition? I couldn't really tell. Emotionally I wanted to say yes, objectively I had to say . . . maybe.

For the next few days, while they did a small amount of foraging, the main thing on the cubs' minds was play. They took great delight in sliding down the crust-covered hill on their backs, butts, or bellies; at one point when I was distracted, LG slid down the hill behind me, knocking my feet out from under me. As far as I could tell, they were still cubs and acting like it. I had no idea how fast all of this would change.

On April 4, after rigging the door so the cubs could get out after I fed them, I walked quickly to my truck and drove back to work. I was hoping they wouldn't follow me, but to be certain of it, after I had driven past the sugar house I stopped to watch them from a distance. As expected, they came right after me. On their arrival at the sugar house, they did as I also expected and tracked my earlier movements around where my truck had been parked, then followed my tracks up the hill to the sap storage tank. Then they returned to the large oak next to the sugar house for security. So far so good. But LB then did what I hoped he wouldn't: He left the tree and went inside the sugar house. I fired a blank pistol into the air, hoping to scare them with the noise, but I was a hundred yards away and the gunshot had no effect; LB didn't come out. I turned the truck around and drove back toward the sugar house, hitting the horn as I arrived. LB came flying out of the doorway with a Woodpecker Cider bottle sticking out of his mouth in the drinking position. He dropped it as he leaped onto the large oak, then thought better of it. By the time I was out of the truck, he was back in the sugar house pawing through a recycling bag of soda and beer cans. Shouting "No!" I rushed in behind him. I yelled at him to leave, I made threatening noises by hitting a piece of wood against the building, and even smacked him in the butt with a piece of plastic pipe. He only became confused, which caused him to moan loudly as he went after the garbage with even more determination.

This wasn't working. I had become excited, because the last thing I wanted for these cubs was to become garbage or nuisance bears. When I finally calmed down, I simply clapped my hands (which I always did to keep them away from things or people), then ran out of the woodshed, and he followed me. LG was much more timid and spent the whole time clinging to a tree.

The next couple of days were incident-free, at least as far as the sugar house was concerned. I brought a road-killed deer carcass for them to eat, and now that they had learned it was food, it pleased them no end. I punctured the carcass in three places: the chest, the intestines, and the rear leg. The cubs went for the intestines first, making me wonder if this was related to the cubs' eating fresh deer scats. Over the next week, they rolled the hide off the deer and ate most of the meat. Black bears, not being true predators, don't have teeth that are designed for cutting into meat. They pull the meat off the bone with their incisors, then grind it with molars, which have broad flat surfaces specialized for processing vegetation. This may explain the affinity that bears have for partially rotted meat. It would be more tender, and, from a bear's point of view, it might smell better too.

But what was it about the intestines that made them a priority over protein, which at this time of year was typically in short supply? My thoughts went back to the possibility that they might be needing organisms to help digest cellulose, and although I had no proof then, the future brought two more bits of evidence to support my suspicions. In a later experiment, I left out a dead mink that I received from the local animal control officer for the bears to find. The mink, a predator, would not have the desirable organisms, but would be a source of protein. The next morning I found a bear had carefully opened the mink's stomach cavity, sampled the intestines, then left the entire carcass uneaten. Perhaps my most succesful experiment would come a couple of years later, with a sixteen-month-old cub that came to us right out of hibernation weighing eleven-and-a-half pounds. For three weeks we fed him the best digestible foods, but he failed to thrive or gain weight. Then, when suitable deer and moose scats became available at the end of April, we gathered some and offered them to the cub. He devoured them and made the sound of contentment as he ate. Almost immediately his appetite improved, and we released him three months later weighing sixty-five pounds.

When I was finished with the day's work in my gun shop a few days later, I drove out to the sugar house to see if Larry Sargent had started the process of boiling. An old friend who has helped us sugar since the very beginning, Larry is a logger, is very capable with his hands, and is someone who has, as he puts it, "sugared all his life." That would be about thirty-five years. Smoke and steam billowed out of the sugar house and the vacuum pump pounded away as I cast my eyes up the slope of the sugar bush, where I caught a bit of movement; it was the cubs awaiting my arrival. Not letting on that I had seen them, I asked Larry, "Have you seen the cubs around today?"

"No," he replied. "But I did see their tracks up by the holding tank."

"Well, I'll go up the hill and see what they're up to and check for broken sap lines at the same time."

When I got to the cubs, they both tried to mug me for food. When they were satisfied that I didn't have any, they followed me up into the sugar bush. In the wet areas where the snow had melted, we were able to walk easily, but everywhere else there was up to two feet of coarse granular snow; the cubs had a hard time going through the snow and would follow in my footsteps whenever they weren't playing with and chasing each other.

I could hear a sucking sound coming from the tubing as we neared one of the junctions. One of the sap lines was lying on the ground. I attempted a makeshift repair, but without tools and a new fitting it didn't work. Just as I was ready to leave, LB found the break in the line and began licking up the sap as it flowed out onto the ground. LG then wanted some, but LB defended his find and drove her off. Not to be outdone, LG grabbed the tubing at the tree and broke off another fitting. The sap now ran freely down the trunk, and there was enough for both cubs as they happily lapped it up. Soon we went back, and I locked the cubs up for the evening, hoping that they would stay in for the night.

The sap had run well that day and Larry was boiling it when I got back from the cage. The sugar house was aglow with light from the lanterns pouring out through the cracks between the boards and billowing steam could be seen where the light was leaking from the upper portion near the roof. Inside were saunalike conditions, with occasional drops of moisture coming down from the condensation on the cold steel roof. Larry had cooked our supper by hanging a rack of hot dogs in front of the doors of the firebox. We finished eating and were listening to country and western music when Larry looked up and said, "We've got company."

I turned to see LB sitting patiently at the edge of the glare from our lights. I knew something was up, so I grabbed my flashlight and headed back to the cage with LB. But not, of course, before he had checked my breath and frisked me to see if there were any hot dogs left for him.

At the cage I could see that they had eaten more of the deer for supper and that LG was gone. I called her, and she showed up from the direction of the ledges. The real problem then became apparent when both cubs demanded suckling, which I realized they hadn't received for at least four days. It was exactly what they needed, but you couldn't say the same for me. The cubs reeked of ruptured deer guts.

On April 12, almost two weeks after the cubs' first exposure to their mother's radio collar, I repeated the experiment. This time when I offered it to LG, she did the usual sniff and lick to identify the smell, but after that her reaction was radically different from before. This time, she rolled on it, then picked it up and lay on her back while holding the collar in her paws, all the while making some of the softest cooing and grunting sounds I had ever heard come out of a bear. Everything she did indicated pure pleasure. Had she recognized her mother's scent? It certainly seemed that way to me. But why now? Were black bear cubs imprinted to their mother's scent in the den? Whereas LB's response was not significantly different from his response to any other bear scent, LG's definitely had been. Was this another indication that LG was adversely affected by the separation from her natural mother?

As we moved through the sugar maples a week later, LG pulled a blue cap off the end of the line and licked the open tee for sap. The runs were over now, but it didn't seem to bother her; she went for a tap that was still in the tree but was unable to pull it out. It's a good thing that under normal circumstances the local bears are still in the dens through most of sugaring season.

At the satellite tree on another day, there were three-and-a-half-inch bear tracks approaching and leaving in the snow, as well as a fresh red pine limb on the ground, indicating that the tree had been climbed. LB immediately climbed the tree while LG carefully sniffed out the tracks, but she didn't display with a stiff-legged walk or do any rubbing or marking. There was only one conclusion to draw: LB had made a trip up to the bear tree by himself, thus announcing his availability to breed. Had the tracks been made by a wild bear, I knew by now, the cubs would have marked over them.

That evening, I planted the other collar Frosty had brought—this one from an adult male—to observe and film the cubs' reaction to it. Both cubs were feeding on the deer carcass in the cage, so I placed the collar about thirty-five yards upwind. LB picked up the scent first and left his meal to investigate. Following the scent in the air with his nostrils, he approached the collar very cautiously. At the collar, he sniffed and licked to identify the scent, then he rolled his head and neck on it for an extended period of time. When he was finished, he went back to his meal in the cage and LG picked up the scent. She became quite excited about it as she swayed her head back and forth as if to collect as much scent as possible. At the collar, she sniffed, licked, and rolled, much as LB had done, but then she went over and marked a small tree with a full back rub. Both cubs had marked over scent when they rubbed on the collar, but it appeared that LG was advertising her availability by marking where I knew no other scent existed.

With LB's solo jaunt to the bear tree, and LG's back rub in response to male bear scent, it seemed that their search for mates had begun. Wild New Hampshire cubs aren't normally sexually mature until June of their third year. But LB and LG were twice the size of wild New Hampshire cubs, raising the possibility that sexual maturity is related to size, not age.

On April 18, we took a walk in the wetland adjacent to the cage. LG muscled her way to the very top of a white ash. As the top of the tree swayed under her weight, she would reach out and draw in the thinner limbs with her paws so she could nip off the swollen buds. LB, meanwhile, was foraging on the ground on roots or tubers and emerging vegetation. He ate several very small horsetail sprouts and two types of tubers that I was unable to identify at the time. I took home a sample of each and planted them in Debbie's flower pots in the kitchen, then waited for them to sprout so I could tell what they were. They turned out to be the immature roots of the tall white lettuce and the tall rattlesnake root, both plants from which the cubs had foraged leaves the year before. To find these, LB would clear the leaves from the soil with his claws, then glue his nose to the ground to sniff for the roots. When he located one, he would use one claw to dig it out, pull it up with his prehensile lips, and hold it in his mouth for positive identification before finally chewing it up and swallowing it. If he put into his mouth something that he could tell wasn't edible, he would simply slough it off with his tongue.

I couldn't figure out how he knew where to dig for the roots in the first place, considering he had to glue his nose to find each individual root. But about a week later, I observed and filmed LB walking along and grabbing dead plant stalks in his mouth. If he identified a stalk as lettuce, he would stop and dig for roots around its base; if it wasn't, he would simply pass it by. To me, this was an amazing testament to the cubs' ability to identify plant chemistry using what I thought—incorrectly, I would later learn in one of my major discoveries—to be the vomeronasal, or Jacobsen's, organ in the roof of their mouths. That major discovery was this: Three years later, after observing this behavior over and over again in bear after bear, I decided to dissect the intact head of a road-killed adult to see if I could figure out what was being used. To my great surprise I found, in addition to the well-documented Jacobsen's organ, a small, never-before noticed one in the roof of the bear's mouth adjacent to the Jacobsen's. At this writing, the anatomy of this organ is being looked at by an independent laboratory. After finding no discussion of its existence in either the bear literature or the literature relating to the vomeronasal organ and other sensory organs in the head, I visited the Museum of Comparative Zoology in Boston to look for evidence of this organ in other species of bears. I found it in all other species except for the panda. The fact that the panda is a specialist that eats primarily bamboo while the rest of the bears are generalists eating many types of vegetation supports my theory that the primary function of this organ is to determine edibility of plant tissue. For lack of a better name, or of any evidence that this organ has been previously documented, I coined it the "Kilham organ."

I hadn't seen the cubs on April 20, so I went to look for them the next afternoon. I called without getting a response as I hiked up through the ledges where they usually spent time. On the third level, I found the remains of a winter-killed deer. Thinking that the cubs might have made it up to this level, I called again. This time, I heard a bear huff from the direction of the oak knoll. The huff told me that I had scared the bear and that it would run and hide. I walked over in the direction of where I heard the huff, and followed my boundary line trail down over the ledges. There was no sign of a bear until I was halfway through the stand of oak. From behind me, I heard LG's distress call. She was hiding in a boulder field to the left of the pass in the ledges; I stayed there until she could catch my scent and identify me, then got her to follow me back to the cage, but there was still no sign of LB. I returned to the truck to find LB's tracks in the mud beside it. On my windshield was a note from Bob Gillie, a friend who was renting our camp until his house was built, asking me to stop and see him. Although I wasn't far from the camp, I drove so LB would not follow my scent trail. I learned from Bob that LB had been on the platform where we put food out for the ravens, apparently attracted to some old rancid fat. The raven platform was about thirty yards from the camp and was elevated to keep the coyotes from stealing the food. Bob fired a .357-magnum revolver into the ground six times in an effort to scare him away, but LB didn't even respond. Bob then let out his two Labrador retrievers, Minnie and Old Dog; LB left then, but not in a big hurry.

While I was talking to Bob about all this, LG must have heard us, and she made her approach toward camp, moving from tree to tree. Bob

tried to scare her by firing shots, with no effect. I was beginning to realize that devising a plan to keep these cubs out of trouble was going to be
no easy task, for methods that made plain sense to me meant nothing to
them. The cubs had been getting bolder by the day, and far more willing
to travel long distances on their own. Raising the cubs up to denning
time had been relatively easy; they never left their own little home range.
Now I needed telemetry or radio-tracking equipment to monitor the
cubs' activities, and I had to worry about the cubs visiting my neighbors.

I got into the truck and drove back to the sugar house, so I could distract LG from the camp. LB appeared from the woods above the pond.
I grabbed his food and made haste to the cage. LB hadn't eaten at the
cage for three days and was ravenous; he bellowed loudly as he tried to
mug me for the food all the way back.

Two days later, I got a call from Dina Cutting, who lives with her
family about a half mile to the north of camp. She told me there was a
bear down by the road below their house. I asked how large it was, and
she said it was a little larger than a German shepherd. I didn't have a bear
that large, but I told her that I would come right over. It was LG. (Long
ago, I learned that people misperceive the size of bears all the time, and
almost always upward.) Why LG was here I had no idea, but I suspected
that she had been following the scent of another bear and for some reason had chosen not to go any farther. While I spoke with Dina, I kept
one eye on LG as a car passed her on the road. She simply hid behind a
tree and let it pass. I drove down to her and fully expected that I would
have to walk her back to the cage, but when I opened the truck door and
greeted her, she ran right over and jumped in. The ride made her quite
nervous, so she suckled on my neck all the way back to my lot. As soon as
she recognized the surroundings by the sugar house, she rocketed across
my lap and out the open window. The troubles were now beginning.

By the end of the month, they were out of control. On the last two
days of April, LG visited two of my neighbors. On April 29, while I was
on the hill looking for them, LG was across the road visiting Bob
Rufsvold while LB, obviously the wiser of the two, stayed on my land
and watched. I didn't find out until I came off the hill and Debbie was
there to explain the situation. She said that a couple of people had
stopped in the road when they saw the cubs, including our neighbor to
the south, who seemed pleased to see them and asked why they had

never visited her place. I was relieved to know that the presence of the cubs was so well received by all of my immediate neighbors. I then walked over and retrieved LG.

On April 30, while I was again off looking for the cubs, I heard a shot from the southern neighbor's direction. It turned out that both cubs had been there, but LB had left. I drove over to see what had happened and learned the cubs had been playing, which was an indication to me that they had been well received and perhaps encouraged. Luckily, they hadn't caused any significant damage; they'd broken a five-dollar bird feeder, then ate seed, suet, and a piece of strawberry cake. But the fact that they had eaten was disconcerting, as there are two surefire ways to encourage bear cubs: to play with them and to feed them. The shot had been fired by Phil Elder, my neighbor's companion at the time, to scare LG off, but she wouldn't leave. I had to load her in the truck and return her to camp. This had been the second time the cubs had been subjected to gunfire at a close distance and had not responded by fleeing, yet the distant gunfire they'd heard on a walk last fall had terrified them.

LG was clearly the leader of these raids on the neighbors. LB had had the presence of mind either not to get involved in the first place or to leave when things got hot. Not LG. Because the cubs had been warmly received initially and, I strongly suspected, fed, LG had quickly decided that she was welcome even while the invitation was being rudely withdrawn. Her obsessive dependency—which had been evident from the day she was rescued from the den—had now manifested itself as a real problem.

Later that week, the ante was upped when I received a call from my neighbor to the south. She had changed her mind about the cubs and now felt uncomfortable about having large "predators" roaming the woods around her house. She explained that strange people had ended up at her place from time to time but she could deal with them. Bears, on the other hand, were creatures she knew very little about and was uncomfortable with. It didn't matter when I explained that she had built her home in the middle of a spring and summer feeding ground full of jack-in-the-pulpit and jewelweed, and that her woods had always been frequented by the wild bears that she just hadn't seen yet. All I could do was to try to reassure her and tell her that I would take whatever action was necessary to keep the cubs away.

What was necessary, I knew, was to catch the cubs in the act and apply negative conditioning on the spot. I called Frosty, and he supplied me with a number of twelve-gauge, nonlethal, bear-control devices that could be fired from a shotgun: firecracker shells, whistler shells, and some B.E.A.R.—humane plastic projectile rounds that were designed to sting a bear in the butt. I loaned Phil a single-shot shotgun and taught him how to use these devices, and I gave him a plastic launcher designed to shoot apples for the same use.

But I knew this problem was going to be hard, if not impossible, to solve. A bear's mind is not so flexible as to comprehend a mixed signal, especially when we as people use our own methods to communicate wrongdoing, methods that are completely unfamiliar to a bear. Bears must have clear signals and methods to control each other, or they would have to spend an inordinate amount of energy in conflict.

Still, I wasn't too worried, and, being an optimist, I was already looking past the solution of this immediate problem. One of my long-term goals was to observe LG when she had her own cubs so I'd be in a position to understand exactly how bears discipline their young. That kind of information would not only come in handy with any future orphans I'd get to raise, but could help make it much easier to control situations where people and bears are in conflict.

CHAPTER 14

A Very Difficult Month

THE TIME HAD come for radio collars to keep track of the cubs. No longer could I arrive near the cage and simply call them out of the nearby woods; not only might they not respond right away, but more and more they might not even be nearby. They were growing up, and grown bears wander. Eric Orff brought me two used collars, which I then tore down to remove the transmitters so I could put them into the new ones that I was fabricating out of two-ply nylon cattle collars. With assistance from Ken Uline, a friend of mine with great skills in electronics, we got new batteries and tested the transmitters to be sure they were working before molding them into their new urethane plastic housings. Since I would need to adjust each collar to the cubs' expanding neck size, I kept the buckle and added a degradable leather "chip" to allow the collar to rot or tear off on its own if I lost track of either bear before I could remove it myself.

It was now May, and I continued to feed the cubs even though it was getting increasingly difficult to make sure that they each got their share. They were now roaming over an expanding area of more than a hundred acres, and although there were plenty of acorns, the supply of lettuce root, sedge sprouts, and wood sorrel was limited. I worried that if I didn't provide an adequate supply of food, they might at any time go back to my neighbors' property, where they had already been warmly received. Both of their earlier visits with neighbors had occurred on days when I had been unable to find and feed them first.

When the collars were ready, I took them out to put on the cubs, even though the receiver hadn't arrived. Might as well be ready to track them when it did, I decided. I climbed up to the third level looking for the cubs, then down the ridge to Cole's Lot, all to no avail. The deer were feeding on acorns on the ridge, and the moose had returned from their winter yard and were browsing heavily in the logged area, but the only fresh cub sign I saw was where they had dug for lettuce roots near the cage. I checked the cage about an hour before dark, but neither of them had returned.

Right after I drove down to the village, I got a call from Bob Gillie that the cubs were back at the sugar house looking for food. So much for a quiet evening at home with Debbie. I drove back to camp to find that LB had eaten all the food and then left, leaving LG hungry in the cage. I fed her and took advantage of the moment to slip on her new radio collar. She made a few attempts to get it off but didn't seem overly bothered by it. LB didn't come back, so I couldn't put on his collar.

The next morning, LG showed up alone for her morning feeding. Without her collar. I searched all her known bed sites and finally found the collar near a leaning pine in Cole's swamp. I refitted the collar, and she cooperated by sticking her head right into it. I left as I usually did, leaving LG in the cage with the door rigged so she could escape.

I returned to work in the sugar house in the late afternoon. When I got out of my truck, I could hear a scolding roar of chipmunks on the second level. That's got to be a bear, I said to myself. Sure enough, LB soon sauntered into view, and when he caught my scent he came right down and walked with me back to the cage to get some kibble. I was surprised to find LG still in the cage and pacing, probably distraught over LB's and my absence. I slid on LB's collar while he was eating.

I took them for a walk across the road to the bear tree by the beaver swamp. There wasn't any fresh wild bear scent at this large spruce, so LG, exhausted from pacing and worrying about LB's absence, decided that it was a good time for a nap; she stretched out across the exposed roots of the bear tree and quickly fell asleep. LB wasn't filled with ambition either; he lay down and fiddled with my shoelaces, pant cuffs, and tried to get at my cameras. The only real effort he made was a vain attempt to remove his collar.

Only half awake, LG started suckling on her paw, a behavior I hadn't seen since the cubs were still in the basement. Back then, it had meant she wanted LB to suckle on her ear, and apparently it still did, at least in LB's mind. He approached her very cautiously, first putting his paw on her back, then nibbling, and finally suckling on her ear. The bond between them had been weakened by LB's two-day absence, and LG plainly needed to have it reaffirmed. Once again we were a family unit, relaxed and content together in one of the cubs' favorite places. Had I known how few of them were left, I'd have savored the moment more than I did.

On May 5, at about three in the afternoon, I got a call from Susie Rufsvold saying that LG was visiting again and that the bear had been treed by one of her dogs. By the time I got there, LG was standing at the base of a large white pine and the dogs were back in the house. She responded when I called her but then spooked when the dogs barked from inside the house. Her butt was all wet with urine, and she peed on herself again when the dogs barked; then she ran for the tree, huffing, whimpering, and letting out her "wwOww" distress call. It took me fifteen minutes to calm her down enough to get her to jump into the truck, and when she finally did, she suckled furiously on my neck. I drove back to camp while she crawled all over the cab and me. At one point she crawled over my right shoulder and placed her paws on the wheel, so I had to peer out to see past her. Had anybody come along, it would have looked as if a bear was driving the truck with no other passengers. But I really wasn't enjoying the moment enough to laugh.

There was a pattern beginning to develop with these visitations of LG's, and it clearly involved LB. He was now showing every indication that he was sexually mature, and was now going off on his own for several days at a time. Much to my frustration, the receiver still hadn't arrived, so even though I had radio-collared him I still had no idea where he went when he left. All I did know was that he was probably with wild bears, because he was sporting new cuts and abrasions each time he returned. But while LB's forays in search of a mate were perfectly normal, LG's resultant anxiety-driven trips to the neighbors when he was gone certainly weren't. These weren't the normal actions of an intelligent animal with a highly evolved survival mechanism. These were the abnormal actions of a needy creature in search of something she desperately wanted. It might have been food, but food was everywhere in the woods and delivered daily by me. When LB was gone, she had to be out looking for company.

But a bear looking for human company is a bear about to find trouble. Even though she wasn't doing any harm, her visitations had now become socially unacceptable. I had given both neighbors pepper spray in an effort to provide some negative response to her visits, but because she had been warmly received at first, I knew it was going to be difficult to break her from this activity, especially now that I had recognized that it was her separation anxiety that drove her to it.

Clearly, Murphy's Law was coming into play; everything that could go wrong was going wrong, and the receiver for the tracking collars still wasn't here. How could I control LG and LB if I couldn't find them? Locking the cubs up in their cage was no longer an option, not only because they had learned they could manipulate the wire until it fatigued and broke, but because allowing the cubs to enter the wild on their own had been the goal of the whole project in the first place. Natural mother bears separate from their cubs in June of their second year; my cubs would reach that milestone next month. I was almost there. The goal I had worked so hard to achieve—an adult life for my cubs—was right around the corner. Things weren't going very well with LG right now, but LB seemed well on his way to full adaptation with the local wild bear community. I hoped things would work out.

Although analysis and problem solving are my strengths, I really was flying blind here. To my knowledge, no one had ever even documented the day-to-day details of raising black bear cubs, let alone actually done it the way I was doing. If there was a solution, it would have to come from me. The natural solution—being a full-time, night-and-day mom—wasn't feasible for me. If it had been, none of the visitations would have occurred in the first place. More workable solutions would have been to have built a much larger escape-proof enclosure, for me prohibitively expensive, or to have a cage like mine on a more remote piece of property so denning and dispersal could take place far away from people. Either option might work in the future, but not for this set of cubs. All I could do now was to spend as much time as I could with them in a effort to keep them out of trouble.

For the next few days that's exactly what I did. LB didn't go off, and the three of us walked every day. When I arrived the morning of May 9, it seemed like any other morning; the cubs came to me when I called, and we took a short walk in Cole's swamp. There the cubs foraged on jewelweed sprouts, willow flowers and leaves, beaked hazelnut leaves, and lettuce roots and leaves. LB marked three times: on a previously marked alder, on a previously marked ash, and he arched his back to mark as he passed under a fallen white birch. The frequency of his marking inside his home range had increased with the advent of the breeding season. When I took him outside his normal home range, the amount of marking he did decreased. I suspected that by marking less outside his home range he would limit his chances of attracting the dominant male. If a female bear came onto his ground, he made sure she would know of his existence.

I returned at about half past four that afternoon to call and feed the cubs, but got no response. I called and searched for them until seven o'clock, but without the still-missing receiver I was helpless. I gave up and went home, only to learn that the cubs had been on the property of my neighbor to the south the whole time. I drove out to see that neighbor and her companion, and listened as they described how the cubs had been there about four hours, playing on the clothesline, climbing trees, eating suet, cake, and birdseed. The woman's description sounded like the play I thought the cubs would only do in my presence, which indicated to me that the cubs had been well tolerated, perhaps even actively encouraged. All of the fun ended when the man of the house returned from work. He immediately loaded the shotgun with a nonlethal B.E.A.R. plastic bullet that I had given him and went outside to confront the cubs. LB left immediately, but LG, just as I had feared, didn't. He then fired, reloaded, and fired again, hitting her twice in the rear with the plastic bullets before unholstering his revolver and firing it over her head. "She left running, and shifted gears every time I fired the revolver," he said.

The cubs had been caught in the act and forcefully driven off, but I was concerned that they had had too much fun before being chased away. I worried that the punishment had not been enough to offset the rewards in this situation, namely, company and food. I really feared that LG would pay these neighbors another visit.

The next morning, I set out to find the cubs, for they hadn't, as I had hoped, fled to the cage after their adventures at the neighbors'. Instead, adding to my worries, I found them only a quarter mile southwest of the neighbors' house on a rock knoll. They followed me back to the cage, where I left them for the day.

I returned in the afternoon to find LB sitting alone below the first set of ledges. It was a little odd to find LB just sitting out in the open like that, and with no sign of LG in the area. He followed me up onto the second level, where he foraged on acorns, nodding sedge, lettuce leaves and roots, and immature yellow birch leaves. Then he did something I had never seen before: he rubbed his head and chin on clumps of nodding sedge before he would lie down to eat them. We made a loop and came back down on the first level, where I found an area where the clumps of nodding sedge had been recently fed on. LB investigated them thoroughly before pulling his head back and moaning in disgust. Something had happened between the time when I left the two of them in the morning and the time I arrived in the afternoon, and now I began to suspect what it was. I checked LB's head, neck, and chest to see if he had been fighting, and I found eight small bite marks. Had an adult wild male been down to put LB in his place? Was that his problem? I returned LB to the cage so I could leave, but the cage was still rigged with latches so he could easily let himself out.

I was surprised to find LB still in the cage when I returned in the morning. I took him on a short walk on the lower sugar road, where we found the four-and-a-half-inch tracks of a wild male with LG's tracks superimposed on top of them. So that was it. Not only had LB fought with this much bigger bear and lost, but LG had then run off with him. LB was taking the whole ordeal pretty hard, sitting out in the open, moping around, and staying in the cage all night and into the next day; although I felt sorry for him, I couldn't help but feel pretty good about it from LG's standpoint. This was just what LB had been doing, and now it was her turn. Here was a natural turn for the better. My prospects for becoming a grandmother were looking up.

In the afternoon I found LB still in the cage, and still no sign of LG. In an effort to lift his spirits, I took him for a walk to the third level. His mood was still down, and I noticed that he was grooming his right hip a lot. I wasn't sure what his problem was, but he was moving slowly and alternating between making a quiet moan and a call new to him but similar to LG's unhappy "wwOww."

When we got to the third level, much to both our surprise and relief, LG appeared. She wasn't hungry but desperately wanted to suckle on my neck. When she then turned her attention to a spot on LB's hip, I knew for sure he had an injury there, but when I tried to examine it, he wasn't very cooperative. I was able to determine that he had a deep puncture wound with a triangular-shaped opening about three-eighths of an inch across. The wild male had got him better than I had originally thought, but not so badly that his mood didn't elevate considerably with LG's return. They played to celebrate, and twice LB tried to get LG into the mating grasp, only to have her squirm and play her way out of it.

On May 15, I finally got the telemetry receiver and antenna from Frosty. Because it was on loan from the Vermont Fish and Wildlife Department, there had been many bureaucratic hurdles to slow its arrival, but at least it was now here. And even though I had trouble keeping LG's collar on her—she would use her two forepaws and one hind foot to wiggle it off—I was eager to try it out. At eight in the morning I hurried out to the sugar house, where I had put the collar the last time she had gotten out of it, only to discover that I now had another problem with the collar: It had originally come from a Maine bear that had dropped it in New Hampshire, and it didn't transmit within the frequency range of the Vermont receiver. I wouldn't be able to track LG even if the collar did stay on. I don't verbalize expletives very often, but I was close to making an exception in this case.

Forty-five minutes later, my dark ruminations were interrupted when I heard shots about a half mile away. It was pretty clear where LG was—at the home of my neighbor to the south—so I got in my truck and drove down there, just in time to see her black shape shoot across the road in front of me as I got to the house. This time, she had received a dose of pepper mace in the face and three shots in the air to scare her more. And as I suspected, there was no sign of LB. The only reason I could think of that LG would submit herself to this kind of continuing abuse was obsession, the obsession that she needed to be with somebody at all times, either man or bear. I was beginning to think that the lack of food from an underweight mother and her subsequent abandonment might have scarred LG for life.

But LB certainly didn't have any such obsession. He had only gone with LG to this neighbor's house one time, and he had shown very little interest since. Where he was now I didn't know, but the neighbors said they hadn't seen him. I suspected that LB had struck out instead in search of more natural companionship.

LG arrived back at the sugar house about half past nine, hungry and eager to suckle, so I took her to the cage and fed her, then went back to the sugar house for the new receiver to see if it would pick up LB's signal from his collar, which he had been wearing all along. I came back in a half hour to find her pacing back and forth in the cage. I let her out, and off we went in search of LB.

LG and I were halfway up the hill toward Cole's landing when I picked up LB's signal. This was my first time out alone with the tracking equipment, and it took a little walking around to get on the right frequency. When I sorted it out, LB's signal was coming from a small ravine that lies below the corner bear tree. We had to climb to get up into the ravine. Once there, the signal was very strong; I knew that he was real close, so I put away the telemetry gear. A steep granite ledge rose to our left, a small runoff brook ran down the center of the ravine, and a small oak knoll was up on our right. At the spot where we stood, the ground was covered with impressions of bear tracks in the leaves; it looked as if two bears had either fought or wrestled. A large fresh wild bear scat was near the base of a large leaning sugar maple.

Soon I spotted some movement on the oak knoll and then saw a bear that I thought was LB coming down to greet us. He stopped about fifty yards away, with his head held alert. I called out my usual greeting, "Hi, guy!" and this bear just looked at me. Then the real LB—obviously smaller and wearing his radio collar—appeared out of the bushes to stand beside the bear I had just called out to. The bigger bear was an adult wild sow. Now I knew why LB had been sneaking off periodically.

LG, meanwhile, had gotten wind of the new bear and scrambled up the large leaning maple. LB then acted like a schoolboy caught doing something naughty and came straight to me emitting a light moan. The wild sow casually followed him down and stopped about ten feet from me. LB was now between my legs, and LG was huffing while climbing farther up in the tree. The sow began making the same chirp or "gulp" that the cubs made when they were nervous, and I could certainly relate to that. She also chomped and huffed at me—signs which I read as defensive but tempered by her confusion about what I was doing here with these cubs. About that time, it became pretty clear to me, and I think to her as well, that we were way too close to each other.

While I wondered how this would all play out, she walked around the base of the large maple that LG had climbed and suddenly came at me.

Swinging and striking the ground with her forepaws, in the blink of an eye she covered the ground that separated us, huffing with each swat to enhance the intimidation factor in a fury of claws, paws, sound, and blurred fur that stopped less than eight feet from me. The intimidation of the false charge worked, sending a flush of adrenaline surging through me, but I held my ground anyway, too focused to be concerned about my safety. She composed herself and walked back around the tree, only to come at me again. Once more, I stood my ground and looked directly in her eyes. This time, she backed off, stretched against the large maple, then climbed it, pushing LG farther out on a limb. I took advantage of the pause in the action and backed off myself, taking what I later measured to be eighteen paces.

After I moved away, the wild sow backed down the tree, and LG backed down right beside her and then came running over to LB and me. The sow had showed no sign of aggression toward LG, and now stood at the base of the tree, watching the two cubs and me.

With time to take inventory of what had just transpired, I found myself still exhilarated and extremely intimidated, but not really afraid. Black bears have no history of unprovoked attacks on humans, and I knew that an animal that puts on a display is communicating its desire to avoid a fight. Like any other animal, a bear must have a reason to fight, because to fight means risking a debilitating injury. To my mind, this bear had no reason to fight with me—she had just gotten too close by following LB down the hill to me. From that point on, her actions were identical to the defensive displays Wobbly Girl would put on every time I would walk into the cage. It also occurred to me that, judging from the intensity of her display, this wild sow might have cubs nearby. But between the foliage and my preoccupation with the moment, I wasn't doing much extra looking about.

LB and LG chewed and played with my shoes and pant cuffs as I stood enthralled with this beautiful new animal. The wind blew directly from me to her as she relaxed and lay down at the base of the tree. I placed her weight at about 150 pounds, and her paw size about the same as or a little bigger than LB's. Her face was round and noble, her muzzle narrow and tan, with a dark brown stripe down the nose. Her fur was a luxuriant and reflective black, with no defects or loss of hair. A distinguishing tuft of brown hair on the upper portion of her left ear could help me identify her in the future, but I knew I wouldn't need to look for it. Her face was indelibly etched in my mind.

For the next hour I could move back and forth, stand or sit, and get just an occasional squared-off lip or chomp from the wild sow. Only when I moved in her direction would she get up to leave, but when I backed off, she would lie back down. For the most part she was relaxed, swatting deerflies, yawning, resting her head on her paws, her ears splayed outward, with a pleasant look on her face. She watched as my cubs played on a log, wrestled, ran, and foraged on beech leaves. I sat there in awe of how this animal, an animal that had never seen me before, was able to go from the fearful intensity of our introduction to a position of relaxed trust, lying there for over an hour by my watch and sharing with me an obviously mutual curiosity. At the end of the hour I got up and simply walked away with the cubs. Just as we were about to disappear out of sight, I turned and looked back; she was at the base of the tree watching us go.

As the cubs and I walked back to the cage, I wondered about the wild sow: Where was the wild black bear's notorious and well-documented shyness toward humans? Had she shown presence of mind in overriding it? This was an animal that certainly had never encountered me before and was, to a near certainty, not habituated to man at all, except possibly as a species to be feared. We were in a heavily hunted area, not a protected park, yet this bear could clearly make the distinction that I meant her no harm. While the presence of my cubs obviously had something to do with her actions, this wild bear was able to overcome an instinct to flee; instead she assessed the situation and determined that it was safe to stay, observe, and treat this one human as an individual instead of a mortal enemy. I couldn't get over it.

By mid-May, the cubs were eating nodding sedge, lettuce leaves, beech leaves, sprouting oak leaves, white birch sprouting leaves, acorns, shad bush leaves and flowers, and black cherry flowers. On one walk, LB flushed a grouse off her nest of eggs, and I was sure the nest was history. But I was relieved to see both cubs walk across the brush pile, passing right over the nest without so much as a sniff.

By the evening of May 18, LB had gone off again, and I had to climb to the third level of ledges before I picked up the signal from his collar. I followed the signal for a mile and a half to an area where I had never taken him. This meant something to me, because I knew the cubs would not leave their known area unless they were with me or a wild bear. I was sure LB was safe and probably with the wild sow, but I didn't think that LG had gone with them, which meant she was probably in trouble.

I got back to my truck and found a note from Debbie, saying that LG had followed an Appalachian Trail hiker all the way from Holt's Ledge to the trailhead near the Dartmouth Skiway parking lot. The Appalachian Trail crosses the top of Holt's Ledge just above my property, and I had always made an effort to avoid it on my walks with the cubs to keep them away from problems like this. LG had, I figured, discovered the attractions of the trail by following the large male bear that bit LB. This incident followed the now-predictable scenario: LB goes after a wild female bear, lonely LG seeks company.

I spent the next day trying to get a location on LB. The nearest I could estimate from two very weak signals was that he was about two miles south of the cage, in rough terrain with lots of small knolls and ravines leading up to some rugged hills—not the easiest country for monitoring bears.

The following morning, I drove right to Cole's landing to try for a signal from LB. To my surprise, I got a strong one from the direction of the cage. I drove back there and called, then waited for him to come out. After sitting quietly on a log near the snowmobile trail for twenty minutes without hearing anything, I decided to relocate. I stood up, and all hell broke loose: LB had been sneaking toward me in the dense sapling cover, and when I moved I startled him. He huffed and took off looking and sounding like a wide-bodied, furry freight train—on a flat-out run, knocking down everything in his way, and huffing every time his front feet hit the ground. He was about fifty yards out before he could hear my call and come to a stop. Back he came, looking tired and hungry. After giving me a thorough sniff-over to be sure I wasn't holding back any food, we headed back to the cage.

I returned in the evening with my sister, Phoebe, who had come home from studying in Hawaii, to find LB still in the cage. His fur was all matted from being in the water, and he seemed to have been pacing the whole time I was gone. Since he could have climbed out at any time through the hole in the roof, which he had used many times before, I suspected he stayed because he was upset that LG was not there to greet him on his return, and was waiting for her to come back. Phoebe and I took him for a short walk to the second level to look for LG and to leave a scent trail for her to follow when she did come back. LB worked hard trying to find her, walking with his nose glued to the ground and slow-licking every foot or so. Unfortunately, the scent trail had grown cold, and LB gave up and went down in the dumps, moaning and slogging along behind us just the way he had after being bitten by the large male bear.

It was eight o'clock in the morning on May 21 and I was feeding LB in the cage when I heard an aerial firecracker go off in the direction of my neighbor to the south. With a sinking heart, I knew LG had returned for another visit. I just couldn't understand why she had gone there first and not here to LB and me. By now, she had been chased out of there with a nonlethal arsenal of pepper spray, potatoes launched out of a homemade PVC pipe gun, plastic B.E.A.R. bullets, aerial firecrackers, and a revolver fired repeatedly over her head. For the life of me, I could not figure out what the continued attraction was, other than the warm initial reception that had long ago worn off into outright—and very loud—animosity. Conversely, LB showed no signs of attraction to other people; in fact, he was showing increasing contempt. It had to be that LG's excessive suckling and obsessive behavior had only gotten worse over time and were largely responsible for her current actions.

I drove down to hear the account of what happened: First LG got sprayed with pepper spray. That made her leave. Then she came back to get hit with the potato gun, and when she didn't run away from that, my neighbor got out the shotgun and shot her with a plastic bullet. This time she yelped with pain, ran off, and didn't come back. That last bit I didn't like; I knew her threshold for pain, and the yelp concerned me. Immediately I started looking for the plastic projectile which should have bounced off.

I couldn't find it.

I went back to get LB so we could look for LG. I was worried now, and we looked hard. We spent close to five hours encircling the area into which she had run off, trying to cut her trail. Three times LB hit fresh bear scent, but only checked it out and made no attempts to follow it. This was really discouraging. LB had stood the best chance of finding LG. I knew it would be virtually impossible to determine her location in thousands of acres of forest when she wasn't wearing a radio collar. All I could do now was hope she wasn't wounded and that she'd return to the cage.

She didn't.

For the next five days, LB waited by the cage, often choosing to stay inside and pace rather than go off on his own. I was feeling anxious and helpless and wanted to do something. But there wasn't anything to be done except to take walks and hope either we found her or she found us.

Finally, on May 26, while LB and I were checking on a small pond I put in near the cage so the cubs could cool off on hot days, I heard soft moans of anticipation through a bed of ferns. It was LG. She looked fine as she greeted LB and me. She followed us back for supper. As we came into the cage, I saw LB sniff her leg and attempt to bite her, and right away I knew she was wounded. As always, she climbed on my knee to suckle on my neck, and while she did I ran my hands over her body and realized my worst fears: There was a three-quarter-inch hole in her left flank. Probing gently and not wanting either to hurt her or cause more damage, I hoped to find that the plastic projectile had done nothing more than just penetrate the skin.

It had gone in deeper.

This was serious and I knew it, but the twin facts that she was mobile and eating were good signs. It had also been five days. Maybe she was already recovering, but I couldn't just leave it to chance. I called Alcott Smith and he agreed with me. He said he would come out the following day with his veterinary kit.

The next day, we arrived at the cage at noon. We locked LB out, and I let LG climb on my knee and suckle so Alcott could examine her. First he pulled a large clump of hair from the wound and probed to feel for the projectile. We decided to anesthetize her so he could remove it and properly assess the damage. While LG was still suckling on my neck, Alcott gave her an intramuscular injection to put her out, and she went to sleep in my arms.

Meanwhile, LB was hanging on to the cage wire and moaning desperately. Had he sensed the gravity of the situation from sniffing and biting at her wound? Could he tell how sick she was from the night they had just spent together in the cage? In every way he was acting empathetic. It seemed to me that he truly was feeling her pain.

The projectile had entered at midflank where her left rear leg and stomach cavity came together. It had traveled inward and downward about four inches before lodging just inside the peritoneal sac of the stomach cavity; fortunately, it had not ruptured the intestine. Alcott removed the projectile and left the wound open to drain.

Then we left her there until Phoebe and I returned in a few hours with antibiotics and dressings to clean the wound. I also brought back her mother's radio collar, which still had a working battery. Frosty had loaned me the receiver for it, so at long last I had a working radio collar for LG. We put it on her and left her alone to fully recover from the anesthetic while separated from LB.

I came back later in the afternoon to check on her and found she had already climbed out of the cage. I called for the cubs, but only LB showed up, so I turned on the receiver. The signal from LG's collar was very strong but very confusing; I wasn't used to this receiver, and I wasn't aware that signals could play tricks when a transmitting collar was so close. As I walked, the signal would be very strong, then get weak, then get stronger again. She must have been right nearby and moving, but why didn't she come to us?

LB, too, was acting very strangely—walking over saplings, marking them with urine, doing a stiff-legged walk, and biting and breaking larger saplings. All of this behavior seemed to me to be way out of place. I fed him some kibble to calm him down and walked off to hide the remainder. When I came back, I startled LB, causing him to huff, literally jump three feet in the air, and at the same time rotate 180 degrees so he was facing me. After that, his mood was a mix of excitement, fear, and, unfortunately for me, a great desire to play. I was still trying to sort out LG's signal, and meanwhile LB would charge me at high speed, tackle one of my legs, and bite it in the process. Next, he would confront me standing up, lunging and swatting at me with his paws. Finally, I had to tip him over with my foot to calm him down a bit, but he just continued this raucous act by himself. Looking back on it now, I realize that I was too confused with the day's events to fully understand that LB was trying to communicate something to me.

Light ran out, and I was forced to go home. I called Frosty, and he gave me some tips for finding the signal at close distance with telemetry. Phoebe came back out with me in the morning to look for LG, and, armed with Frosty's advice, we followed the signal right to her.

LG was dead. Lying in the fetal position in a bed near the game trail, she must have died shortly after being operated on. The strange changes in yesterday's signal that I thought were her movements could only have been her ghost.

But LB had found her. An area of flesh around the wound had been removed, and LB now showed how that happened as he came over to lick the wound and bite at it to remove infected tissue. I eased him out of the way and picked up LG's body to carry it out so I could give her a proper burial, but LB would have none of that. He stood up and wrestled LG's body from my arms. I knew enough to leave them alone. Burial could wait. As we walked away with tears in our eyes, Phoebe looked back to see LB suckling on LG's ear.

The permanence of the situation really overcame me later as I came back to lock LB in the cage, then returned for the melancholy task of removing LG's body for burial. The word *tolerance* kept repeating itself in my mind. If there had been just a little more tolerance for LG's weakness, she might have survived her teenage months. She was close to making it to adulthood and the freedom she deserved. This really was hard to take. She had given me so much in the vibrancy of her life, and now I had to endure the sadness of its passing.

But even as I bore the heavy weight of what I had let happen to LG, I already could see that my personal failure to keep this one deserving bear alive was only a mirror of a much bigger problem. Black bears everywhere were reinhabiting their historic range, and conflicts with humanity could only increase. Already I had the sense that tolerance—or the lack of it—would determine the fate of many black bears for many years to come.

CHAPTER 15

Moving On

FOR LB AND ME, June began as a time for mourning, bonding, and a new beginning. It was also a time for me to reconsider whether I had done the best I could have for LG. Her death had come as a direct result of her unhealthy dependency on others, an affliction that I was able to recognize on the day I got her but didn't have the ability to fix no matter how hard I tried. In April I had called a leading expert on separation anxiety in dogs, whose name escapes me now, who didn't have time to talk about a bear. I then turned to the literature, but there was nothing I could find that was even remotely related to her problems. The only other route I could have taken would have been to bring her permanently into caged captivity, but, after experiencing her life in the wild, she would have done poorly in such an environment.

As for LB, I think he knew she was gone. The day after we buried LG, he made one brief visit to the house where she had been mortally wounded, and after that he never went back. On the walks we took for the next ten days, his suckling was much gentler and he no longer raked his teeth across my ear prior to quitting. When he was done, he often rested his head in my lap and went back to sleep. But this was now June, and he was a year-and-a-half-old bear. Soon it would be time for him to go.

In the few days that we had left together, LB showed all the signs of a maturing male beginning to take seriously his role in a community of wild bears. We were fast approaching the height of the breeding season, and even though at only seventy-five pounds he was years away from directly challenging any of the three-hundred-plus-pound dominant males, LG was clearly—but cautiously—in search of a mate. His approach to the problem was pretty sneaky: He wasn't rubbing over the major mark trees; he was instead dragging himself over the fresh scent of the females that were responding to the dominant males' marks. Thus he made sure his own marks of urine and semen, which communicated his desire to mate, were subtle, making it less likely that they would be discovered by the adult male. The odds LB would be caught by the dominant male were not that high, though, since the dominant male would have a large breeding territory to cover, and if the bigger bear had engaged a receptive female, he might not come by a particular mark tree for a week or more.

One day at the beginning of the month, we found a new bear tree that was being heavily used near a wallow to the west of my lot. There was a worn ring around the tree, sunken footprints, in addition to fresh scar-ring and bite marks on the bark—all indicative of recent use. On our way back, we crossed through the logged area adjacent to my property, where we found fresh tracks about the size of LB's made by a bear feed-ing on jewelweed and jack-in-the-pulpit. Then, lower down in a twitch road, we came across two sets of bear tracks: one, four inches; and the other, three and three-quarters. Normally solitary, bears start traveling together as couples just prior to breeding. It looked as if LB had lost out on an opportunity.

When I arrived the next morning, LB was still in the cage pacing back and forth. Something was bothering him to keep him inside the escape-rigged cage. (He hadn't spent the night there since LG was missing.) I wondered if he knew he had lost a prospective girlfriend to that four-inch-tracked male. I decided to take him for a walk to cheer him up, but when we got up into the ledges he found a comfortable spot, curled up, and went to sleep. I let him sleep for an hour before dropping back down through the sugar bush toward the cage. I tried to pull some taps that had been accidentally left earlier, but LB felt obligated to undo everything I did. I tried to discipline him and told him "No!"—only to have him open his mouth wide and roar back at me. Well, I couldn't blame him for being testy. I was still a bit down in the dumps myself.

In the evening, Frosty came over to try and lure LB out of the woods to a parked car with its radio on. The idea was to try teaching LB about the dangers of man, so if LB were to come to the car, Frosty would fire a black powder blank over his head to try to scare him. Frosty had the telemetry equipment with him and knew LB was in the vicinity, but after an hour and forty-five minutes LB had come close but not within sight. Frosty gave up. LB hadn't fallen for the trap.

The next day, I took LB back up to the third and fourth levels of the ledges. For about an hour, he fed on jewelweed on the fourth level, where another bear had fed recently; then he followed me down to the corner bear tree on the third level. He checked the tree for fresh sign but found nothing of interest. As we traveled, LB fed on beech leaves, red maples seeds (which he climbed for), blueberry flowers, and ants; he also tested a moose scat, then rejected it because it was too old. At the bear tree by the wallow on the Cole property, LB drag-marked over scent a dozen times, did a stiff-legged walk in the line of sunken footprints that led up to the bear tree, and did a full back rub on a small red maple prior to getting to the main bear tree. He was still advertising.

We crossed from the wallow onto a knoll covered with spruce and oak, where LB lifted his head and sniffed, which indicated to me that he had caught the scent of a wild bear in the vicinity. Judging from the amount of drag-marking he had been doing, the bear was probably a female he wanted to find. Since I didn't want to spoil his fun, I attempted to leave, hoping he would stay behind. He definitely wanted to stay but felt obligated to follow me if I left. He knew from our other walks that any time he would stop to nap, I would stop with him, so in a clear effort to prevent me from leaving, he lay down in my path and pretended to go to sleep. It was getting late, so I stepped around him and continued down the hill. His tactics changed accordingly. Now he decided to stop me by grabbing my calf muscle from behind. This worked a little too well, for he grabbed my calf just as my leg swung forward and his canine tooth plunged deep into my flesh. Not only did it really hurt, but there on my leg was the same triangular puncture wound that he had gotten on his butt when the wild male bit him. LB's wound had healed completely in nine days, but the one he gave me didn't completely close for twenty-nine.

When I found that LB was gone the next day, June 4, I guessed he had headed off to make contact with the bear on the hill. With the telemetry equipment I picked up his signal across the road from the cage and about a mile away. He returned to the cage on the fifth, only to leave again on the sixth. I couldn't find him on the seventh but picked him up again on the eighth with a signal coming from the oak-and-spruce knoll. On June 9, he was back on the oak knoll where I had first seen him with a wild bear. I was confused. Was he with the same bear? Was she the same female whose tracks we had found traveling with another male? I decided to go in and see.

This time, I grabbed my video camera and climbed up through the ravine to the knoll. When I got there, a large animal rushed off through the brush ahead of me, then a second one. I called out to LB, and he responded with the moan of recognition and appeared from the brush. He was happy to see me and immediately solicited suckling. I was sure I wouldn't see the other bear again, so I walked up the knoll with LB to see what they had been doing. About all I had discovered was a bed site and that they were feeding on acorns when I looked up to see the wild bear running toward us. The bear stopped about thirty yards away and began to circle us cautiously. LB tried to approach her—I could see now it was a female, and not the same one as before—but she chased him away. After a moment of indecision, LB returned to my side, and the sow cautiously made her way back to her previous position. A small bear—I estimated her weight to be between 120 and 130 pounds—she wasn't much bigger than LB but appeared to be more solidly built; her chest was broader, and her face was that of a mature bear.

With her head held low and swinging from side to side, she started toward us for the second time. I was trembling with excitement as I looked at her through the viewfinder of the camera; I had read about this very behavior in popular hunting magazine articles, and it was supposed to be a precursor to an attack. But to me it looked as if she was just trying to sort out my scent. I held my ground and kept taping. When she was eighteen feet away, LB started another approach to her. This time, they both stretched out to sniff each other's noses, the same means of greeting and recognition that LB and LG had used. But the whole time, the sow's eyes were fixed on me, and, perhaps because the confusion was too much, she started chomping and making the nervous "gulp." Then she swatted LB, hitting him on his collar and behind his left ear. In his response, LB rose up on his hind legs, arched his back, and lowered his head with his chin forward, upper lip extended, and ears pinned back. It looked as though he was going to fight back, but then he made a hasty retreat. His reaction was one of surprise and anger, or perhaps even betrayal. I had never seen anything like this before, but was well aware that I was responsible for the conflict. LB had been with this sow for at least three days before my intervention, and I'm sure they had been getting along very well.

LB came back by my side, and the sow moved over to the base of a large oak tree about twenty feet away. For the next hour and a half, he never approached her again while they both fed on acorns and took short naps. Occasionally she would "chomp" and "gulp," and he came over to suckle on me at least five times. During all this time, I kept filming the sow with my video camera, at one point getting within fourteen feet of her. That was a little too close—she stretched up the trunk and finally climbed into the oak tree. It seemed that we'd all had enough. I finished shooting the sequence with her sitting up in the tree, then left the area with LB following me.

It wasn't until I got home and was showing the tape to my brother Josh and some friends that somebody yelled out, "Look—another bear!" Sure enough, there was a small cub sitting out on a limb beside the sow in the last sequence.

This explained a number of things that I had thought strange. While I was filming the sow, she kept looking up; I thought she was looking at the blue jays that were mobbing us. I never even entertained the thought that LB would be able to travel with a sow that had a cub.

(As it turned out, I was able to get a glimpse of this sow's life over the next few years on the remote video camera that I set up later, a Trail-Master 700v. I filmed her that summer with no cub, and the following summer with two cubs of the year, so it appeared that she had lost this cub before the breeding season was over and had been bred in time to deliver cubs the following winter. The cub I filmed in the tree seemed to be small for a cub of six months, so maybe it was malnourished. Or it may have soon thereafter fallen prey to a large male.)

On the morning of June 10, I got LB's signal from across the road; he appeared to be disappearing over the first ridge. The area across the road is a difficult area in which to radio-track because of the rugged terrain. Knowing this, I returned at noon to get another signal and was surprised to find him walking out toward the road with some rock climbers. He was moaning softly, and his ears were back, but the climbers assured me that he had been a perfect gentleman. With the group of people around, he didn't recognize me until I lowered my head down to his, and he gave me a quick lick to the chin. I opened the door to my truck, he hopped in, and I gave him a ride back to the lot. He sat relatively still until he recognized his surroundings by the sugar house, where he jumped out of the truck.

LB was still nearby when I got a signal on him in the afternoon. I didn't know that anything special was going on with him, so I took my bulldozer up the hill to put in some water bars in my woods roads to prevent erosion. As I worked my way down the hill toward the sugar house, LB jumped out in front of the 'dozer and zigzagged back and forth to get me to stop. This was strange, so I got off the 'dozer and walked with him down the hill. I knew he was trying to tell me something when I got to my truck and found he'd left a message: I had left the window partway down, and he had climbed in and bite-marked the interior of the truck; then he had crawled out and marked the plastic tool box in the bed of the truck with urine (the urine had a sour smell and left an oily residue on the tool box), and in the final part of his message he destroyed the seat on the three-wheel all-terrain vehicle. Although I had no inkling of it then, I now think that LB was trying desperately to tell me he was leaving.

Despite the long odds of having been raised by a surrogate human mother, LB had now graduated and declared himself a bear. Dispersal time was here. On the morning of June 11, I received the last signal I would ever get from LB in the town of Lyme.

For the next two weeks, I searched for LB by climbing all of the high ground in the area and driving around with an omni-directional antenna that Ken Uline had rigged on the roof of my truck. Things seemed pretty futile, especially when I read that male cub dispersal could be anywhere from 5 to 240 miles from where they were raised. A break finally came when another friend of mine, Hank Buermann, offered to fly me to search for LB from the air.

I met Hank at Lebanon Airport early on the morning of June 19, and Frosty joined us to rig Hank's Cessna 180 with the telemetry equipment. With an antenna on each wing strut and selective switches for right, left, and both, we were ready for an aerial search for LB. Flying at about

3,500 to 4,000 feet, we searched the area over my property, north to Mount Cube, east almost to Mount Cardigan, and back to Lebanon. We had covered a land area of nearly one thousand square miles without getting a signal, and I was done for the day. All that low-level turbulence had left me a bit peaked, but Hank was ready to keep flying.

Between poor flying conditions and Hank's schedule, we weren't able to fly again for two weeks. I maintained a daily vigil with the antenna on my truck, but the wait for more flight time was arduous, leading to all kinds of dark speculation. The first thing I thought was that the equipment had failed, a real possibility as my handiwork in rebuilding telemetry collars hadn't been rigorously tested. Without a working collar, LB could be anywhere and I would be unable to contact him. When I was able to put away that anxiety, I used logic to try to convince myself that he was all right: If he were nearby and his collar failed, he would probably show up at the cage. If he were hurt or killed by accident, I would certainly be notified. The fact that the phone hadn't rung meant that he was behaving himself by keeping himself out of sight like any other wild bear.

Meanwhile, I had contacted Ken Elowe with the Maine Department of Inland Fisheries and Wildlife to find out what procedure he used to find wandering cubs. He had studied dispersal of male black bear cubs for his master's thesis and said the trick was to fly at 10,000 feet in expanding circles. On July 3, Hank took the plane up to 9,500 feet, and we had visibility of about forty miles as we flew north over Mount Lafayette in the heart of the White Mountains. We turned and flew down over Interstate 93, which runs up through the center of the state, and followed it south all the way to Concord. I had a hunch that LB would be near Mount Cardigan because it was the most significant landmark he could see from the ledges near the cage. I asked Hank to fly right over Cardigan. Sure enough, we picked up his signal on our approach about five miles south of Cardigan and located it on Melvin Mountain, just south of Cardigan in the town of Grafton. If that was LB, he was about twenty miles from the cage.

I hurried home and picked up Debbie to monitor the receiver as I drove, and we left to locate LB on the ground. Once we were in the Mount Cardigan area, it didn't take long before Debbie picked up a faint signal off the west side of Melvin Mountain, just northwest of Shepard Hill. We drove around Shepard Hill to Grant's Pond before we got a second signal. That placed him between the peaks of Melvin Mountain and Shepard Hill. Now we had his precise location: LB was eighteen miles from the cage as the crow flies, and twenty-four by road.

The following day, Debbie and I returned to find LB had moved a mile to the top of the ledges behind the village of Grafton, crossing a road in the process. We went home, and I made plans to come back the next day and try to walk in on him. The country was fully wooded and would be hard going, but I was determined.

I hadn't seen LB in a month. I had a lot of questions that could be answered if I saw him: What condition was he in? Had he been fighting? Why did he stop where he did?

On July 5, I got a location just northwest of Grant's Pond on the base of Melvin Mountain. He was about five hundred feet off Wild Meadow Road, but the closest place that I felt comfortable getting the truck off the road was a mile and a half farther, at Alexandria Four Corners. I took the abandoned Orange Road in and parked at an old log landing. I headed off with a backpack containing bear food, my 35-millimeter camera, my video camera, and the telemetry equipment, comprising a handheld directional antenna and the receiver that I carried slung over my shoulder. The load wasn't very heavy, but it was awkward, a real problem in the poor footing and dense cover of the deep early summer woods. I could get no signal from where I parked the truck, so I traveled south through a freshly logged section that looked as though it would be a popular place for bears when the blackberries ripened. Navigating by terrain, I cut west to the base of the mountain as that angle should have taken me toward LB's last known location. When I finally picked up his signal after an hour, I was a third of the way up the mountain and in a mixed stand of spruce and oak. It showed heavy usage by both deer and bear. I was trying to get a bearing on the signal when I heard a twig snap behind me. I turned to look and saw a large white-tailed buck with a nice ten-point rack still in the velvet. He was traveling on a run and hadn't seen or smelled me. I took care of that when I made an unsuccessful attempt to get out my video camera.

I followed LB's signal for about a mile through long stretches of hardwood, across small ridges and ravines made by the many small brooks running down the mountain. As the signal got stronger, the bear sign increased. When the signal told me I was very close, I stood on an oak hardwood knoll that had a path of sunken footprints, indicating an important bear place. Running beside the knoll was a spruce-and-sphagnum swamp in a small ravine. The signal indicated that LB was down the ravine, so I sneaked along the opposite side being careful not to snap any twigs. In order for me to see him, I would have to be close enough to hear him go, so I could call him back. As I came out into a small opening I heard two quick huffs and the sound of brush breaking as the bears ran off. Immediately I called out "Hi, guys!" LB stopped running and circled back to me with his greeting moan. I knelt down, and he came right up and suckled on my ear. I don't know if *joyous* is the right word for our reunion, but it had been a long time for both of us.

LB did joyously gobble up the apples that I gave him and worked on the dog food almost as enthusiastically; he was hungry but not ravenous, and while he ate I gave him a thorough going-over. He was thinner than when he left, but it looked as though his frame had grown. He had one new puncture wound in his hind leg that was smaller than his first one and was completely healed. There were a couple of minor cuts on his head and neck that were still crusty, little nicks just like the ones he used to get from LG in their food fights. He had no ticks, fleas, or other ectoparasites. His mood was relaxed, not anxious as he had been when he left. His penis was clean and dry, indicating that he was no longer dragmarking or advertising for a mate as he was when he left. The double huff and the double bed site indicated that he had been with a mate when I disturbed them. The fact that he was still getting erections indicated that he and his mate were consummating their relationship. They had been bedded in a softwood thicket at the base of a large hemlock tree across the ravine from where we now were.

Unfortunately, it was two in the afternoon, I was a long way from the truck, and it was unfamiliar territory. It was apparent that LB would follow me, so I needed to allow time to handle whatever might happen when we separated. It was time to start back.

LB started to follow but let himself get easily sidetracked, digging in stumps for no apparent reason and lying down in front of me and pretending he was tired. This was like old times. Then he spooked to scent with a high head and looked back intently in the direction of the bed site. I knew what was up: his mate had come back and was close by. The same series of events had taken place that time LB sunk a canine into my calf trying to keep me from leaving the hill after he had scented a bear. I knew she was near us. But curious as I was to see his mate, I wasn't sure she would come out with me there and I didn't have the time to spare. I kept moving. LB started to follow me at a reasonable pace, but he continued to stop and look back.

It was a long hike. I get thirsty fairly easily and have a habit of kneeling down to get a drink out of almost any mountain stream where I can trust the source. In this case, when I knelt down, LB came up and suckled on my ear. And when I bent down lower to get a drink, I felt a paw slide seductively over my back. I stood up to break off his advance.

With black bears, ear suckling and nuzzling are bonding behaviors between siblings and between mother and cub. During the mating season the same behaviors are bonding behaviors that allow two otherwise solitary animals to stay together long enough to breed. Also during the breeding season, these are sexual premating behaviors. A parallel in our own behavior would be that in a family, hugging and kissing are bonding behaviors, and in a human sexual relationship they serve as both bonding and presexual behaviors. Always a gentleman, LB did not make a fuss when I stood up, and he continued to follow me back to the truck.

Near the logged area we came upon a tremendous white pine, nearly four feet in diameter. It was a bear place, with sunken footprints encircling the tree, and beside the circle of tracks was the largest bear scat I've ever seen. It seemed recent. LB did a modified stiff-legged walk as he placed his feet carefully in the sunken footsteps. He sniffed and slow-licked the tree and the scat before we headed out. I wondered: How did LB, large for his age but still just a yearling, maintain breeding status with this sow with a large male right in the neighborhood?

We got back to the truck about half past four. When I opened the truck door, LB jumped in. I had parked in the sun, and I wanted to move the truck to the shade so I could visit with LB a little before I left. LB was calm when I started the truck, but just before I got into the shade he leaped across my lap and bailed out. Once I parked and turned off the engine, he climbed back in.

We had a relaxed forty-five minute visit and one last suckle on my ear before it came time for me to go. He had the opportunity to return with me—we were together in the truck, and he knew what riding in it was all about. I started the engine, and he bailed out the window. It was clear he wanted to stay. I got out and left him a big pile of food in the woods, more than he would normally eat in two days. As I drove off, he stepped into the road to watch me drive off, making no effort to follow.

I came back the next morning but was unable to get a signal on him at all. The food was all gone. I checked the mud in the road to see if he had made any attempt to follow me. I was pleasantly surprised to find two sets of tracks in the road, LB's measuring three and a half inches and his mate's measuring four. Those were the tracks of an adult sow. It was clear that she was following him, not the other way around. Their bond had been strong enough for her to follow us a mile and a half to the truck knowing he was with a human every step of the way.

As I drove back, I continued to wonder why LB at a year and a half was able to maintain a relationship and breed with an adult wild sow. Was it possible that the female bear had picked LB for reasons other than his size? Could she tell from his smell that he was from another gene pool? The trip that LB's mate had made knowing full well that there was a human involved demonstrated that she was willing to go to great risk to protect her investment in and commitment to LB. I fully expected that there would be some little LBs around in the spring.

That day, I hadn't gotten a precise location, but the signal I did get was about four miles from the log landing where I had left LB the day before, a distance probably determined by the wild sow's reaction to my interference. From July 7 to 11, LB stayed in what I came to consider the female's home range, but none of the signals came from anyplace where I might get good enough access to try another walk in. Plus it seemed wise to leave them alone.

After my visit with LB on July 5, I had stopped to see Ed Landers, a fellow gunsmith who owned the place at the start of the Orange Road. I went in and introduced myself and started asking about bears, but all I got back was rather a stern look over Ed's half-glasses and not a word. Realizing I wasn't communicating what my interest was, I explained. His face relaxed. "I thought you were a bear hunter," he said. "I wasn't going to tell you anything. We like our bears around here." We went on to exchange bear stories and talk about our trade. He did allow that this area was heavily hunted by houndsmen.

LB left the area on July 12, presumably moving on to fatten up for the winter. I guessed he had been with his mate for two or three weeks. That's based on the fact that he left Lyme on June 11. He traveled roughly twenty miles, which he could have done in a day, but probably took a week or two because he would have been finding females and checking on their receptivity along the way. Because he was relatively free of scars when I finally found him, I guessed he hadn't endured much conflict and possibly made it over to the Mount Cardigan area within a week to find his mate.

I lost track of LB for the next month and a half. I made a number of futile attempts to locate him by driving around, but I had no idea which direction he had gone. I figured he was nearby, but that could be any-where in a twenty-mile circle. Or larger. The terrain was so rugged in the area around Mount Cardigan that it would be hard to pick up his sig-nal from any of the roads. But I was comfortable in knowing that he could take good care of himself in the wild and assumed that as long as the phone didn't ring, he was behaving himself. I did want to locate him before the bear-hunting season opened so I could make contact with him to check the tightness of his collar and assess his condition.

We were unable to fly to look for LB until late September, and when we did it was with only one antenna functional on the tracking receiver. Hank Buermann was the pilot and John Bressette was the copilot. On our westerly ascent we hit the signal at about six thousand feet and roughly six miles from Mount Cardigan. When the signal was the strongest, we descended to two thousand feet and flew a cross pattern over the area just north of the big mountain. Using the ridges and smaller mountains to shield the signal, we were able to get a very good location.

The next morning, I stopped and picked up Ken Uline. All three of the receivers that I had been using were old, and Ken was able to keep at least one going at all times. We spent a long day trying to get a signal on LB. I knew about where he was. The problem was that he was in a very remote location with the nearest road two miles away. With the terrain as mountainous as it was, getting a signal was not easy. On our way up the road to the AMC lodge, we took a road north to the Potter cemetery, where there was a nice vista of Firescrew Mountain over an old hay field. On the way out we got nothing, but on the way back, we picked up a weak signal and I got out to get a reading. The signal was in the direc-tion of the base of Firescrew, and the intermittent transmission led us to believe that LB was moving. We kept going to get a second location so we might pinpoint his position.

I saw a dirt road going through a farmyard that looked as if it would take us to high ground. As we pulled into the yard of this remote home-stead, an elderly gentleman greeted us and figured we were probably lost. I don't think the old guy got much company, so when I told him what I was up to, he regaled us—after numerous nonrelated stories—

with his rendition of the long-standing belief in these parts that bears communicate by hooting back and forth. He assured us that there was a healthy bear population because you could hear the bears hooting on the ridges in the evening and you could hear them as they moved down to feed in the valleys at night. This fellow was a good storyteller and quite entertaining, so I asked him what these bears sounded like. He let loose with a robust "Who-who—whowhoooo!" I was impressed, but to this day I haven't yet heard a bear hoot. When he was all done telling stories and calling bears, Ken and I drove down the dirt road and tried to get a signal. We weren't successful, though, and were unable to get a second location from anywhere.

On October 9, I found an old town road that led to the height of land near Cilleys Cave. From there I made a short hike to overlook where I thought LB might be. When I turned on my receiver, his signal came in immediately. I climbed partway up Firescrew to get a second location, and with it I was able to determine that he was moving toward the base of Mowglis Mountain. I was very tempted to go down and see him, but the abandoned road I was parked on was now being used daily by bear hunters with hounds and it was likely LB would follow me out. Leading LB directly to the hunters wasn't something that I wanted to chance. But his present location was very remote with limited access. I thought that if he stayed put, he would be relatively safe for the duration of the bear season.

On October 18, I was unable to get a signal on LB from Cilleys Cave or anywhere in the vicinity, so I decided to drive over to Grafton to try for a signal from Grant's Pond. I got what could have been a partial signal about a quarter mile south of the west entrance to Mount Cardigan. I came across a hunter I know named Guy Sanborn, who was running his bear dogs there. He said the dogs had split and were on two bears. If LB were running, it could explain the partial signal I received. Guy knew all about LB and me, so I showed him some pictures and then left him to try to regather his hounds.

A couple of days later, I climbed Firescrew and was unable to get a signal in any direction. This was very unusual, but he could have been run out of the area by the hounds or just been behind a ridge from me.

On October 29, Hank called for me to meet him at the airport at two in the afternoon to go fly and look for LB. We flew until dark, with no success at all. The only thing close was a strange-sounding signal that had the right pulse and which came in and out again very quickly over North Dorchester or Rumney. By then I was suspecting the worst. It was completely possible the funny signal was LB's collar hanging in someone's garage or vehicle. It was getting dark, and we needed to get back to the airport with some light to spare. Hank was remaining optimistic and volunteered to come back out the next day.

We never got the chance.

That evening at home, I picked up the phone to hear Tom Dakai, our local game warden, on the other end. My heart sank. I knew what the call had to mean.

Tom told me LB was dead. He had been shot in Hebron, a town just to the northwest of Mount Cardigan, by a logger who was working in the area. He had seen LB one day and brought his rifle back into the woods with him the next day. He sat and waited for LB to reappear and then shot him when he did. It was the legal season, and the logger was a hunter with a license. LB had lived a short but complete life, dying the way many a wild bear does.

I guess it's my English heritage that allowed me to receive the news with a stiff upper lip, but as the days passed my self-imposed repression gave way to growing sorrow for the loss of nothing less than a true friend. A sorrow brought on by my voluntary investment in his life, an emotional investment with no measurable value in the cold reality of the ongoing relationship between humans and bears. I had known and understood that reality when I took on LB and his twin sister twenty-two months earlier, and had tried without success to keep my attitude dispassionate, my relationship to the cubs free from the kind of attachment that would only make me anxious for their safety.

Now my anxiety was gone, but unfortunately so were the cubs.

CHAPTER 16

Between the Bears

THE BEARS WERE gone. It was now late in the fall of 1994, and after a year and a half of increasing commitment, growing fascination, and a deepening personal attachment that I had tried to avoid, I found myself suddenly cut off from all three. I had lost my cubs and with them went my attachment to the daily lives of bears, a painful void that I knew could only be filled by another set of cubs. But I had no way of knowing whether any would ever be offered or, if the opportunity did arise, whether I'd accept them. It's one thing to go into a project blind, filled with enthusiasm and naïveté. It's another thing altogether to do it with your eyes—and your heart—wide open.

In the weeks that followed the news that LB had been killed, I went back in my mind over all the time I had shared with the bears, and as I did, I felt both a sense of failure and a sense of accomplishment. Failure because I had been unable to control the inevitable effects that the bear-human conflict would have on my cubs, and accomplishment because these two animals had provided me with a wealth of insights into their lives. I now had time to compile my field notes, comprising 215 pages; my photographs, more than a thousand of them; and the video I shot, nearly twenty hours. This was my first wildlife research project, and, not being an academic or professional and feeling a bit intimidated by formal science, I had made sure I had thoroughly documented everything I had observed. From my notes I knew I had observed the cubs react to wild bear scent 157 times, and to known bear scent on the used telemetry collars eight times. I had watched them identify and eat over 125 different food items, and I had the calendar dates when these items were eaten. Two of the things they ingested were of particular interest: the fresh deer scats and the soil. I thought it likely that the cubs swallowed these two for reasons other than as food: the scats possibly as a way of obtaining digestive organisms, and the soil to buffer toxins in the plants they ate. If this were true, the possibility existed that with their apparently sophisticated ability to identify plants by mouthing, black bears could be using plants for medicinal reasons as well. But at this point these were just guesses.

Over those cold winter days that gave way to the warming springtime weeks and hot summer months of 1995, and as I read back over my notes, categorized my pictures, and watched the videos, all those hours with the cubs came vividly back to life. It became obvious to me that despite the hardships and emotional trauma of raising LB and LG, if another set of cubs were offered I would have to take them in and do it all over again. For one thing, observing another set of cubs would allow me to differentiate the quirks of an individual bear's actions from the representative behaviors shared by black bears in general. For another, it would give me a chance at my unfulfilled goal of placing an adult female back in the wild so she could have cubs of her own someday. Should I get the chance to foster more orphans, those would be my twin purposes: to put at least one female successfully back into the breeding population in the wild, and to add to our own knowledge of the black bear in the process. My mind was made up, but it wasn't just up to me. First someone would have to find another set of orphans.

Meanwhile, I had more than enough work. Aside from continuous trips to the Dartmouth library to research bears and try to determine what the significance was of certain behaviors I had recorded, I went back to work in my gun shop as usual. I was also the chair of the Lyme Planning Board, which oversees zoning in our town, and over the previous two years had been telling bear stories in our slow moments. The board members now began encouraging me to give a public lecture on my adventures with the cubs. This was a fine idea, but the last time I had made a public presentation was in college, and all I remembered of that horrendous event was my freezing up right in the middle of it. Regardless, I made plans to give a talk in our small town library. When the day came, the room was packed to its fifty-person capacity, and somehow I got through it. Debbie, who had already seen the slides and heard the stories more than once, seemed to get a chuckle out of it anyway; she said I spoke too fast in run-on sentences, was as stiff as a zombie, and didn't stop to take a noticeable breath through the entire talk. She was right, but the townsfolk had loved it anyway. The next week I was invited to talk at the local Upper Valley Land Trust's annual meeting, and not long after that, Noel Perrin, the well-known author and Dartmouth professor, invited me to speak to an environmental science class. And so it went. I've averaged twenty-five public-speaking events a year ever since. What had started off innocently enough when LB and LG arrived was not only turning into a real education for me but for many others in the process.

Still, I wanted to do more with what I had discovered than tell stories to interested general audiences. I wanted to impact the scientific and academic communities as well, but without affiliation with a government agency or scientific institution to guide me I needed advice. I knew exactly where to turn: to my father and his library. And in their turn, both my father and his extensive collection of natural history books sent me to the man I wanted to talk to first. I wrote to George Schaller.

Schaller, the director of science at the Wildlife Conservation Society, whose legendary observational studies on lions, mountain gorillas, and pandas have made him the top field biologist of his time, was greatly admired by both my father and me. So even though I had never met him and knew he had certainly never heard of me, I wrote to him, outlining what I had been doing and explaining my background and current situation. Weeks went by with no response. I knew he was a busy man, and I wouldn't have blamed him if he tossed my letter. But then in the middle of September a letter finally arrived; it was from George B. Schaller.

The letter wasn't long, but in it he was very gracious and apologized for his late reply, explaining that he had just returned from several months in Tibet and Mongolia. He said in the letter, "I was most interested to read about your detailed investigations on bear cubs. As is so often the case when someone devotes him or herself to a subject with open mind and dedication, startling new insights emerge."

He invited me to call him. He gave me encouragement and good advice on the phone and suggested that we stay in touch. The call was a real thrill, and I especially remember his advice on writing about animals. "People aren't interested in just bears," he said. "They're interested in people and bears." That was perceptive—and very good—advice to someone who was more concerned with bears than with people.

In January 1995, I drove to the state capital and gave my slide presentation of the results of raising the cubs to the biologists and staff at the New Hampshire Fish and Game Department in Concord. Of the slide shows I had given so far, this might have been the most important one; I was well received and garnered support for future projects.

That year, 1995, was one of drought, and the long-term lack of rain had caused severe food shortages for wild bears throughout New Hampshire and Vermont. It was October before the rains came, right about the time we received a telephone call from Fish and Game saying that Rob Calvert was bringing a cub our way. He delivered this cub in a medium-sized Havahart trap, the humane wire-frame cages that lure an animal in with food and then drop a door to close them in. The bear was a little female weighing just twelve pounds. She was ten months old and had been caught panhandling hikers at Pinkham Notch. She wasn't malnourished, she just hadn't grown, giving her the appearance of a miniature bear.

I named her Little Girl 2 as an homage to LG. She was standoffish but tolerant of my touching her. Like all bears, however, she had her limit, and not long after she arrived she let me know where it was when I touched her one too many times. Most animals bite when they get annoyed, but she just grabbed my hand in her mouth softly but firmly, moved it away from her body, and released it. That winter, LG2 hibernated in a wooden packing box that I modified for her and could access from the wood shed at our house in the village.

While she was deep in her winter sleep, I got the call I had been waiting for.

On February 17, 1996, Eric Orff called to say that a den had been disturbed by a logging operation in Twin Mountain, a town to the north near the famous old Bretton Woods resort in the White Mountains. The logging was going to continue, so the bears needed to be relocated, and to do that the Fish and Game folks would have to capture the sow so they could move the family as a unit. But catching a wild sow in the middle of winter when she isn't eating is far from easy; she can't be tempted into a trap, and in the wide visibility of the snow-covered, leaf-barren woods it's almost impossible to sneak close enough to get an anesthetic dart into her. "If we can't catch her right away," said Eric, "the cubs will be heading in your direction."

In fact, they already were—the field team had no luck with the mother and wanted to take no chances with the cubs. Later that afternoon, Conservation Officer Todd Bogardus arrived with three seven-week-old black bears: two females and a male weighing about four pounds each. These cubs were healthy and had been separated from their mother for only six hours; they were neither malnourished nor abandoned, so already I was ahead of where I had started with LB and LG. But this time, there were three of them.

As I braced myself for another fifteen-month commitment, everyone around me knew there was no way for me to do it alone. Not with triplets. And not with how much Debbie and Phoebe had come to love the bears that were now in our lives to stay. The days of "my" bears were gone. From here on out, this was a family effort.

CHAPTER 17

The Triplets Arrive

FOR THEIR FIRST twelve hours with us, the triplet bear cubs were very vocal, waking us up in the middle of the night with their terrible squalls until we decided that their shivering as we fed them was from cold, not tension. Debbie solved that problem by setting an electric heating pad to medium and placing it in the bottom of the trunk-sized basket that was their den in the upstairs bedroom. Cubs in wild dens apparently get heat from their mother, for after that there was no more squalling. The three slept hard all through the night from then on.

Days were a different story. At only four pounds each, they were active bears nonetheless, even if what passed for a walk that first week was more of a wobble. Just like older bears, though, they could square off their lips and huff when upset. Many of their initial vocalizations were the same as they would be when they got older: irritated moans when uncomfortable; the sound of contentment when happy; a bully's roar when hungry; a sigh when content. Other times they'd render even quieter sounds, including faint squeals and a variety of small chirps. My brother Josh commented that one of these chirps and corresponding nudging, made when the little bears were searching for a nipple, sounded a lot like the one his kids had made when they were tiny and still nursing. After feeding, the little bears would make a pigeonlike "coo" that changed to a soft sigh as they serenaded themselves to sleep.

Because we had two females this time, we needed names to distinguish them, so we named one Curls for the curly hair on her forehead and the other Squirty because she was the smaller of the two. The boy we left at just that: the Boy. The names at this point were more for our own convenience in referring to them than for telling them apart; like all the bears I've ever raised, they began almost immediately to show not only their physically distinguishing marks but their personalities as well. Within a month, while the cubs were still upstairs, the Boy began escaping from the pen, a three-by-eight-foot corral with two-foot-high sides that Josh had built out of plywood, and letting loose with a series of distress calls as soon as he found himself separated from his sisters, who would then try to dig out through the plywood to join him. Already the Boy was showing himself to be the explorer of the group.

One of the immediate differences I could see between raising these new cubs and the first two was that I could now recognize their behaviors as they developed. Whenever they were scared either by a sound or a smell, they would "tree" to the highest pillow on the bed or on me if I were with them, all the way up to my head and shoulders. They suckled on my ears and fingers and wrestled to bond with each other and with me. (In my case, they wrestled with my hand, but I knew what it meant. Even today, in her sixth year and at times well over two hundred pounds, Squirty initiates wrestling with me every spring to get reacquainted when I find her again in the woods. It's not quite as cute as it was back then.)

At the end of six weeks, we moved them down to the basement, where I had built a climbing gym out of ash logs. They took to it readily, attracted to the climbing opportunity after only a few moments' tentative hesitation, during which there was much audible sniffing and cautious exploration.

Although their climbing skills were unformed, the cubs knew immediately how to go about developing them, especially how to reach down with their feet to find a footing, and were very tenacious about practicing and learning how to deal with the obstacles I had built into the log structure. Whenever one would get into a jam and loudly panic, I'd help the little adventurer out. It only took them three days to become fully adept at climbing, and by that time they had also gotten comfortable with the cold basement as a new home, sleeping together in a warm circle with their heads buried under their bodies to conserve heat.

In the middle of April, I took them out for a test run in the woods, carting them together in one large pet carrier in the back of my pickup truck. Parking in the open area at the Turnpike Lot camp, I let them out and stood nearby while the scared cubs cried and made distress calls. Expecting them to follow, I started walking toward the woods, where I knew they'd be more comfortable, but only two of them came with me. Squirty wouldn't budge, choosing to hang back by the truck and bleating a distress call until I came back and rescued her. As expected, when we all finally made it to the cover of the still-leafless woods, all three cubs became much more relaxed, running, climbing, and exploring without inhibition. Again their behaviors were consistent with those of LB and LG, especially now that I could recognize them. Right away, they began mouthing vegetation, testing it with what I still thought to be their Jacobsen's organ, and they did slow licks as well, combining them with much audible sniffing. If there had been any question as to the dominance of olfaction in the way cubs explored and categorized their world, it was now being rapidly answered while I observed.

Midway in that first walk, the cubs took off by themselves, something that LB and LG had not done, and when I walked through the dry leaves to catch up, all three treed. The Boy huffed and chomped at me as I approached, while the girls just huffed. None came down until I sat on the ground to make myself less threatening, and when they did they still approached cautiously until they got my scent to confirm it was me. After that, it was an easy walk back to the truck and an uneventful ride home. All in all, an almost perfect first outing, making it easy to look forward to the many more to come.

By the end of April, the cubs were already up in the pipes in the basement, a full month ahead of when LG and LB had done the same thing, leading me to conclude that their development even at this very early point seemed to be related more to size and condition than to age. In any case, they were plenty ready to move outside, and on May 2, my father, Phoebe, and I took them out to the Turnpike Lot cage. They took to it happily but didn't understand that they couldn't walk right through the cage wire when they could see through it just fine. Later that evening, Debbie and Phoebe went back out to check on them and to bring from the basement all their familiar toys, which they responded to right away. In the morning when I arrived, they were nowhere in sight, and it wasn't until I had searched for five minutes, wondering how they had escaped, that the Boy appeared from behind the den entrance. They had been inside all along, hiding in the same place that LG and LB had sought for security when they had lived there.

As the sparse greens of the May woods progressed toward the full canopy of spring in June, the triplets and I fell into the same visit-feed-suckle-walk routine that had been the staple of my time with the twins. Feedings were as spirited as ever, marked with the predictably ferocious but short-lived bouts that I coined "fights over something desirable in short supply," a description that also applied to their sometimes three-way scrambles over who got to suckle on my fingers. After all, I only had two hands, and in the middle of more than one of their odd-bear-out squabbles it seemed possible that number might go down.

While these fights were the same as those between LB and LG, they were much less frequent. I would learn much later on, when Squirty had cubs of her own, that the frequency of these fights was based on how much milk the mother bear could produce. For their first six months, the only food available to newborn cubs is the amount of milk produced by their mother. The shorter she is on resources, the harder the cubs will fight for what she has. This competition, just as it does in birds of prey, will lead to young of different sizes, a strategy that enhances the survival of at least one offspring in years of food shortage.

My definition for these fights applies to adult situations as well: two bears fighting over a fishing position on a salmon stream; two similar-sized males fighting over a female; two females fighting over territory. The fights themselves are focused, practiced, and while they sound horrific they usually result only in superficial wounds to the head, neck, and shoulders. Of course, *superficial* to a bear may mean removing an ear, tearing out a patch of skin, or suffering a deep slash from a powerful claw. This is not at all to say that bears will never kill other bears intentionally, but rather that it would make very little sense to the system as a whole for individuals to settle routine disputes with injuries that could result in death.

But if the fights were always predictable, the walks rarely were, at least not in the specifics. Some days the cubs wanted to stay near the cage, on others they'd be off and covering great distances. Some walks were mostly play, others mostly exploration. But always there was climb-ing, and lots of it as they slowly learned what kinds of trees had grippable bark and dependable limbs. They fell all the time. One time, I watched them tumble to the ground six times in a half hour, and still they kept at it undaunted—even an eight-foot free fall into standing water bothered the Boy not in the least. At the end of a long walk, I would leave them behind to an evening chorus of New England birds in the spring: wood-cock "peenting" in their mating flights in the pond clearing; robins, ovenbirds, and various warblers singing nervously just before dark; downy, hairy, and pileated woodpeckers drumming against tree hollows.

There are advantages in not being the firstborn child; parents get over their fears as newness wears off and experience takes its place. This was definitely the case as I left the cubs out for the first time on May 13. I had learned from LB and LG that as long as a cub was well fed and healthy, it would be fast enough to evade any adversary by escaping up a tree; and as long as the cubs depended on me for food, they would stay close to the cage even when threatened. The older they got and the more independent, the farther they would travel, but that time, I also knew, wasn't here yet.

Toward the end of the month, the cubs and I took an afternoon walk to Merle Wilmot's lower log landing, and on the way back, just as we were about to cross the Grafton Turnpike, a motorcycle came racing by on the dirt road, sending the cubs up two large pine trees. Before the sound of the motorcycle had faded, a car came by in the same direction, followed by another and then another before it dawned on me: it was the last Sunday in May, opening day for the asphalt-track races at the Canaan Speedway, and the spectators were all going to the races. I counted thirty-five cars in forty minutes, and, knowing that the cubs would stay spooked for a while, I went home for supper.

When I came back in just over an hour, the cubs weren't in the two trees and they weren't in the cage. I went back to the twin pines and called and called until finally, twenty minutes later, I heard a twig snap. They were about forty yards away at the base of an even larger pine tree. Curls climbed up on my shoulder and suckled my finger, then the cubs followed me cautiously across the road and back to the cage where I knelt down and soon had all three suckling on me for reassurance. The bond had been tested and needed to be reinforced.

By the middle of June, the cubs had grown to forty pounds for the

Boy and thirty-five each for Squirty and Curls. Their familiarity with their range around the cage was growing, too, and soon they learned to follow the scent trail that I or Phoebe would leave behind as we went to the truck after feeding them. On June 15, I found the trail of a wild bear in the mowed grass of our pond berm, where a quick backtrack confirmed that it had been nearby, feeding heavily on jack-in-the-pulpit. I guessed that this was the same male that had visited the cage the week before; he had left a four-and-a-quarter-inch track on the path into the cage.

When I came back to camp, where Debbie was transplanting flowers in her garden by the pond, we both heard large animal noises in the brush, coming from the end of the pond. I ran to get a heavy shirt and my camera just as Curls and the Boy came into the clearing to greet Debbie. Then, when I went to lead the two cubs past the pond and back into the woods where they'd be more at ease, Squirty appeared on the opposite bank. With very little coaxing, she walked right in and swam twenty yards across the ten-foot-deep pond to join us.

I kept a very detailed record of everything the cubs reacted to on our daily walks, whether it was by scenting, mouthing, or eating. On an afternoon walk on June 16, for instance, the cubs reacted to scent on the Tyler Ridge bear tree by sniffing, slow-licking, and olfactory huffing, which is different from the alarm huff they make when threatened; by a stiff-legged walk; by marking with urine; and finally by climbing on the tree. Later, they did all the same except climb on a coyote scat that contained the fur of a domestic animal that I couldn't identify. They mouthed buttercup flowers, red clover leaves and flowers, blackberry leaves and flowers, blue-eyed grass, pink corydalis flowers, Indian paintbrush, and a plant unknown to me. They actually ate blue-eyed grass flowers and seed pods, jack-in-the-pulpit (only Curls did this), unripened sarsaparilla berries, and ants four times.

On that same walk, I tried a demonstration of how a sow bear could teach her cubs to eat a specific food. I had noticed that whenever I got down on the ground to get a drink, the cubs came over to me and started a chorus of audible sniffs, so keying in on that behavior I got down on all fours in a patch of clover and ate some. The cubs came right over and individually stuck their noses in my mouth while sniffing and olfactory huffing, after which they got very excited. They proceeded to search for and then eat the clover. Does a mother bear have a mechanism to get her cubs to come over when she wants to show them a specific food, or do the cubs just do this whenever she eats? What would be the advantage of this behavior? These were still big questions. At that point, there were three major bear foods that the cubs had not yet eaten: jewelweed, lettuces, and clover. Do cubs have to be taught to eat these plants, or will they take to them on their own later, when these plants flower? Curls was the first to eat jack-in-the-pulpit, something she had learned when we had followed the hot scent of a wild female that had been digging them; the other two started eating it within the week. Was this social learning from an unrelated bear? Can bears learn from any other bear?

A few days later, I got a chance to try the experiment again, this time with Indian cucumber root in Cole's swamp. The cubs were definitely predisposed to this behavior: Once again, they came right over and checked my breath after I chewed the root, which doesn't have a very distinctive flavor. This time, the Boy and Squirty tried mouthing the root, and Squirty immediately picked up that she should eat it and began digging where I showed her the plant. Curls then joined the dig, but both bears ended up with clintonia instead. The clintonia root is smaller and has a more bitter aftertaste, but the girls seemed to like it, enthusiastically digging up about a dozen of them. It was clear to me that smelling my breath and digging the root were separate learning experiences. The cubs were already eating clintonia leaves and were imitating me in the root digging. Eventually, they were digging the Indian cucumber roots as well.

An opportunity for another experiment came at the end of June when Gene Thorburn, the animal control officer for Hanover, stopped by with a recently killed beaver. I cut the wide, flat tail and some flesh in one piece from the carcass and tied it to a length of string to make a drag, then carried it to the cage. When I got there, the cubs were nowhere to be seen. It's tricky to run an experiment without the subjects, so I set out to find them, eventually locating all three at their favorite climbing pine. After a quick suckle to say hello, they followed me back toward the cage in their usual meandering, playful manner, but as soon as they encountered the strong scent of the beaver tail, they turned very serious. All three circled cautiously, then came up to the tail and examined it using sniffs, slow-licks, olfactory huffs, and an upper-lip flick that I hadn't seen before, while rolling it over and over with their paws. This was all business. Finally, the Boy bit at it, pulled back quickly, then grabbed the whole two-pound treat in his mouth and ran off with it, with the other two in hot pursuit. He didn't get far before Curls grabbed it from him and ran off into the woods, with the others giving chase.

I caught up with them at the leaning oak. By then, the Boy was left out and the girls had the beaver tail. I picked up the trailing string and began dragging the beaver tail toward the swamp. Curls started following immediately, but not by sight; instead she used her nose to track the scent, even though the moving tail was still visible. I stayed ahead of her and the other two cubs all the way to the snowmobile trail. By that time, all three were trying to catch it and help me out by lightening the load. First one and then another would pick it up by mouth, turn and run for the bushes with it, only to have it jerked away as the string came taut. The string gave out before they did, so I retied it and resumed my walk. As we continued the game for another circuit around the swamp, Curls figured out that she could wrap her arms and legs around it on the fly and stop me cold in my tracks. Back in the cage I hung the tail up by the string so they could only get it from above. I wanted to see if they would pull it up from above, but they didn't.

By the Fourth of July, the cubs had grown so confident in their home range that they were beginning to expand it through longer explorations on their own, a natural-enough process that unfortunately included the need to cross roads and the increased chances of encountering other people, sometimes in their own backyards. It was time for some teaching about the dangers that lay ahead.

With LG and LB, I had been hesitant to be the one to apply adverse conditioning for fear of alienating the cubs. But handing out bear-repelling devices to the neighbors so that they could do it for me hadn't worked very well in keeping the cubs at bay; moreover, the supposedly safe plastic bullet that struck LG had been anything but. Now, after rethinking that decision, I concluded that this time I had to be the one to do the adverse conditioning, both to achieve a more effective result and for the safety of the cubs. If in the process the triplets decided my scent had to come from my evil twin, so be it. It ought to make them even more distrustful of humans if they couldn't even be sure about me.

On the afternoon of July 12, I drove out to see if the cubs were near the road. My father, who had been cutting brush by the road, said the Boy had walked up to him, while my neighbor Bob Rufsvold said he'd seen them from the road while he was jogging. Armed with a .22-caliber pistol loaded with blanks, I drove down the road until I found them playing in a hemlock tree. I parked the truck and watched until they climbed down, and then I fired the blanks. It had little or no effect on them, so I got back in the truck and drove away, waiting until I was out of sight, then turned around and drove back till I saw them running up the road. I gunned the engine and leaned on the horn, sending them scrambling off into the dense roadside brush. Then I drove away and parked before walking back to see three black shapes bouncing along through a thicket of saplings. I fired another volley of randomly spaced blanks and watched them disappear.

This experience hadn't been very satisfactory, so I went home and prepared some bigger, louder blanks. An hour later I was back. Taking a position on the bank where I could see them across the road, I called and was pleasantly surprised to have them come to me from behind. They were nervous and demanded bonding by grabbing my hands and suckling on them. That was enough for one day. We went for a walk.

The next day, I came back for another round of adverse conditioning. This time, I decided to invade their sanctuary and confront them as a hunter might. But I really was apprehensive this time, knowing full well that I might be singled out as the villain, especially if they saw me and could add my visual image to the negative picture I wanted to paint in their minds. Still, this had to be done, and I knew I was the only one who could do it properly. To minimize the negative impact from these scare lessons, I planned always to approach silently, in contrast to the regular vocal greetings I always gave the cubs in my maternal role.

Armed this time with a twelve-gauge shotgun loaded with black powder blanks I had put together specially for the purpose, I approached stealthily and began checking their safe trees. Hurricane Bertha had gone by to the south, and it was raining hard, not the best conditions for primitive firearms, but I wanted to shoot the black powder because it was ideal; along with a very loud report, there's a thirty-foot column of smoke and the rotten-egg stench of hydrogen chloride in the air for a long time afterward. But after a fifteen-minute search without finding them, it was time for me to go. Since I knew there was a chance that they were observing me while hiding, I fired two well-spaced shots from different locations before I walked back to the road and left.

It was still pouring rain when I came back four hours later and proceeded to call the cubs from near the cage. After a half hour of no response,

LB giving me the eye

LB and LG suckling my ears at Wallow Bog

Squirty, Curls, and the Boy swimming

Squirty, Curls, and the Boy sniffing ants in the moss

Squirty, Curls, and the Boy climbing a dead tree

Nose to nose with LB (*Courtesy Forrest Hammond*)

Squirty soliciting breath from Curls

Yoda and Houdini having a water fight

Yoda and Houdini wrestling

Yoda at four months

Houdini mouthing poplar leaves

Squirty and Curls out on a ledge

Squirty at two months

Squirty and Snowy

Object play: LG playing with a piece of wood

Social learning: Curls coming to see what Squirty has

I finally heard the Boy roar from the direction of the water hole I had recently dug for them. I spotted the cubs on the ground, but when I approached and greeted them, all three huffed at me and went up three separate trees. I walked under the trees and got nothing but a chorus of distress calls, huffs, and moans; not one of them wanted to hear anything I had to say. The Boy finally backed down out of his tree, only to bristle up, huff, and run to the tree Squirty was in. By now, I had begun to think that they had seen me shoot the black powder while I was wearing this rain suit, so I went back to the cage, took it off, and came back in the coveralls they normally saw me in. They were still less than impressed as I stood at the base of their trees trying to coax them down while getting thoroughly soaked by the torrential rains. I went back to the cage, put my rain gear back on, and came back, this time armed with their bottles. I sat at the base of one of their trees and waited. After an hour and a lot of coaxing, Curls climbed down into my arms and started to suckle. The other two quickly followed.

On July 26, I decided to attempt a night out with the cubs, even though the weather was partly cloudy and threatening thunder showers. After feeding and suckling at the cage, we started out on our trek to the third level of ledges. It was just after noon; the pack on my back contained a sleeping bag, my camera gear, and food for the cubs. But no food for me. I could survive the night without eating—in fact I could spend several nights out without eating—and even if I had brought food for myself, I would have had to share it with the bears. Not a pretty picture; I'd seen their snarling version of "sharing" often enough, thanks.

The cubs took the lead, and I followed them straight up the hill to the boundary path and on up into the ledges, where the cubs quickly went out of sight. Snapping sticks as I traveled to let the cubs know where I was, I moved at my own pace. A moist gentle wind was blowing from me to the cubs, giving them my location even when I was walking silently. They followed me through the first pass and swung wide into the base of the next ledge, where they picked up my scent trail and rejoined me as I climbed onto the third level. At the bear tree the cubs reacted to fairly old scent with a mild set of stiff-legged walks, sniffs, slow-licks, and olfactory huffs. The Boy marked a spruce by pulling the boughs down and rubbing them over his shoulders. After a thorough search of the area that turned up only one three- or four-day-old scat, the cubs started playing, running, climbing, and chasing.

After the bear tree, the cubs left me again to climb the next set of ledges. When they didn't come back, I started searching. I found them stranded and emitting persistent nervous moans on a ledge, clearly afraid to come back down. I climbed as far as I could to offer them encouragement. Curls approached the escape path I was trying to show them, and just when I thought she would slide down to my legs she chose instead to leap onto my shoulders, a forty-pound surprise in a precarious spot. With her on the ground, I backed off and coaxed the other two to follow—on their own four feet. But by the time I had the Boy and Squirty safely down, Curls was gone. I had seen her going around the base of the ledge to my right, then had lost sight of her.

I called and called for her. Finally, I got an answer from high above and way over to the left. She was more than halfway back up the ledge and calling in long sorrowful moans. The other two cubs and I had no choice but to climb up after her for the rescue and continue upward from there. Even after we got to her, the rest of the ascent was no easy task; the face of the ledge was covered with low bush blueberries and stunted red pine, forcing the four of us to pick our way to the top, literally and figuratively.

But it was worth it. Once there, we looked out on expansive views to the east, south, and west. Equally impressive, unfortunately, were the thunderheads looming all around in the midsummer afternoon. In a matter of ten minutes, they were on us. First thunder and lightning, then heavy rain; we had to move rapidly to find shelter. I led the cubs to the main pass to this level and down to a rock shelter halfway down the ledge. Once under the outcropping and beginning to dry, the cubs demanded suckling, never fun in a crowded place with 150 pounds of nervous bears scrambling for only two prime positions. Fortunately, I had the empty bottles from their earlier feeding, so Squirty and the Boy suckled on them and Curls settled for my finger.

But the peace didn't last long. Anxiousness from being away from the safety of their own home in this nasty weather made them demanding, and twice I had to back them off by clearing my throat. Then, when it became clear that even threats weren't going to work, I broke down and gave them the food I had brought for their breakfast. The bribe worked beautifully. After they ate, Curls went out in the rain and climbed a nearby ash tree to pick out a bed for the night, and soon the other two went up with her. When the rain broke at half past eight, there were three soaking-wet cubs trying to sleep up in a tree and one pretty damp human hunkered under a rock. We were outside their home range, and they were clearly nervous. With just enough light left to make it back to the cage, I decided to call it quits.

Some of my experiments weren't planned at all. On July 30, after cooling off in the frog pond, the cubs took off on a tree-climbing tear before disappearing up the ledges. When I caught up, they were eating sarsaparilla leaves and exploring the well-worn animal path along the base of the second ledge. When they came to an impassable outcropping farther up the ledge, Curls came to me and stood on her hind legs, apparently soliciting a boost, which she happily accepted. The Boy watched, then came over and did the same, a seeming example of imitation that was at least partly verified when Squirty, lagging behind as usual, arrived too late to see how her siblings had gotten up there and tried to go directly up to them by a different route altogether. Only when that failed did she come back to me. I helped her up, then grabbed a tree to lift myself and follow, but it uprooted as soon as I pulled on it. Forced to try Squirty's alternative route, I was partway up the twenty-foot face with precarious footing and slippery handholds when all three cubs came over to help out, which in situations like this usually meant jumping on me. I hastily cleared my throat to back them off, then clambered back down before one of my fifty-pound Flying Wallendas decided to jump and knock me off the ledge.

I had to find another route along the base of the ledge, and by the time I did and got up to the cubs' level, only Curls was there to greet me with her "I missed you" moan and a brief touch on the lips. The other two had gone back down the ledge to follow my scent trail, and by the time the Boy met us halfway, Curls and I were looking down at him from a six-foot-high sheer ledge. Inadvertently I had set up a "detour test" for animal thinking.

As soon as he saw us, the Boy abandoned the scent trail, came straight to the ledge, and tried to scale it. When he couldn't, he hesitated for a moment, then followed the ledge south for fifty more yards until he found a route up.

Next on the scene was the ever-lagging Squirty. Doing exactly what the Boy had done, she left the scent trail as soon as she saw us, and just like the Boy tried but failed to get up the sheer rock face. But instead of running the base of the ledge, she climbed a nearby oak tree, and only when she decided it was too far to leap to us from there did she go back down and select her brother's route to us.

I wanted to practice tree climbing, hoping to see what it was like to be in some of the trees the cubs so effortlessly scampered up. Early one August afternoon, figuring that the cubs would follow me to the climbing pine, I set out to do my ascent and descent, hoping to get it done before they got there to "help." But the whole time I was up in the tree, there was no sign of them, leading me to think that they had followed the morning's earlier wild bear scent out of their range. With plenty of time to search for them, I returned to the cage to find no sign that they had been there either, so I headed back to my truck to get my camera pack before looking for them. From fifty yards away I could see the truck windows were just as I had left them on this hot day—half open. Only now they had muddy paw prints all over them.

The rearview mirrors were bent out of position, and the interior of the truck was a disaster area. Everything had been disturbed. The tear in the roof upholstery that LB had started when he popped in to say good-bye was now expanded to an area eighteen inches square. On the plus side, it was clear from the lollipop wrappers spread over the front seat that the perpetrators had placed a higher value on candy than expensive video equipment. That evidence—not to mention the muddy prints—pretty much narrowed the field, but even though they were the only bear cubs around, I thought I would give my guys the benefit of the doubt. Until I could find more evidence to link them to the crime, of course.

I called the cubs, and they filed up from below the sugar house, talking to me in a variety of moans as they arrived. The Boy solicited attention by reaching up, putting a paw on me, and conversing in soft talk, while the other two brushed by my legs as a greeting. While they did, I checked them over, and it didn't take long to spot something yellow on Curls's muzzle: a chip from a lollipop.

We were now in the energy-sapping heat of deep summer, and the cubs were lethargic. Walks were short, and I made sure we stayed near the cage so they could swim and feed without much effort. One mid-nineties afternoon, I was down on all fours filming Curls feeding on the ground when Squirty wandered over and climbed on my back. I thought she just wanted to play and be friendly, but Squirty—ever the planner—had another motive: she stood up on my back, grabbed one of the larger hazelnut bushes she hadn't been able to reach on her own, stepped off me, and rode it to the ground. In this kind of heat, planning for minimal-effort feeding apparently wasn't entirely my department.

Seeking some cooling air a few days later, the cubs and I climbed to the third ledge lookout, where we didn't get the breeze I had hoped for but took in the thirty-mile view anyway. First the Boy and then Curls stopped for a quick look at Mount Cardigan in the distance before moving on, but Squirty lingered as the rest of us started on our way. My bears have always loved this view, the same one that LB used to stare at before leaving on his own. He had gone off on his first big adventure in precisely that direction, cruising through the same country that he spent so much time viewing from up here on Holt's Ledge. Coincidence or not, that's the route to their open world that most of my male cubs have taken ever since.

When Squirty didn't follow right away, I went back to find her still at the edge of the ledge, lying down and feeding on something pretty much the way she would on any other occasion. Only this time, there were sixty or more angry hornets wildly orbiting her head. Her concentration was so strong that she would merely swat her muzzle to disrupt a sting and casually lick up the culprit as its punishment. This was one tough little bear.

The Boy and Curls soon arrived, and when they saw what was up, they joined right in. Curls quickly dug out and ate a section of the larval chambers of the hornets' nest. There wasn't much room for the Boy because of the placement of the nest, so he chose another plan of attack. First walking farther along the ledge, then climbing down to a narrow shelf below the nest, he came back over to a small spruce tree growing out of the ledge face. Breaking the branches as he climbed, he made an attempt to leap over to the action. That didn't work, so he scaled the rock face itself, but by the time he got there, the girls had finished off all the good parts. He pawed and stuck his nose in the entrance of the nest, only to realize he had missed out on most of the treat. Meanwhile I was trying to video the remaining hornets going back into their nest when the Boy walked into the frame and stood with his left hind foot casually covering the entrance to the hive. Yet even with that disruption, the angry hornets directed their wrath exclusively on the bears, allowing me to film as close as three feet from the hard-fought entrance of the nest without being stung. As in other hornet and bee campaigns, the only real risk to me was when one of the cubs attempted to lose a few attackers by scooting between my legs. (Not always, though. There was the time I found a paper hornets' nest in a pile of leafy green brush and sat down to film the cubs as they found it for themselves. When the Boy approached, he stepped on one of the limbs holding the nest, triggering the defense. The hornets swarmed and attacked the only intruder in sight: me.)

Pondering why these attacks were usually directed at the bears and not at me, and remembering that bees and hornets are more likely to attack dark colors than light ones, I now recognized the selective pressures that probably led to their behavior: Most of the world's bee and hornet eaters are black or dark brown.

By the third week in August, I decided to try a well-known awareness experiment, one that I had read a great deal about and had planned since the beginning to try out with these cubs. It's called the mirror self-recognition test, and it goes all the way back to Charles Darwin himself, who conducted the first one in the 1870s. Here's what he wrote:

> Many years ago, in the Zoological Gardens, I placed a looking glass on the floor before two young orangs, who, as far as it was known, had never before seen one. At first they gazed at their own images with the most steady surprise, and often changed their point of view. They then approached close and protruded their lips towards the image, as if to kiss it, in exactly the same manner as they had previously done towards each other, when first placed, a few days before, in the same room. They next made all sorts of grimaces, and put themselves in various attitudes before the mirror; they pressed and rubbed the surface; they placed their hands at different distances behind it; looked behind it; and finally seemed almost frightened, stared a little, became cross, and refused to look any longer.

Modern researchers have pretty much dismissed that first experiment as a good idea but an inconclusive test. Yes, the orangs reacted to the image in the mirror, but how could a human observer tell if they thought it was of themselves? Then in 1970 an American comparative psychologist named Gordon Gallup devised the now standard solution. Starting with Darwin's test, he let some chimpanzees get accustomed to seeing their images in the mirror, then, while they were sedated, he put dye marks over one eyebrow and one ear. When they awoke, they were given the mirror again. If they noticed the mark and touched or rubbed it with their hand, it indicated that they had recognized the image in the mirror as their own. Since then, the test has been widely applied to creatures ranging from elephants to dolphins to pigeons. As far as I could find, neither Darwin's nor Gallup's test had ever been tried on bears, and of those that had been tested, only chimpanzees, orangutans, and humans over the age of two had ever conclusively passed it. Could black bears stand on that high pedestal as well?

Debbie and I picked up a full-length mirror at a yard sale, and I set it up by simply wiring it to the sides of the cage. The cubs were out on patrol when I arrived at the cage, so I was able to set up the mirror without their knowledge and wait for them to arrive. Unlike many of the primate trials I had read about, where the chimps are given repeated opportunities to "pass" the test to the researchers' satisfaction, this would be the very first time my cubs had ever been exposed to any mirror.

Coming back alone, Curls was the first victim. Upon spotting her image, she squared off her upper lip, walked a cautious semicircle, then approached and came nose to nose, slow-licking her counterpart in the looking glass. These were all behaviors I recognized: The squared lip and cautious behavior were both consistent with seeing a strange bear. Next came the approach and nose-to-nose touching, which was a normal greeting, and then the slow-lick to identify the other bear. She knew as soon as she slow-licked that this was not another bear. Next she tried to figure out what she was seeing but not smelling: she looked behind the mirror from the side; she stood up and looked behind it from the top; and finally she pulled the mirror over and walked on the back of it.

I reset the mirror before the Boy arrived a few minutes later. He approached it cautiously, just as Curls had done, repeating her sequence right through the slow-lick. Then he looked at the reflection, looked beyond the mirror, then back at the reflection, then beyond the mirror again, repeating this sequence several times in quick succession. In "Monkey in the Mirror," a documentary on the PBS *Nature* series that I later watched, there's a nearly identical scene with a chimpanzee doing the looking.

Arriving after the Boy, Squirty spent the most time in front of the mirror, licking her image and eventually putting her paw up repeatedly against its reflection. After about a half hour, I put the mirror away and tried to analyze what I had observed.

All of the cubs had reacted to the image as they normally would to the sight of another bear, responding in all of their instinctual ways until they slow-licked the image for identification. At that point, the identification process failed; what they were seeing wasn't another bear because it didn't smell like one. But the image they were seeing was still a bear—their eyes clearly told them that. As I watched them, it seemed apparent to me that eventually they realized it was their own image. It still does, even though I now know how hotly debated a topic this is. It wasn't my intention, but I had now plunged into the world of behavioral-science controversy.

Rigorous scientific researchers all say I can't make a general statement like that—that the cubs knew they were seeing themselves in the mirror—based on such limited evidence. But my conclusion wasn't nearly as uncritical as it might seem, especially as I thought carefully about what did or didn't take place when the cubs first saw themselves in the mirror. For starters, I got to observe it three times, each with a fresh cub, and in each case the reaction was essentially the same. Each cub treated the image as a stranger bear until a slow-lick—the final arbiter in virtually everything they tested—told each that they were dealing with something different. But that "something different" was no extraterrestrial. It was a black bear, and they knew it; all their actions up to the slow-lick demonstrated that that's what they saw. The big question at that point was: Did they recognize the bear as their own image? Initially I think the answer was pretty definitely no. The experience was just too novel to them individually, and there couldn't be any evolutionary selection for wild bears dealing with mirrors, so they would have no instincts to guide them. So they looked around the mirror the way they would explore any obstacle that separated them from another bear. Whether or not they were trying to see how another bear got in there, or whether or not they were trying to figure out what was blocking the scent, or what any of the possibilities were, nobody can say for sure. But Squirty's paw-for-paw behavior (which demonstrated that in the end she was on the right track) and the Boy's sequence of looking at his image, then looking behind the mirror repeatedly were both—at least to me, who had at that point spent well over two thousand hours watching bears learn their way into their world—examples of behavior directed at themselves, not at another bear. Continuing these experiments sporadically over the next several years, I saw a number of additional examples that I thought to be self-directed behavior. Curls, for example, started bi-pedally rubbing herself against a post in their shelter, then turned toward the mirror to watch herself. Another time after she had been gone for a couple of weeks and the mirror had been covered for the winter, Curls ran back into the cage, tore the cover off and sat down to watch herself as she swayed back and forth in front of the mirror. Houdini, who you will meet later, lay down in front of the mirror after eating some beaked hazelnuts I had provided. With his eyes on the mirror, he repeatedly picked up a husk in his lips, raised it about four inches off the floor, then dropped it.

Although with these three and with other bears I did try several more mirror tests, all of which reinforced my conclusion that their actions in front of their reflections were self-oriented, I never tried Gallup's actual mark test on any of them because I felt it had a bias toward animals that were visually oriented and had fingers to point with, and I didn't want to drug my bears for anything other than their own safety and survival. My charge was to foster and release functioning black bears into the wild; any research I might do along the way needed to conform to this plan. Which was fine with me; I believe that all wildlife research is better in a natural setting anyway, delivering higher-quality results across the board. For the time being, this would have to be enough new ground broken in this area, a conclusion apparently shared by Curls. The next time I tried to set up the test, she broke the mirror.

By the end of August, we were in an extended drought, and the cubs were getting harder to find. It was perfectly normal for them to be expanding their home range and spending their nights farther and farther away from the cage, but this mother bear wasn't going with them. When it became difficult and time consuming to call them to me every day, I knew it was time to put a transmitter collar on one of them so I could go directly to wherever they had wandered. I put one on the Boy. He was the most adventuresome and, as a male, the most likely to leave the area.

Actually my timing for rigging up the telemetry wasn't all that random. I wanted to be sure I could find them the next day when an important pair of visitors was due. George and Kay Schaller were coming to take a walk with the cubs.

George called me the next morning and said that he and Kay would be there in the amount of time it took to drive. I assumed they were driving from their home in Connecticut, which would give me most of the morning to work in the woods, but they were coming instead from their summer place in Vermont, only forty minutes away. When they got to my house, I wasn't there. But my father was, so he and George had time to compare notes and to get to know each other, a great treat for my father. With great embarrassment I arrived an hour late, but if George and Kay were annoyed they didn't show it. Instead they were very gracious, warm, and friendly as we all rode together out to the Turnpike Lot to find the cubs. On the way out, George described his recent trips to Tibet and Laos while telling us what he knew about Asiatic black bears, pandas, and a previously undiscovered species of deer.

Out at the lot, Kay waited by the cub cage as George and I followed the Boy's signal with telemetry. The cubs were a quarter of a mile south of the cage eating blackberries when we caught up with them. Curls tried to climb George as if he were a tree; otherwise the cubs were well behaved on the half-hour walk. George and Kay had a long drive back to Connecticut, thus limiting our walk to a short one, but I was honored nonetheless. That someone of George's experience and acclaim would take notice of what I was doing in my backyard was really gratifying, especially at that early stage of my work with the bears. We've stayed in touch ever since.

The drought stretched on toward September, driving the cubs to great distances in search of food and water and making them hard to find even with the radio collar. On the last day of August I spent all day getting weak signals—or none at all—until I gave up and headed back to my truck, only to find all three back inside the cage cheerily eating apples from the pile I had left there. They were so exhausted and hungry that the Boy soon collapsed into a deep sleep with his face right in the apple pile, so I secured the cage with three locks to keep them in and went home. When I got there, a fellow from Hanover called to say that he and his wife had been hiking the Appalachian Trail and had run into three bears north of the Holt's Ledge lookout, two miles from the cage. He was quite exhilarated by the encounter, and when I asked him to describe the bears, he said he and his wife estimated them at 150 to 160 pounds and guessed them to be three to five years old. One, he said, had been wearing a radio collar. I told him the cubs actually weighed about sixty pounds and were nine months old. Now I knew not only why I hadn't been able to track the cubs by radio but why they were so tired and hungry. Considering how far they had traveled into completely new territory, I was both amazed and pleased that they had made it back to the cage on their own.

Misjudging the size of a bear is not uncommon. Hikers who spot one in the woods usually guess a bear's weight on the high side because they tend to look at the body alone. More experienced hunters, who see them more often than hikers, soon learn that the size of a bear's ears relative to its head is a better measure. By the time a bear is a year old, its ears will already have reached their full size; thus when yearling cubs are still growing, their ears will look big, and as they mature and their heads grow, their ears will look small. Another misjudgment people often make is to mistake fat for big. Bears with legs that appear short are simply fatter than those with legs that seem long. Recognizing this, the Boone and Crockett scoring system measures a bear's head, not its weight, to determine the record-book ranking of a hunter's trophy. Most black bears shot by hunters weigh less than 150 pounds and are under five years old; in fact the highest-scoring bear ever shot in New Hampshire had a skull that measured twenty-two inches (adding together the length and width of the skull), but weighed only 189 pounds. The most vulnerable to hunters are the dispersing males like LB.

On the first of September, Josh and I started building a new cage on the Lambert Lot. The cubs were beginning to travel, and I wanted a place to move them before they found my neighbors. For two hundred dollars, I bought three hundred feet of ten-foot-high chain-link fence from a scrap metal dealer, and with the help of Josh and a couple of friends from Lyme, Ken Uline and Tony Ryan, we used it to enclose a sixth of an acre, complete with three large pines and pool with running water, leaving the top open. From this base the cubs would be a full mile from the nearest occupied house, with many more miles of uninhabited forest stretching away in every direction.

Meanwhile the drought continued unabated. On a hot and dry September 6, Craig McLaughlin, the biologist who oversaw Maine's bear rehabilitation efforts, arrived as a guest to see my methods. We led the cubs down the lower skid road into the Cole logged area, then in sequence to the midlevel bear tree, up to the broken spruce bear tree, to the one on the upper skid road, and finally to another near the Tyler Road wallow. Together Craig and I formally observed and recorded all the standard reactions: sniff, slow-lick, and olfactory huff; stiff-legged walks; urine marking; scat marking; rubbing and climbing. It was a full day, and on the way to the final bear tree we got a couple of hundred yards ahead of the cubs. All day, Craig had been fascinated by the bear trees and the cubs' reactions to them. While we waited for the cubs to catch up, he asked if I had been able to determine how often bears visited a given tree, and I answered by showing him how I removed the bear hairs from the bark every time I checked out a tree; if there were more the next time, it gave me at least a rough hint. Seasonal usage could also be shown by the fact that bear hair oxidizes, turning from black to brown over time. After about ten minutes Curls showed up alone, with her nose on my scent trail. She checked out the tree and then started looking back up the trail for the other cubs.

"Her bond with her siblings is too strong to leave them," I told Craig. "She'll go back and get them if they don't show up soon."

She did, disappearing back up the trail. In less than five minutes she was back with Squirty and the Boy.

"What do you suppose she told them?" I whispered to Craig. He just smiled.

A couple of days later, Phoebe was in the cage with the Boy and Squirty when a tiny short-tailed shrew popped out of the den box, where it had been stealing the cubs' dog food. The two rough and tough black bears, each outweighing the shrew by a ratio of 900:1, reacted in perfect accord with their intrinsic natures: The Boy jumped straight backward, and Squirty ran all the way out of the cage and up a tree.

September passed relatively unremarkably into October. The drought passed, and hunting season arrived, keeping Debbie, Phoebe, and me vigilant and somewhat on edge. The cubs would be safer in the new cage on Lambert, but it wasn't yet fully finished.

On October 16, in the middle of peak fall foliage season, Harvard primatologist Richard Wrangham drove up from Cambridge to see the cubs in action. This was a little bit like a blind date, since Richard was a friend of a friend of a friend, but we had a common interest in animal behavior and I had read a great deal about his work with chimpanzees, so

I invited him up. Born in Scotland and esteemed as one of the world's authorities on primate behavior, Richard had worked with Jane Goodall at Gombe before establishing his own study area in Kibali, Uganda. But bears were new to him. "All I know about bears," he told me as soon as he got to Lyme, "Walt Disney taught me."

We spent the day in the field together with the cubs. Our discussions were all about behavior, and the cubs performed as if on cue. Was the Boy's selecting a half-rotted log to float in the frog pond an example of tool use? In an exhibition of insight, each of the cubs attempted to climb a cherry tree but stopped when they could see it was too dangerous to continue; Richard said he had never seen his chimps change their mind once they had committed to climbing a tree. At the end of the walk, near five in the afternoon when we had come back onto very familiar ground for them, the cubs came to me to suckle on my fingers. I told Richard that was their way of letting me know they were going to spend the night out here. Then they quietly walked away. Richard was impressed that by saying good-bye the cubs had indicated that they planned ahead not to come all the way home to the cage with us. I had earlier told him that one way the cubs communicated their location to each other and to me while walking or feeding was to make noise as they walked; if I wanted to leave without them following me, all I had to do was slip away quietly.

"Do you think the cubs do the same thing?" he asked. "Intentionally?"

"Just listen," I answered.

Though they were still within easy hearing range of us, the cubs weren't making a sound.

It was a pleasure spending a day with Richard, since he more than understood everything I was talking about in terms of behavior. As we walked down the hill toward the sugar house, he said, "Ben, whatever you have to say about the bears, I will believe." As he was leaving, he invited me to come to Harvard to give a seminar on my findings, not just to his graduate students but to his colleagues as well. That was pretty intimidating, but I said I'd be honored to accept.

On October 20, the new cage was ready on the Lambert Lot, and it was time to cart the cubs over there. Josh had built a custom transport box for the journey, so all we had to do was get all three of them inside it. But the Boy was weighing in at well over a hundred pounds, and even Curls, the smallest of the three, was close to seventy. Force was therefore not on the agenda, nor, if we could avoid it, was anesthetization. But following Rule One of bear motivation (that is, food wins every time), an onion bag full of donuts lured them into the box without any fuss.

To keep the cubs from climbing out the open top of the cage we built, I ran two strands of smooth electric fencing through the chain link and dabbed some cooking grease on it to get the cubs' attention, then went home to let them learn about electricity the hard way. I returned the next day to see how they were doing. When I walked around to the back of the cage to see if they understood the electric fence yet, Squirty started to come up to me, then stopped. Her eyes drew together as she focused on the fence five inches from her nose. With a disgusted look on her face, she turned around and walked away.

It didn't take the three cubs very long to get accustomed to their new larger enclosure on the Lambert Lot and to the surrounding range as well. For about a week they continued to scent-mark the trees and boxes inside the twenty-five-yard square cage by rubbing their fur against them and walking over saplings. In our walks in the new territory outside the cage, both with me and with Phoebe, Curls seemed the most intent on exploring the lay of the land, while Squirty seemed more focused on checking out individual trees and casually pulling over dead stumps, once again demonstrating the astonishing strength that so often stayed hidden beneath the gentle natures of these half-grown creatures. The Boy pretty much went with the flow, checking out the various scents between bouts of wrestling with his sisters and halfheartedly trying to get them into the mating grasp; they never had any trouble rolling or twisting away from him, even though he was, at well over a hundred pounds now, noticeably outgrowing them. That he was maturing showed not just in his size; after these sisterly rebuffs, he would sometimes sit and orally masturbate. For their part, the girls were showing maturity, too; Curls had for the past several weeks been showing her increasing dominance over Squirty, taking precedence in both feeding and suckling by fiercely taking her turn first, a superiority she didn't try to establish against the Boy, who returned the favor by staying neutral during his sisters' disputes.

On their initial forays into new territory, the cubs went out of their way to find and examine all the large trees, especially the white and red pines. At every big white pine, they would stop at the base of the trunk and look up, admiring and cataloging each as a future haven, proving to me later that that was their intention by unerringly fleeing to the nearest one whenever something spooked them on a future walk.

This late in the fall, the cubs were feeding primarily on beechnuts and acorns, and in their attempts to find them in this new range, the dominance of scent became even more apparent to me than it had been before. They didn't appear to hunt for beech and oak trees with their eyes as much as they seemed to smell them from afar. On one of our initial walks into a new zone, the Boy suddenly went off the trail and ran forty yards to an abundance of fallen acorns under a tree he had never been to, and on another walk Curls led the other two away from me for more than three hundred yards into new country with her head held high, arrowing in on an abundant crop of beechnuts under three large trees. Could they have smelled the food from that far away? It surely seemed so, although it was possible that they were following bear scent instead; either way, it was their noses that drew them.

Once they had found a good food source, the cubs readily remembered it, often sprinting a hundred yards or more in anticipation of the spot on future walks. Their spatial orientation was evident and impressive, since they sometimes did this from a completely new direction and from distances of two hundred yards or more. While these distances may not seem great to someone unfamiliar with eastern woodlands, they do represent genuine navigational difficulties for a human with a compass, let alone a "lesser" animal. Even in winter when the leaves are gone, the tree trunks and limbs are so thick, it's unusual to be able to see more than seventy yards; in the spring through fall, one travels through the woods as if submerged in a sea of green, with visibility ranging from zero to just a few yards even on the marked trails, let alone the dense thickets sought out by black bears. On top of that, the land itself is anything but flat. Cognitive mapping is the only way to stay oriented, and the cubs were demonstrating to me that their ability to employ it was well developed.

Deer hunting in New Hampshire overlaps the bear-hunting season for most of November, so it wasn't hard for me to obtain excess carcass parts for the cubs. On a rainy and warm afternoon early in the month, I arrived at the cage with the cubs' dinner and four fresh deer legs. When the cubs appeared from wherever they had been, Squirty was the first to notice them, shying cautiously away from the new smell. The more aggressive and dominant Curls grabbed one and ran to the big pine, and the Boy grabbed another and backed with it into the den. Even after seeing her siblings' reactions Squirty never took one while I was there. Meanwhile the other two issued warning moans while enthusiastically chewing on the legs.

A couple of days later, I noticed Curls paying close attention to the empty apple bucket in the cage. Some of the cooking fat I had initially spread on the electric fence to draw the cubs' attention to it had apparently splattered on the apple bucket, and Curls had finally decided to investigate it. First she made a wide pass around the bucket, then she stepped closer to cautiously sniff it—and explosively swatted the bucket off the lean-to deck and across the cage. Not a bad clue that she had associated the smell of the fat with the shock of the fence, and an even better one into the nature of a bear's sudden reaction when displeased. The speed and force of the blow were impressive, to say the least. But then, pushing the situation a little farther, she continued her investigation of the chastised bucket until she decided it was safely neutralized. She licked off the spot of fat and walked away.

An unexpected benefit of the open-topped cage showed itself when I arrived early in the afternoon of November 17 to find a half dozen ravens had been feeding with the cubs on the road-killed deer carcass I had put in the cage two days before. The ever-alert ravens had flown off as I came near, and at first the cage looked empty when I came into it, but then the Boy and Curls walked up to me from the corner where the deer carcass was, followed by Squirty, who was hiding behind the big pine. Two snowy days later, I came up to the cage, and this time at least thirty ravens lifted off from inside the cage. The cubs had now learned that ravens would be with them on any major wintertime food discovery. I could see Squirty sleeping in her perch halfway up the big pine, indicating that she still hadn't taken on the taste for venison that her siblings had. The other two cubs were pacing rapidly at the pond end of the cage; from the tracks in the snow, it seemed they may have been startled when the ravens spooked.

As November drew to a close, food got scarcer and scarcer, driving the cubs to forage for nuts in depressions, beside rocks, close to the base of the tree, and in even less likely locations; it reminded me of digging for clams in Maine when the flats had already been well combed and I had to look for those special spots where there might still be some. On one walk, following the cubs quietly in the wet snow, I stayed back and leaned against a tree to watch them forage until Squirty and the Boy circled to look for me, sniffing their back trail as they did. Only twenty yards from them, I wasn't noticed until I moved; if they had been able to see color, my red plaid jacket surely would have given me away. I then made my move toward the cage, and Curls took charge, running into the lead, followed by the other two and then me.

On November 27, the cubs were in the big pine in the cage when I arrived, Squirty and Curls together sixty feet up and the Boy twenty feet above them. They climbed down to greet me but stayed at the base of the tree until they were sure it was me, either by recognizing my smell or through a combination of my verbal greeting and body language. I gave them hickory nuts and a frozen deer leg before they suckled, then I tried to weigh them. But they were now getting so big that with a cub on my shoulders I couldn't see around their grasping arms and legs to view the scale. So I picked up Squirty and held her so that I could read the window when I stood on the scale, but she took advantage of the opportunity by reaching up and snagging the bag of kibble I had put on the high shelf. I put her down and grabbed the dog food from her and put it back, then tried a second time to weigh her. But this time, she decided to climb on my shoulders and stand on my head to get at the kibble, at which point the other two cubs saw what was happening and joined in what rapidly turned into a clambering, roaring frenzy. I gave in and fed them the kibble. Two days later, I finally got the job done: Curls weighed 80 pounds, Squirty 90, and the Boy 140.

Although they weren't showing any real signs yet of seriously wanting to go to den, they had at least started some prep work on the three-chambered den that Ken Uline and I had built inside the cage with the chambers stacked one on top of the other. The bottom den they selected had one big chamber with tunnels for use as bathrooms and entrances, and already the cubs had blocked the smallest of these tunnel entrances with straw. They'd also tried to drag the deer carcass into the den, but it had gotten stuck, so I cut it up into more manageable pieces for them. Another sign that they were beginning to slow down was that only about 40 percent of the cage had tracks in the snow. Their pacing trail still went to the back of the pond but wasn't heavily used; most of the action now was at the base of the big pine.

The last day of November was the first one since they had been in the new area that I didn't spend time with them; instead, while they were away from the cage I hung a set of orange "Keep Out" signs on it. The day before, I had found two sets of unscheduled visitors' footprints in the snow next to the cage; they were made by someone wearing small boots and by a dog. The cubs, apparently scared by the intruders, had been in a tree and slow to come down even when they knew it was me.

After I got the new signs attached, I rode my snowmobile to the top of the lot and hiked into my deer stand, passing fresh deer, moose, and (four-inch) bear tracks in the snow. As I was walking back out near dark, a ninety-pound bear broke into a run beside me, then stopped in the road as it crossed twenty yards in front of me. It was a fat little bear with a short body and short hair, indicating to me it was probably a two-year-old, since a yearling would have had fuzzier hair. Its three-inch tracks joined the bigger set in heading toward the heavily wooded bowl on the other side of Lambert. Now I knew that my cubs weren't behaving unnaturally in still being active and not yet in their dens.

I left them alone for six days, in an attempt to see if that might induce hibernation. No such luck; I arrived on December 5, to find the three cubs very anxious to see me. They mugged me for the bottles, then all suckled at once, nearly burying me under three hundred pounds of fattened-up bears. When they were finished, I could see that they expected food, so we all went on a walk for acorns.

On December 7, we had a sixteen-inch snowfall, a pretty decent blizzard by our standards. LB and LG had finally gone to den after a heavy snow, but it had also been near zero degrees when they did; now the temperature was between twenty and thirty. Curious to know if temperature or a heavy snow was more important in driving bears to their dens, I went out to the cage the very next morning to take a peek. There were no bear tracks in the snow, and the cub door was tightly in place; the cubs had pulled it closed behind them. I quietly went away and left them alone.

But if I thought that would be it for the winter, I was mistaken. Two days later, again heading up by snowmobile to my deer stand on the high ground, I cut a three-inch bear track headed in the direction of my clearing. It was late in the day, so I didn't have time to follow it.

The next day, I did. It was made by one of my cubs all right, probably Curls. I found that she had followed my tracks from the cage when I had sneaked up there the day after the storm. Then, skirting the clearing to avoid that open space, she ran down the half-mile path I had bulldozed several years before to connect my clearing to Jasper Day's road, then up his road, across his brother, Roy's land, through my oaks on the hill, and back to rejoin the other two cubs in their safe area. By the time I got there, all three were gone.

I called from the cage with no response, then took the snowmobile up the hill to see if they had fed in the oaks. They hadn't. When I got back to the cage, all three cubs were in the nearby log landing. I had originally come out here to feed apples to the deer, but now I gave them to the cubs instead. When the best of the apples were eaten, the Boy stood up on his hind legs and body-searched me; first he sniffed and pulled on all of my pockets, then rotated me with his paws making sure I wasn't hiding anything. Squirty then checked my pockets and climbed to the upper shelf to make sure no food was hidden up there. Clearly, their metabolisms were still in full eating mode. Later that afternoon, Phoebe went back with bottles and food.

But eventually they started to slow down. It was a rainy day in the low thirties as I trekked back on December 12 for a late-afternoon visit with the cubs. They were all in the den when I arrived, and it took ten minutes or more for them to come out. After eating their kibble and suckling, they took turns picking my pockets. The Boy and Curls liked having their chests scratched, unusual for bears; Curly even showed a scratch reflex. Squirty lay against the den entrance, grooming and playing with her genital region. The Boy went and got a football-sized clump of snow, first sharing it with Squirty, then attempting to take it into the den with him. He and Curls both deliberately relieved themselves before crawling back into the den, Curls by backing herself in and raking an armload of bedding material with her. With all three cubs back in the den, I lay down next to it with my head just inside the door and listened to a chorus of sighlike moans reminiscent of when they were young and going to sleep after nursing; I stayed until the song subsided, transformed to quiet suckling sounds as it slowly faded away.

By December 20, the cubs were staying in the den full-time. On my last visit before leaving them to their winter's hibernation, they crawled out to greet me, suckle some apple juice, and eat kibble. Inside, they had used straw to wall up all of their entrances, and I brought up carpet to help keep the wind out of the tunnels. The cubs assisted in this last bit of insulation, then crawled back into the den.

CHAPTER 18

Public Notice

Now that I had gone through a first year in the woods with a second set of cubs, I was beginning to form my own theories about their social structures and ways of communicating. Many of the astonishing things I had seen LB and LG do, I had now seen done in the same ways by the triplets. Patterns of very complex behavior were beginning to reveal themselves. It was time, I figured, to see how their methods of adaptation stacked up against the competition. So while the cubs hibernated that winter, I returned to the two extensive book collections available to me, my father's study here at home and Dartmouth's Baker Library in Hanover.

My father's, as it turned out, was not only handier but far more complete. On his lovingly maintained and subject-classified shelves, I found every major title I needed, from his 1952 edition of Konrad Lorenz's classic *King Solomon's Ring* to the much rarer Niko Tinbergen's *Social Behavior in Animals,* all of them dog-eared from repeated use and filled with my father's endlessly questioning underlinings and handwritten marginalia. For someone trying to play catch-up in the world of research into animal thinking, it was a treasure house.

But in the meantime, while I tried to study, people were beginning to want to study me. Back in 1995, Sy Montgomery, the well-known nature writer, had come up to Lyme to interview me for a story in the *Boston Globe Magazine*. That story, which ran in March 1996, turned out to be an unexpected catalyst for something much bigger: That same month, as soon as she came back from filming a documentary based on her book *Spell of the Tiger* in West Bengal for a *National Geographic Explorer* TV special, she called me to say that she had told the National Geographic people about me and my bears. "Guess what?" she said. "You're next."

She was right. Not only did they decide to shoot a TV special, but they hired Sy to write the script. In April, the first *Explorer* crew had arrived to begin the yearlong filming process, starting when the triplets were still in the basement and continuing well beyond. In fact they weren't finished yet, a situation about which I had mixed feelings. On the one hand, it was gratifying to be recognized for the work I was doing, and I knew that national television exposure could be a great way to give people at least a glimpse into the true lives of these shy and wonderful creatures. On the other hand, it was a lot of distracting work, some of it fun but much of it less so.

Because the final TV show had to tell a seamless story, we spent hours repeatedly filming what to me were mundane and barely noticed daily details: I had to be filmed getting in and out of my truck, walking to and from the cage, mixing food (not just me, but Debbie and Phoebe too), looking for the cubs, feeding the cubs—you name it. When it came to filming the cubs in action, nothing ever happened quickly, and rarely as everyone wanted, since the cubs tended to go wherever the action seemed most interesting to them, which most of the time was with all the new people and the potentially edible toys—tripods, video cameras, microphones—they brought with them. If the plan was to film me crossing a brook with the cubs and the camera crew went ahead to shoot us coming at them from the far side, the cubs would invariably go ahead with the crew, leaving me standing alone on my side of the brook staring at a full camera crew and three bear cubs on the other side staring back at me.

But we had all gotten used to the situation by that point. A good thing, too, since it has never gone away. Squirty, who was to grow up with the recurring visits of television and magazine photographers, would later have to devise methods for dealing with her own cubs in their presence, a process that she would handle with an amazing mix of tolerance, force, and adaptability. For now, though, this was all new to me and to the bears, and I was already scheduling filming dates for the following spring.

CHAPTER 19

The Triplets Grow Up

SOMETIME AROUND THE end of March, the triplets came out of hibernation. Debbie, Phoebe, and I had all been busy with maple-sugaring work—and Debbie with her full-time job as well—so it wasn't until April 3 that Phoebe and I walked up from Tony Ryan's house to find the cubs weren't in their cage. The trees were still bare, but so much snow had already melted that we didn't even need snowshoes. On our way into the cage, we could see from the tracks in the receding snow that the cubs were already up. After putting out the food we had brought with us, two large Ziploc bags full of dog kibble, I called for the cubs, and after a few minutes they filed down off the hill, roaring with hungry moans as they scrambled for their food. They all had adult teeth now and had apparently forgotten how to suckle; when it came time for their bottles, they destroyed the nipples. Working together after they'd been fed, Phoebe and I weighed them: Curls was fifty pounds, Squirty sixty-five, and the Boy an even hundred. They had wintered well but were plainly ready to start regaining their lost poundage. In a neat solution to the teeth-on-nipple problem, Phoebe made up some apple ice that was a big hit when we came back two days later.

The cubs' lives as minor media darlings kicked back into gear almost as quickly as their appetites did. On April 8, a CBS television crew arrived to shoot a *Coast to Coast* segment that eventually ran at the end of July, not long before the show itself went off the air. Maybe the problem was over-staffing, since a six-person crew had been sent to tape the short segment.

We met the cubs on the road up to the clearing, and, just as I had expected, the arriving crowd drew the cubs before the cameras were ready. I told the crew not to move and then sent Phoebe ahead with the food, and when that didn't lure the cubs back to the cage where we wanted to start the filming, I tried to keep them from rushing up to the crew by clearing my throat. Only Squirty responded by staying back; Curls and the Boy went ahead anyway to investigate the strangers. They got within twenty feet of them when somebody moved, which sent the cubs fleeing. As soon as they hit Phoebe's track, they followed her scent back to the cage. Things were just getting under control when Curls decided to get territorial by squaring off her lip and taking a wide defen-sive stance to prevent Shari Levine, the producer, from going into the cage to set things up with Phoebe. We got Curls calmed down as the rest of the crew arrived in time to each get their faces closely examined by the Boy, who was so attracted to Shari's eye makeup that he sniffed and slow-licked both of her closed eyes to check it out. Quite an encounter for a Manhattan-based television person.

The shoot then proceeded at various locations inside the cage, and after a session by the big tree, I joined the cubs for what I expected to be a chance to videotape them at play with me. But they had another mes-sage. The Boy gave me a shove and an irritated moan, while Curls played inside my jacket and kept grabbing and twisting it while moan-ing, too. The cubs were telling me that they had had enough of these strangers. It was time for the shoot to be over.

It took almost a week after the television mob had left for things to settle down between the cubs and me. The Boy even bit me one time, and it wasn't until the four of us had a good round of play and wrestling on April 13 that it dawned on me that up to that point the cubs had been growing suspicious of me. In the years that have followed I've seen the pattern repeated, especially with Squirty but with other bears as well; a necessary ritual of rebonding and reestablishment of mutual trust is the annual bear-initiated wrestle in the woods.

April is a nasty weather month in New Hampshire, and this one was no exception. A nor'easter dropped several inches of heavy, wet snow on the eighteenth, driving the cubs to take refuge in the dense spruces uphill from the cage. Some days, the cubs declined to leave the cage at all, even when I tried to coax them out for a walk; other times, they would head out on their own, watching from places of hiding until they were absolutely sure who I was before coming out to say hello—and to mug me for food.

Ken and I had built a lockable storeroom in the shelter so I could keep food there and not have to lug it in every time. I used a nail slid through two holes to keep the door secured, a system that I thought the cubs couldn't undo, since I knew they'd have no trouble smelling the food through the cracks in the wall and would try to get inside. But after watching me put the food away a few times, they began to try. Bite marks appeared in the wood around the nail head, showing me that they had been paying attention not only to the fact that there was food behind the door, but specifically to how the lock worked. Since my scent was all over the door but the chewing attempts were only at the lock itself, it was obvious to me that they had figured out by watching me undo it that the nail was the key to opening the door.

Toward the end of the month, I tried another experiment. I wanted the cubs to make contact with the resident wild bears the way LB and LG had back at the Turnpike Lot. But this new Lambert cage, unlike the old one, wasn't in a year-round cover of nearby pines, spruces, or ledges; instead, we had located it in an open hardwood stand that wouldn't provide much natural bear cover till the trees filled out in May. Knowing that wild bears wouldn't be likely to come near the cage anytime soon, I decided to take the cubs on several long marches up to higher elevations and softwood cover. The first trip was to Snow Hill. All three cubs walked over saplings all the way out, but not on the return trip. The cubs didn't show any interest in scent and were at the cage the following day when I arrived. The next trip was to the northeastern end of Lambert. Again they marked only on the way out as they had done on the other trip, but this time they did show some interest in scent near the top. Maybe I was making progress.

The next morning, the cubs were nowhere to be found. With only a faint signal from the cage, I started climbing up the hill after them, and when I finally caught up with the signal, I was just above where I had taken them the previous day and they had found some interesting scent. That had been the only time they had ever been there, but the cubs had no trouble finding it on their own by following the scent trail they had left by walking over saplings on the way up with me. As I marveled at that navigational ploy, I also realized that by leaving the trail in the first place, and marking it only on the way out, the cubs had planned to come back even as they went out for the first time.

I called repeatedly and tried to close in on the signal, but got caught up in a mess of blown-down trees which were hard to get through. I couldn't help but make a lot of noise, which should have been okay since that was how I approached the cubs normally to let them know I was near, but the signal just disappeared. The cubs had run away from me, over the top and down the far side of the ridge. This wasn't normal; I knew I'd been close enough for them to hear me, and they'd run anyway. All I could figure out was they had to be with another bear, and if that was the case, following them would be futile. I turned around and trudged back to the cage.

The next day, after they still hadn't been back to the cage, I went back up, got a strong signal from the top of my lot, and decided to track them down. This time, I wasn't going to call them; instead, I wanted to try to sneak in to see what they were up to and who they were with. It was wet and misty with clouds covering the ridge top when I reached the beech stand where my land abuts Jasper Day's. The signal strengthened, and I slowed down. The ground showed sign of heavy feeding by deer and bear; I spotted several fresh wild bear scats.

As I moved cautiously toward the signal, I spotted the Boy and Curls before they saw me. They looked up when I snapped a stick, but they still didn't recognize me as the wind didn't carry my scent in their direction. They huffed, and chomped, then treed up a large maple. As soon as they did, I heard a third bear slap a tree and snort about a hundred yards away in the woods above me. As the two cubs climbed, they continued to complain, adding an undulating moan to the verbal mix. When she heard this, the unseen bear, a 130- to 140-pound wild sow coming more than a hundred yards from where she'd swatted the tree, rushed to the base of the large maple, looked up at the two cubs, and then turned and made a quick false charge at me before retreating back the way she had come while repeatedly looking back at me. Just as she went out of sight, the cubs moaned again, and the wild sow came rushing back to their tree. She repeated this defense a third time before the Boy finally got my scent and started down from the maple with a moan of recognition. The wild sow heard his moan and moved away in a new direction, where I could see her walking back and fourth in the distance, probably trying to pick up my scent. The Boy approached me slowly, then, with his sister not far behind, ran the last few steps for a greeting.

Curls suckled on my closed fist while the Boy made a feeble attempt to do the same; then both cubs stood and body-rubbed me with their heads and necks. The Boy became suddenly irritated and bit my forearm hard enough to leave large bruises, and I reacted harshly by pushing him over with my foot. His response was immediately submissive, as he made no effort to retaliate and stopped moaning. The rubbing on me was unusual, something my cubs have only done in the presence of a wild bear, a behavior that I now think is meant to tag my scent with theirs so I won't scare off their wild friends. The bites to my forearm were message bites to punish me for interrupting their social encounter.

Through it all, the wild sow had been sitting up on the bank below the Appalachian Trail watching us, but when I tried to walk up to her with the cubs following, she wandered off over the ridge. After thoroughly checking out where she had fed, marked, and snow-bathed, the cubs followed me until they recognized my road up the hill, where they relaxed and began to play. Back on the ridge, while the cubs had made their investigation I had made one of my own, searching until I found the spruce the wild bear had swatted; she had hit it so hard, her paw had left an impression on the tree trunk.

Meanwhile, Squirty was among the missing. I suspected that she was off with a wild friend of her own.

I came back that afternoon just in time to see three little black bodies climbing up the door and into the cage; Squirty was back. I took them all out for a short walk to the pines by the brook, where they played dominance games and suckled before we all took a nap at the base of a large pine, each bear touching me while they slept. Squirty gave me a kiss on the lips, something she hadn't done in a while.

The next day, I arrived at the cage to find neither cubs nor any signal from the Boy's collar. After I had gone uphill to try to find them, I turned to see Curls step out onto the road fifty yards below me, following my tracks with her nose to the ground. When I called out a greeting and moved in her direction, she spooked, huffed, and ran back into the woods; I had to work my way upwind of her before she recognized my scent. While we walked back toward the cage, she did a stiff-legged walk, then stopped at the pines play area by the brook not far from the cage and wouldn't come any farther. I saw Phoebe in the cage and she told me the Boy had spooked on my arrival and run out of the cage and down over the bank to sit at the base of a large pine. When he came back and we went to get Curls, she was very wary, huffing at us before running to a large pine. But eventually she came in, and both cubs stood and rubbed me with their heads and necks, as if to reaffirm their claim on me. We all went back to the cage so they could eat. All the cubs' reactions—rubbing on me, stiff-legged walking indicating strange bear scent, and the fact that Squirty was gone—indicated to me that a male bear had been in the vicinity and that Squirty had gone off with him.

While Curls and the Boy ate, I pondered all the new questions that had arisen just this month: Was Squirty attracted to this particular male? Why didn't both girls go with him? As to the wild sow, why did she try to defend the Boy and Curls from me? She had only known them for two days. Why did she let them travel with her? Was she partial to these cubs because she knew they were without a wild mother? Even if she knew that, why was she being altruistic toward unknown bears? After all, Curls was a potential competitor for her space.

After they ate, I took the cubs up to the bear tree on the other side of Perkins Brook, where they rubbed their backs on the tree before the three of us took an hourlong nap and started back. The Boy was persistent and anything but subtle in his advances toward Curls; she took this for a while, then fought him off with a snarl. Back at the cage I gave them more food. As I walked away, I looked back to see both of them watching me go.

In the morning, I followed the signal up the hill, coming into the beech stand from the south. Walking as quietly as possible, I sneaked in among the beeches, where I got a location on the Boy below me but still out of sight. There were a couple of fresh wild bear scats in the beech stand, so I decided to wait quietly and see what might happen.

It had just started to snow when I caught movement up on my back trail. It was Curls, cautiously tracking me with a bleating "ww-wo-ww" of distress. After a short rub on me and a quick irritated bite to the same bruise on my left arm that the Boy had given me, she ran away, huffed, and treed. Standing on a burl about halfway up the maple tree, she scanned the beech stand by sight and smell for signs of other bear. Back on the ground, she marked frequently by walking over saplings, then suddenly huffed and treed again, climbing up to a bend in the trunk of a different maple, and this time she stayed there while I now scanned carefully about me, trying to see what was bothering her. It had to be another bear, and soon enough I spotted a black shape moving about seventy yards off, a small adult that made just that brief appearance and then vanished.

I stayed there for another half hour before moving down to try to find the Boy. At the bottom of the beech stand, I got a signal that turned out to be false from the upper left, near where I had seen the wild bear. Curls relaxed and fed as I walked ahead of her on my way back uphill. And then, just as quietly as it had before, the wild bear reappeared, a female peering out at me from behind an oak trunk. At first she retreated uphill, then she stopped, came back to the oak, and called down two small cubs. This time, she left for good with her cubs following her out of sight. She was about the Boy's size, and she hadn't put on any displays at all.

Almost as soon as the three wild bears were out of sight, two other bears appeared from down the hill. They were the Boy and Squirty. After a quick greeting, we all headed back to the cage.

By the end of April, my efforts to make contact with wild bears had paid off in spades for the cubs, but the result was a growing independence and wanderlust in each of them as the spring days lengthened toward June, the natural month for dispersal. And the prime month for mating. It was time to put radio collars on the girls, too.

As May blossomed toward June, the cubs grew both bigger and more independent, rarely staying together, and extending their separate ranges in all directions. The Boy wandered out of telemetry range on May 13 and didn't come back for almost three weeks; Curls began to show signs of wanting to establish a territory of her own; Squirty found a wild boyfriend, who stayed out of sight whenever I tried to get close enough for a look at him.

I came close to catching a glimpse of the wild male on May 1 when I climbed Lambert to get above Squirty's signal thinking I might catch her with him if I came quietly downhill. I caught sight of her just in time to see her running rapidly away. I called to her with no avail, so I found a comfortable place to sit down and track her with telemetry as she circled uphill and then stopped. I waited about fifteen minutes before calling "Hi, guys!" in my usual way. Her signal then got louder, so I went in that direction until I could see her moving from large pine to large pine toward me, but as soon as she saw me, she snorted repeatedly and went up a tree, then hid on the opposite side of the trunk when I came toward her. She didn't recognize my scent because the wind was coming from the wrong direction. I stood still until she started back down from the tree; then I got down on my knees and offered her my face as she approached. We came nose to nose; she smelled my breath and finally let out a moan of recognition. I stood up, and she rubbed all over me, a behavior consistent with the presence of another bear in the area. Then she high-headed scent and flicked her tongue, and as we started walking away, she kept stopping to look back and smell her back trail; I had no doubt the other bear was nearby, especially when she walked over saplings and arched her back to rub on overhanging branches to mark her trail as we moved toward the cage. Several times, she even stopped to scratch, conveniently facing the rear so she could check the back trail. We traveled three-quarters of a mile before reaching the plateau above the cage; here Squirty attempted to punctuate the path she had left for her male friend to follow by marking it with scat. Any doubts I had about the intentionality of her scat marking were removed when she squatted to mark with scat, but nothing came out.

The next day, I met Squirty farther up the hill. Not only did she come right to me without running, but she followed me all the way back to the cage without marking once.

In my mind, Squirty had intentionally left a trail of scent marks for her male friend to follow. This behavior has great significance for I can find little evidence in the literature that any of the great apes have demonstrated it. Such direct olfactory communication also implies that planning, insight, and theory of mind were involved, all which I will discuss at length in Chapter 26, "What Is It About a Bear?"

Meanwhile, as if I didn't have enough on my hands with the looming dispersal of the triplets, we were about to get four more cubs in early May. The first, a tiny, undernourished cub of the year, came with the name Teddy after Ted Walski, the New Hampshire Fish and Game biologist who brought him to us. When a turkey hunter in Washington, New Hampshire, had found this abandoned cub, the bear had a piece of skin missing on his foreleg. The feisty little guy—in addition to his bad leg he had a bite across the bridge of his nose and snorted and swatted a lot—weighed only five pounds.

The other three, a healthier set of orphaned triplets from Vermont, arrived two days later. Healthier physically, that is, for their story was very sad. The mother was shot out of season, apparently so the shooter could give the cubs to his uncle as pets, all very illegal. The uncle then took one of the female cubs to work to show off, and one of his coworkers turned him in. The story then hit the newspapers and television in Vermont. There are rarely convictions when a bear is shot out of season because the shooter usually claims self-defense and is given the benefit of doubt by the courts. In this case, the shooter had to pay $1,500 toward the cost of rehabilitation, and the uncle and everybody else who handled the cubs had to get rabies shots at over $300 apiece, so there was some justice. Needless to say, these cubs had a genuine dislike for humans, including me.

While Phoebe and Debbie took on the brunt of the workload with all the new cubs, I still had all I could handle keeping tabs on the big three. I couldn't tell where they might be, not only from day to day but sometimes from hour to hour. On the morning of May 14, Frosty and I arrived at the cage earlier than usual, about nine, only to find it empty. Signals came from three different directions, with just one of them anywhere nearby, so I took Frosty to show him the bed site the Boy had built out of leaves at the base of their favorite large pine. (The Boy didn't exhibit this behavior until he started running with wild bears.) Spring beauty was in bloom, and red trillium and trout lilies were not far behind, so the walk wasn't going to be a bust even if we didn't find the cubs, but then we saw Squirty's tracks in the oak stand heading back toward the cage, and when we arrived, all three cubs were there. They were a lot bigger than the last time he had seen them, and Frosty's nervousness at being this close to bears this size apparently showed, because the Boy swaggered up to him, stood on his hind legs, and nipped Frosty on the shoulder. When we tried to leave after that, the cubs boiled out of the cage with us, so Frosty took my truck back and I stayed with the cubs to satisfy their bonding demands for wrestling and suckling.

But if I thought that happy session between the three and me would settle things down for the scheduled return of the National Geographic film crew the next afternoon, I was in for quite a surprise. Curls joined us shortly after we arrived from below the clearing at about half past two. I got a strong signal on Squirty from the cage area but nothing at all from the Boy. After hiding the food, we proceeded to the wrestling pit, in the process walking right by Squirty, a fact that Curls with her nose couldn't have missed. But instead of greeting her sister, Curls snorted and ran away toward us, so I went to investigate and found Squirty standing at the base of a tree. Curls returned and chased Squirty up a large pine, not a playful chase at all. When they came down, Curls chased Squirty in front of the camera, where both bears stood up, faced off, and scolded each other with resonating moans. Then they relaxed and greeted, wrestled, and suckled each other. Finally, they lay down together in a nearby brook to cool off.

Where had all this come from? I had never seen this behavior before and immediately suspected it might have had something to do with the fact that the Boy was missing. Perhaps his wild sow had run the girls off this morning, but the reality was that this was the beginning of the family breakup for the girls.

After the National Geographic shoot, with bear scent from the girls still on me, I went in to see the new Vermont cubs. The blond male and female checked me out with sniffs, slow-licks, and huffs. Then, having figured out what I was, I got squared-off lips and a rendition of snorts and stand-up swats from the safety of their den. They backed off when I did the same.

For the next several days, only Squirty stayed close enough for me to find. I was sure that all three were having regular encounters with other bears, a suspicion confirmed by the overnight appearance of an incisor bite on one of Squirty's forelegs. It didn't seem to bother her very much, but she was spooky and seemed to catch scent in the air on our walks. So many mysteries would be cleared up if only I had the nose of a bear.

A week after that, the tables were turned. Squirty went off with her boyfriend again just when I found Curls, which I did by getting a good line on her coming from near a road-killed deer I had set out close to the white pine bed tree. I sneaked in just enough to see a very black, very heavy bear about Curls's height, but much broader, run off at high speed toward the clearing. Curls's signal, on the other hand, was getting stronger from the other direction, so I called and heard her moan of recognition as she followed my scent trail to me, then rubbed her scent all over me for about five minutes. The deer carcass had been moved and chewed, but the hide hadn't been broken into, and I couldn't interest her in it even when I cut the hide on a hind leg. She did bite-mark a sapling over the carcass. By the red pine, Curls marked with a vegetative scat and started the same "mew, mew" call the Boy made when he was missing the girls earlier. After checking the tree for fresh scats, Curls led me to the cage to eat. Then we returned to the bed tree, and Curls snuggled up to me and slept for an hour.

In the morning, Curls was gone. That afternoon, I found the four-inch tracks of her boyfriend—a heavy animal who had completely "disappeared" the dead deer. He must have eaten some and carried the rest, for there was no drag mark. I looked around and found that Curls had slept in her nest and he had slept on the other side of the tree. Then they had apparently gone far away; when I drove up past the height of land to try to pick up Curls's signal, I got nothing at all.

For the rest of May, I played electronic tag with the girls as they traveled in wide circuits with their mates. Some days, I'd get just telemetry signals; other days, I'd catch glimpses of them rushing off with the male as I got close; and occasionally I'd get a timing message from the trail timer I set up at the cage, learning that Curls had been in to feed at five in the morning or at half past two in the afternoon. So I knew roughly their whereabouts. But the Boy was nowhere to be found. It was beginning to get unsettling.

On May 27, Debbie, Phoebe, and I took the Vermont cubs and Teddy to the Turnpike remote cage. Five days later, Phoebe and I took the four of them on a walk that seemed to be going well until they got to Cole's swamp and decided to go off on their own. Phoebe grabbed Teddy, and I had the option of grabbing one of the Vermont three and returning that one to the cage with Teddy, or letting them all go together. They were giving me incredible stink-eye, so I decided to let them go, thinking that I knew the country pretty well and could find them later. I also knew, according to an article written by Albert Erickson from Minnesota, that cubs of this age could fend for themselves, at least until winter.

On that note, the yo-yo ride of bear tracking swung into even fuller form. That same day, both Squirty and Curls showed up at the cage to eat. But it wasn't the joyous reunion I might have imagined; Squirty, now the dominant one, chased Curls until they faced off in a cat fight, swatting each other before standing to face each other with their heads down while making their resonating moan. Eventually, they calmed down and came back into the cage to eat, but kept a safe distance from and an eye on each other the whole time. When I tried to take both of them for a walk, Squirty chased Curls back, so I led them back to the cage and Squirty treed Curls up the big pine and lay at the base of it, keeping her from coming down until I gave them another bag of food, which they both shared. With that, I left.

On June 1, Tim Bixby, a local bear hunter and houndsman, brought his old hound to try to locate the missing Vermont cubs, but it didn't work. All of the scent led back downhill toward Cole's swamp and the cage. We did find tracks of other bears using the area: the three-inch tracks of a yearling and probably those of a sow and cubs.

The next day, back on Lambert with the big bears, I got Curls's signal from Roy Day's sandpit on the way up the hill. I didn't find her, but Squirty was by my pond with another bear.

It was the Boy. He was as glad to see me as I was him. First he greeted me by checking my breath, then went for my backpack with the food. It was like old times. After the bears ate, we walked over to the sleep tree, where Squirty suckled my fist and the Boy gave me kisses and chewed on my fist before falling asleep. I gave them one more bag of food at the cage and left. I hadn't gotten out of earshot before I heard a commotion back at the cage and suspected that Curls had arrived to complete the reunion. The Boy had been gone nineteen days, but he was fit and strong, with no apparent wounds. Dispersal time was here, and he seemed ready.

Their reunion didn't last long. The three bears were together on Winslow's Ledge the next day when I picked up all three signals coming from nearly the same spot near the Dartmouth Skiway, but a day later only Squirty's signal still came from there. The other two had gone back to the area near the cage on Lambert, and when I went to check on them, the Boy met me at the clearing and Curls came down from higher up to meet us at the cage. It was the biting height of blackfly season, and I had sprayed myself with bug repellent before going into the woods, an olfactory addition to my personality that the Boy apparently disapproved of, for as soon as he sniffed it, he climbed on my lap and urinated all the way down my leg—not a dribbling mark but a full-length soaking. (Debbie didn't think the Boy's addition was much of an improvement when I got home. "That's a real strong smell, Ben," she said, a pretty good understatement even by her standards.)

But his being in my lap gave me a chance to check him over. I found two puncture wounds, one several days old just below and to the left of his sternum and another in his right hamstring that was very fresh. I suspected it happened when the three of them went over to Winslow and Squirty's larger mate sent these two packing back the way they had come.

Meanwhile, we kept looking for the missing Vermont cubs, and it wasn't until June 12 that I finally found fresh sign. We were in a mild drought, and experience told me the missing cubs would have to be near water to survive, so I had systematically followed perennial streams and visited the small spring-fed wetlands I knew in the area. It was along one of these small brooks that I discovered numerous trees with fresh rings of disturbance around their trunks and cub claw marks on the bark. I noted the location of the tree with the most sign and returned to tell Debbie and Phoebe what I had found. On June 13, I returned to explore the area and climbed the ledges above where I had seen the cub sign. The ravens there had been diving and making the "Pruck, pruck!" sound they use when chasing invaders, so I had my hopes up that the cubs would be nearby; but I found instead that the ravens had a nest in the cut where I used to hunt deer, the first raven's nest I had seen on those ledges. In that situation, they might be diving at anything that moved.

Phoebe made up a batch of cub food—milk replacer, applesauce, and baby cereal—to place at the tree in hopes the renegades would find it and stay near the food supply, which for the next several days in a row it appeared they were doing. On June 22, an adult bear took the food and the large plastic bowl we served it in. In the morning, I walked down the hill looking for the bowl and found an ash tree really torn up with bite marks by a wild bear. Large patches of bark were removed up to the four-foot level, and there was a ring of disturbed ground all around the base of the tree. At first I thought it was an extravagant attempt at marking, but on closer inspection I could see incisor marks on the tree that indicated the bear was eating the cambium layer between the bark and the sapwood. In all the thousands of hours I've tromped around New Hampshire's forests, this was only the second time I've seen this behavior. In the states of Washington and Oregon, cambium eating by bears is considered a major nuisance by the timber companies. Since it's so rare here in the food-rich environment of the Eastern woodlands, it seems likely that the agricultural mono-crop approach to forestry has a lot to do with their problem out West.

When I rode my three-wheeler back to camp, I saw bear prints in the tracks it had left where I parked. I knew it was Curls, since she was the only one of the cubs that had ever returned to camp. My hunch was verified by turning on the telemetry equipment and immediately getting her signal from the pond clearing. I put food in the unfinished cage that we had started in case Teddy had needed to be separated from the Vermont cubs, and called her. She came up, checked out the food, then marked with scat in front of it. I tried to introduce her to Teddy, but they scared each other. Teddy wouldn't come out of his box and kept making the gulping vocalization; Curls marked with urine on his scent and continued to drip even while she was eating.

I came back in the afternoon to call Curls up to see Phoebe and a couple of girls from Lyme she had brought out to see a bear. Teddy and Curls had a snort and run fest, and again Curls kept urinating as she ran, perhaps out of fear. Teddy would huff and then bleat, causing Curls to huff back and then look interested. When they were calmer, I followed Curls to the pond to get a drink, then I lay down by a stump and Curls came over for a nap. She was a cuddler. When we woke, we went back to the cage, but as soon as Curls started to eat, Teddy came out of the den box and huffed at her, sending her scurrying out to short-tree and look back at Teddy. I went in to see Teddy, knowing I was covered with Curls's scent. He sniffed me all over while climbing on my shoulders and standing on my fanny pack while Curls watched. That seemed to calm them both down; Curls went in to eat, and Teddy was quiet when I left.

But the Vermont cubs were still missing, and I wasn't going to stop trying to find them. The next morning, I checked their food site a little later than usual. Nothing had been eaten, so I took the camera and went downhill to photograph the ash bear-bit tree, and from there I went further downhill to cross the brook. I caught a flurry of black movement to my right and looked up to see what had to be the three renegades climbing some small hardwoods. I got excited and, forgetting how they felt about me, called out a greeting; they reminded me by effectively dropping out of the trees. I recognized the Vermont cubs' blond face markings. Their feet hit the ground running. They were joined by a fourth cub and an adult female. All five bears disappeared into the understory. I now realized what must have happened: a wild sow had adopted the three cubs. It was equally clear to me that this female's resources would be stretched to the max and I needed to come up with a supplementary feeding program.

I set up a camera site where I could access it with my three-wheeler and placed a road-killed deer out to see if I could attract the female to feed so I could identify and monitor her. She responded quickly. Then I placed a gallon-sized Ziploc bag of the cub mix out for her cubs. The next day, I filmed her feeding on the deer carcass, then picking up the bag of cub food and taking it with her. For the next seven weeks she carted off a bag of cub food every day, stopping only when the blackberries ripened. When she stopped coming, the bags were eaten on site by coyotes and raccoons. We never did find the forty-nine bags she lugged off.

With that problem solved, I turned back to the Teddy and Curls saga. Curls had traveled four miles overnight to the cage on the Lambert Lot, a fact I deduced from the dog-kibble scat in the cage there, but had returned to the Turnpike Lot, where Teddy now sported the new radio collar I had put on him. Phoebe and I set out on a walk, and Teddy chased Curls several times in a circle around us. When he got too close, Curls would moan at him with disdain and sometimes run and huff, but she showed no real animosity. Once when they came face to face, she made the resonating moan and simply put her paw on Teddy to hold him back. They were making good progress, but if Teddy had his way, he would have adopted Curls already.

Squirty, meanwhile, had separated from her mate, and I was able to meet with her several times on Winslow. For three days afterward I got a very strong signal from what appeared to be exactly the same location near the Lambert cage. I drove up to investigate and found what I usually call a dropped collar signal—a loud tone and no bear. I tried every trick in the book with the telemetry receiver, but I couldn't locate the collar. Finally, it dawned on me: the collar was in a tree. I used the roof of the shelter to trim the signal and spotted the collar hanging from a limb eighty feet up in the big pine in the cage. My first reaction was that one of my friends had pulled a prank on me, but the collar was just above the whorl of limbs Squirty liked to sleep on. I fitted out a new one and spent most of the next week looking for her the old-fashioned way.

On the Fourth of July, Phoebe drove me to the Appalachian Trail so I could walk back to the Dartmouth Skiway through Squirty's territory. There were bear trails in a wet area on a plateau above the trail; they led to a nice little brook, then across it, and into a beech stand where bears had been feeding, and finally to a small rock summit with a large red pine bear tree. From there I hit a marked snowmobile trail with a fresh vegetative bear scat right in the middle of it. After going downhill for a quarter mile, I cut back up toward the ski trails, passing several wet drainages with lots of jack-in-the-pulpit along the way. As I reached the first ski trail, I heard a moan behind me and saw Squirty walking up my back trail. I gave her a snack and fitted her with the new collar. She played and rolled on the slope with me, then we went for a walk while she ate strawberries, rattlesnake weed leaves, ants, grubs in white birch, jack-in-the-pulpit, and clover flowers.

In the middle of July, the Boy began to get himself into a bit of trouble. I got a call from Charles Bridges, the chief biologist at New Hampshire Fish and Game, saying that the Boy had relieved a hiker of her knapsack on the Appalachian Trail on Lambert. At the time, I had very little information on what had happened, but that wasn't acceptable behavior and I knew I had to act quickly to correct it. I called Gordon "Peanut" Wilder, and he agreed to run him with his hounds the following weekend. The idea was to demonstrate to the Boy that not all humans were passive, and some could be quite aggressive.

Early that Saturday, we were out with the dogs looking for the Boy. He wasn't on the front side of Lambert, so I drove ahead to check by the Beal cemetery and picked up his signal on the Winslow side between two log landings. I parked my truck and got out of the cab to wait for Peanut, and the next thing I knew, the Boy appeared out of the woods; he must have been close enough to smell me. I yelled at him, got back in my truck, revved the engine, and scared him across the road, then drove back to Peanut and related what had happened. He and Jerry Robinson, a Lyme-based hunting dog editor and writer (and a longtime friend of mine) who had come to help, then drove off to where I had seen the Boy, and there he was, standing in the middle of the road. When the truck slammed to a halt, the Boy ran ahead and stopped at a large pine to look back just as the hounds were turned loose. Before they caught sight of him, the Boy cut north into the woods toward Smarts Mountain, and the dogs took his back trail south toward Winslow. They were gone about ten minutes before correcting their error and chasing back toward the Boy in the right direction, where they soon treed him on the upper part of Jasper Day's lot, holding him up that tree for over an hour before the fellows arrived. I didn't have the heart to go in on the tree, but when I talked to him later, Peanut said the Boy gave a good account of himself.

"I didn't think your hand-raised bears would give the dogs much of a chase," he said. "But not only did he run hard, he came down the tree and took a swipe at the hounds."

That was quite a compliment coming from an experienced houndsman.

That evening, I located the Boy down at Tony Ryan's, a mile from where he had been treed.

But it wasn't just the Boy who was beginning to make problems for us. I got a call from Cindy Swart, saying she saw Curls crossing the road twice by her house, and that her dog chased Curls both times. She thought that Curls might have chewed on her window sash, but there were dog prints on the building when I went out there to have a look. The next day, Curls was at Josh's and was treed by Famous, his sister-in-law's Australian shepherd. I wasn't comfortable with Curls near houses, so I supplied Frosty and Josh with twelve-gauge shotgun blanks to scare her. When they went back, she ran out of the section of woods in front of them and crossed the road into a fenced pasture. They caught up with her on the back side of the field and fired the gun three times. But Curls had absolutely no reaction to the gunshots and then followed the men down the drive and across the road. Frosty finally drove her off by throwing stones at her. She popped her jaw at him and ran off into the woods.

But if I was beginning to think that my hand-raised bears were going to be more than normally troublesome around people, I soon learned otherwise. On the last Friday in July, I got a phone call from the Hanover police saying they had a bear cornered on Rayton Road, a residential district less than a mile from the Dartmouth campus. When I arrived, the bear was gone, but it was easy to see that the young bear had been living in fifty-yard-wide strips of cover behind the houses where the ground was almost perfect bear terrain—thick with low brush and tall white pines, featuring an abundant supply of large female jack-in-the-pulpit and attached contiguously to large wooded tracts on nearby Balch Hill and Velvet Rocks. We found a bed site at the base of a pine tree only forty feet from a house; there were two scats and a piece of bird feeder by the bed site. The cub was probably a yearling and by all the accounts I heard from the neighbors was less afraid of people than my cubs. The police officers had shot at her with plastic bullets with no visible effect or reaction. They promised to call me if she reappeared.

The dog days of August took on a more specific meaning for my bears as we continued to hound them whenever they showed too much interest in a human dwelling or in crossing well-traveled roads. On the fifth of the month, Jerry Robinson called to say Curls had been on the deck of his house, one of the more remote in Lyme and not far from one of the regular wooded routes used by bears, mine included. Just four days earlier, Debbie and I had spent time at this house (having dinner with Jerry and his wife, Sherry), Curls might have caught my scent and decided it was okay to look for food there. I called Peanut Wilder and had him give chase within a half hour, and with Peanut and Jerry following the dogs, it didn't take long to put the bear in a tree. It turned out that it wasn't Curls after all; it was the Boy. Jerry had fired a gun on the deck and again while the Boy was treed; the bear had lurched in reaction only to the first shot. After he was treed, Peanut called off his dogs, and they all pulled out and left him there. I drove out several hours later and found his signal coming from some distance away.

When I got home, I had a phone message from the Hanover police, requesting that I meet them again on Rayton Road. I drove down to find a small female bear surrounded by police officers with twelve-gauge shotguns loaded with plastic bullets and cracker shells, and a distraught homeowner insisting that bears have no place in residential areas and demanding that this one be shot. The police had no interest in harming the bear, so I was called to break the standoff, which I did by simply walking toward the bear until she turned and left. The officers joined me as we walked her back to the forest.

One of the police officers later told me that before they called me, they had fired a cracker shell at the bear and didn't realize until it was too late that they had hit a tree and the shell had ricocheted back behind them. He said that they heard a hissing sound that didn't register, then a BOOM! that sent them all leaping forward—toward the bear. Who didn't react at all.

On the morning of August 7, I was back in my own territory with Peanut and his dogs when they struck scent at Jasper Day's, and again on the ledge crossing, but nothing hot enough to run until finally they got a fresh strike on the Boy at the two log landings above the Beal cemetery. The Boy went up a tree, and the dogs took off on what Peanut thought was the Boy's back trail. But it turned out that Squirty and the Boy had been together, and the dogs were now running Squirty, who was too wily for them here on her own home ground. She drew them up on Lambert and lost them on the ledges on the far side. Meanwhile, the Boy was terribly nervous in the tree, since Peanut had another dog that he put on the tree to hold him there until the other hounds could be regathered and he could pull the whole pack out.

I had never spent much time around bear hounds before this, and it was something of a revelation to compare the way they track as opposed to a bear's methods. The dogs seem to follow airborne scent, making it important that the scent trail be no more than one or two hours old. Bears follow both airborne scent and the smells left behind by fur brushing against vegetation. Wind conditions, slope, and the seasonal state of vegetation all affect how long the scent trail can be followed in either case.

Curls didn't escape the hounds' attention; in fact she was run three times. The first time, the dogs didn't push her hard at all, but it was enough to send her on the four-mile journey to camp to be consoled. The next two times she was run, she found that she could lose her pursuers if she climbed up through the ledges, where the dogs couldn't travel. She used the same set of ledges each time, staying inside her home range and keeping a comfortable distance ahead of the frustrated hounds.

After the monthlong flurry, the dog-running action slowed down. For one thing, it seemed to have achieved its effect of making the bears more shy of roads, and for another, the Boy decided, after being held in the tree when Squirty was run on August 7, that it was time to leave. The next morning, he was eleven miles away in the woods behind the summer-closed elementary school in Canaan, where two employees of the Soil Conservation Service surveying the school property awakened him out of his bed. Thinking they were friendly (for they had approached him in much the same way I would have), he followed them, making his soft appeasement moans. Nevertheless, they were terrified and got hold of the Canaan police, who called me. By the time I arrived, the Boy had gone back into the woods, and although I picked up his signal, he was way ahead of me, traveling rapidly back north, toward Pollard Hill in Dorchester. But the next day he was still in Canaan, the signal coming from near some beaver ponds that I knew, and the day after that, I got nothing at all.

The rest of August was relatively calm, punctuated by the occasional call from the Hanover police whenever a raiding bear reappeared. On August 24, for example, Sergeant Larry Ranslow and I caught up to one crawling onto a porch on Morehead Lane. I treed the eighty-five-pound yearling male, then jabbed it with my jabstick, injecting enough sedative to get it to drop out of the tree onto a soft embankment and try to run away. I ran him down and grabbed the bear by his hind foot to keep him occupied while I waited for the drug to take effect. Then I drove him home in the front seat of my truck and put him in the cub cage; two hours later, he was up and about. Conservation Officer Tom Dakai came by the next morning to relocate him.

September arrived with still no sign of the Boy; it now seemed certain that he had gone off in search of his adult territory. Knowing that he could range a hundred miles or more in the process, I wondered if even with his radio collar I would ever see him again. What I didn't know was that as I worried about him now that hunting season was open, he had been reported thirty miles away in Andover, New Hampshire, a report that was never passed on to me and which I only learned about after the fact. That only made it all the more poignant: the Boy was shot near a cornfield by a hunter ten days later in Boscawen, a town even farther away to the southwest. The hunters reported that he had weighed 120 pounds field-dressed, and that they had broken his collar when they tried to use it to drag him away. I have to give the one who actually shot him some credit, though; he made a full public accounting of the incident in the first nationally televised film on my work, "Mother Bear Man," which ran on *National Geographic Explorer* the following April.

The girls, happily, stayed out of any rifle sights for the rest of the long season. They stayed away from hikers and homeowners, too. As Squirty and Curls fed through the rest of the fall and readied themselves for denning time, I thought about ways to ensure their futures. We had made strides in that direction with all the dog-running, and it occurred to me that I could further protect them by posting signs in the back country informing hikers and hunters about the lives of my young bears. I've done this ever since, with great success.

Furthermore, my recent experience with the problematic Hanover cubs of the same age told me what I had long suspected, that it's not so much the bear but the circumstance that brings on the difficulty. We live in a heavily populated world, where even "remote" areas like the north woods of New Hampshire have a high level of human activity; bears and people will always come together, but in relative terms it's not that often. In writing this book, I know I have tended to do what everyone does in recounting a personal history: I've written about the exciting times when the cubs needed educating or got in a little trouble. But what's left out is the 99.9 percent of the time when they lived and acted as functioning wild bears. That's what I remember most, even if it's hard to convey in a book.

CHAPTER 20

Squirty Stays Close

WITH JUST SQUIRTY and Curls under my close scrutiny—and Teddy being tracked and tended to mostly by Phoebe—1998 turned out to be a year of unexpected calm before the mostly unanticipated cub storm that was to follow a year later. For the whole of 1998, in fact, I would never even see Curls. The radio collar I had made for her died two days before the bear-hunting season ended, giving me reason for concern. Although no female bears were taken in that part of town, I wanted evidence of her survival anyway. I believed she was around, but for reasons that I didn't put together until later, we failed to connect. Three years later and after two sets of her own cubs, she's still around. Without the assistance of a radio collar, five square miles is a lot of area to cover when you're trying to connect with a bear. I've had to settle for a few unverified sightings and one good video shot of her in June 2001 by my friend and neighbor Alfred Balch.

Squirty and I, on the other hand, have stayed close in both senses of the word. When she had gone to den that winter, I knew only approximately where she was. Her home-rebuilt collar had gone dead over the winter as well, but when she started moving again in the spring, the signal came back to life. I first heard it on April 4 coming from the top of

Lambert and immediately headed that way. As I walked along, I could see tracks where the deer had begun to move out of their winter yards to feed heavily on the acorns that had been protected by the heavy snows; a group of five ran out ahead of me as I followed Squirty's signal toward the stand of spruce on the Norris Lot. The signal didn't get strong until I could see the top of the ridge ahead of me. I knew she was close, probably in the low spruce understory ahead of me, but I saw nothing. I waited and watched for several minutes before finally calling to her. She seemed to materialize like a ghost, soundlessly standing about forty-five yards away. I called again and she turned, did a stiff-legged walk, marked with urine, and approached me with a soft repetitive moan. I greeted her, nose to nose, and offered her a bag of kibble. She sniffed it and went to my pack and removed the other bag in her mouth, then ran to a more secure spot at the base of a spruce tree to feed.

She got up, walked off, and left a scat—a scat full of what looked like parasitic worms. I took samples to identify so I could medicate her if they were harmful, then followed as she wandered into the ice-damaged beech stand. The stems of the beech were broken halfway up, leaving a five- to ten-foot layer of treetops and limbs covering the forest floor, nearly impenetrable to me but heaven for a bear. Still lethargic from her winter's sleep, Squirty stretched and walked lazily ahead of me. She stood up with her back to a tree and solicited stand-up play with me, a means to reinforce our relationship. We crossed to the top of my lot, where she rolled up the leaves that fell last fall and revealed old egg cases and hundreds of recently hatched insect larvae, which she then licked up. So that was how she got the worms. Walking over saplings, she marked the rich food source on which she would feed for another week. Back home, I floated a section of her scat in water and counted the remains of the larvae, which I identified as larvae of the March fly. Each scat contained the remains of seven thousand or more, a real bonus to a protein-hungry bear just out of hibernation.

Over the next two weeks, a pattern began to develop. If I went out to see Squirty alone, she would allow me to find her, even if sometimes it took several hours of patient tracking, but if I tried to include another person, we wouldn't get to see her. With the aid of telemetry, I knew roughly where she was, and I could track her as she moved away from me on the few times someone else was along. Teddy, on the other hand, wouldn't let me make contact even if I was alone; only Phoebe could get close enough to see him in April. She said he looked thin but larger-framed.

The first evidence of Curls's survival I found at her mark tree, a split hemlock at the base of Snow Hill where Squirty would nervously react to airborne scent; here I found fresh pieces of bark that Curls had chewed off the same way she had the previous fall. But I also could tell that Curls was around if Squirty made a sudden departure from the area around my Lambert clearing and the cage. One day when that happened, I moved in to make contact with Curls. I placed a bag of food in the cage, a place where I had never had any evidence of wild bears going, hoping Curls would climb in and get it. I called a few times, waited for a while, then left. Two hours later, I returned to find the food gone, so I put more down, called, waited, and left again. I came back two more times, and each time the food was gone. I even marked the nearby ground with my urine to make sure it wasn't a wild bear. I couldn't understand why she wouldn't come to me

By late April, my reestablished bond with Squirty was strong enough that she came and found me one day, a real surprise since I had picked up no signal. Her collar battery, it turned out, had gone dead. I gave her some kibble and was able to change the collar without any resistance from her. We wrestled, then she followed me out through a rocky ravine, where she mouthed and then ate a couple of expanded beech buds. I kept moving as the wind blew down off Snow Hill. Squirty, with head in the wind, departed my company and climbed up the boulder field toward the top of the hill.

When I had originally walked in looking for her, I had noticed fresh bear activity on either side of the trail I had been using: a chewed-up log and a pine stump missing some bark. I thought Squirty might have done it, even though she had no reason to follow me out that far. I got in my truck and drove home. It wasn't until the next morning that I noticed bear tracks on my truck; Curls had climbed in the bed while I was up on the hill with Squirty.

When I came down off the hill on another day, I ran into Roy and Mary Etta Day, who said they had just seen two cubs crossing down near Tony Ryan's property line. By now, I had begun to realize that the most likely explanation for Curls's shyness was that she must have cubs, so I ran in to find them, making a lot of noise but catching up to them anyway. It was a sow and two yearling cubs, but the sow was smaller than

Curls. They stood and faced me, then ran off together. There was bear-feeding sign in the area, and there had been a sweet acrid smell in the dew-laden air for several hundred yards before I caught up to the sow and cubs. I still haven't figured out what I think is bear scent; I can only get faint wisps of it when I wrestle with my bears, but what I smell in the air, like the scent I picked up while chasing the sow and her cubs, is stronger and more distinctive.

In early May, I found where an adult male with a five-inch front pad had left tracks and bit a three-by-five-inch patch out of a red pine. This first sign of the mating season corresponded to the lengthening of beech buds into leaves, a factor to be compared next year to see if it was annually consistent and could be used as a predictive indicator. By the end of the month and into June, the most dependable indicator showed: People all over Lyme were calling me to report seeing bears on the move.

One day Frank Cutting said that a good-sized bear got his bird feeders at three in the morning, then left in the direction of Holt's Ledge.

On another day Ronald Baker saw a small bear cross the skiway.

On May 25, Luane Cole called to say a young bear was at her parents' and had taken suet and a bird feeder. I arrived to find a dark-faced yearling that looked like a male. The cub seemed to be in good condition but was smaller than Teddy. I followed him up into the woods and was able to get less than twenty feet from him without even spooking him up a tree. He was obviously exhausted from traveling. As he lay beside a log in front of me, his eyes would drift off to sleep; then suddenly he would awaken because of my presence to chomp, huff, and swat the log before drifting back to sleep. Jack-in-the-pulpit and both types of lettuce grew in big numbers on the bank behind the house; I suspected that he found the natural food first, then noticed the bird feeders.

We went out to the camp on the Turnpike Lot on May 30, and Debbie walked around the back of camp and encountered a male bear heading for the barrel she stored birdseed in. She called for me, and I ran up to see him on the bank above camp. The bear, who weighed about two hundred pounds, snorted and false-charged at a distance of thirty yards, then left. He returned the next morning to clean up the seed we had left on the ground.

The following day, Nancy Grandine called at eleven in the morning to report a bear in her backyard right in the village, less than a hundred yards from my own house. She estimated its weight at about eighty pounds. She had no food out, and the bear just left.

That afternoon, at a quarter to six, Bill Piper phoned to say a yearling cub was in his backyard having a smorgasbord with his bird feeders. When I arrived, the same cub that had been at Luane Cole's parents' house was eating from the bird feeder three feet from Bill's window. I walked after the cub, and he would go a short distance then stop; I pursued him down into the woods until he let out a snort and took off. Ten minutes later, he reappeared; this time, I stared hard at him and took two steps in his direction, and he took off. His track measured only three inches.

On June 1, Roe Pillsbury called; there was a "large" cub in her yard. I went right over and identified it as the same one that had been after Bill Piper's feeders the day before. I was wrong about this bear keying in on natural food; he was keying in on the highest-quality food available, sunflower seeds in bird feeders. While I was there, I filmed an interesting encounter that the yearling had with Roe's husband Gerry's full-sized archery bear target. The little bear responded to the styrofoam replica as though it were another bear, running to the base of a tree when he saw it, making several cautious moves toward it until he came nose to nose. Realizing it wasn't a bear, he then left it alone. Here was the mirror test with a twist.

And then I got the phone call I had been hoping might come. Kathy Larson called to report that she had seen a bear with a cub below the Smith Mountain Road not far from the cage. There was a good chance that this bear was Curls. And if she had a cub with her, that would explain why she wouldn't come to me that day I tried to connect with her in the cage. Other things fell into place as well: the last time I saw Curls, in November 1997, I was impressed by her weight—at over 250 pounds, it was an indication of pregnancy.

I got out there five hours after the sighting, at about four in the afternoon, called up Squirty, and the two of us climbed up the basin until we hit Curls's track, where Squirty did a full back rub on a dead three-inch tree, followed the track while checking scent, then marked nearby with scat. I moved on, and she followed, hesitating at the edge of the trail, then moaning and continuing to follow the scent down the trail. It appeared that Curls had crossed over to Lambert, for when we got to the cage Squirty hit live scent and sprinted past me, becoming visibly more nervous. But if it was Curls, we never made contact.

As June progressed, Squirty began to show signs of wanting to breed. On June 20, I met up with her as she made her way to the Pout Pond Brook beaver ponds. After eating her snack, she marked me twice with a back rub and once by rubbing her side against my leg. It seemed possible that she was ensuring that I would not scare off any potential suitors, as she normally didn't intentionally rub on me.

Four days later, her signal told me that Squirty was at the cage, so I approached as usual, and when I was in full view of the cage, I saw the hindquarter of a bear going in. It looked a little large, but I assumed it was Squirty. Because she hadn't seen me and I didn't want to alarm her, I called out a greeting. Squirty came out the door in my direction—with a large male right behind her looking over her back as though he intended to mount her. His head was large and round, his shoulders were about six inches above hers, and as they stood I could see six inches of him on either side of her. He must have weighed 350 pounds. He had a dark stripe down his nose with brown panels, markings very similar to Squirty's.

I didn't move, but I was only twenty yards away. He spotted me immediately, then turned and fled back into the cage, running full speed into the chain-link fence on the far side and bouncing back, then charging in a panic back and forth before climbing up and out at the end by the pond. Squirty then bolted and ran to the left of me through the brush. When I was sure he was gone, I turned to see Squirty standing ten yards behind me. She now had my scent and approached me. I expected her to be agitated, but instead she was completely calm, far more relaxed than she had been the times I walked in on her with her mate the previous year. But I was a third wheel here, and I knew it. I went home.

When I later returned to make plaster castings of tracks, I found the male had come back to search for her. He had gone back to the clearing to remark his sunken footprints with a stiff-legged walk and to walk over saplings as well. I could also see where he had fed on clover and rolled around in the log landing.

Not wanting to disturb her chances of mating success, I left Squirty alone for the next several weeks, tracking her from afar with telemetry to see that she was still okay and staying in her home range. The few times I did see her in August were when she found me, once when I shut down my bulldozer after working on an erosion problem. She simply appeared, a real surprise as I hadn't even had a signal in quite a while. Her coat seemed dull and disheveled, and she had lost enough weight that her spine now showed. I fed her at the cage and then walked with her for a bit until she lay on her back scratching with her fore- and hind paws, pulling out great gobs of her winter's wool. I searched her body for evidence of fighting and found a fresh claw mark on her chest. After she had been asleep awhile, I quietly left, but after a short hike, I heard something behind me. It was Squirty. It seemed she had come back for what appeared to be a short period of reassurance; then she jumped across the road and disappeared up the hill.

She recovered her weight and good health quickly, though. By October 1, she was quite large, weighing over two hundred pounds with a forty-inch girth, heavy enough to sink into the duff when she walked, leaving noticeable tracks.

But she still kept her sense of caution, even with her intimidating size. On October 3, I took Debbie with me to the Lambert Lot to see if she could get pictures of Squirty and me together. We followed the signal to a thick area near Perkins Brook, where I called out as we approached, but Squirty erupted out of her bed and took off huffing and chomping for a full fifty yards. Debbie stayed back, and Squirty held while I approached her, but when I told Debbie to come on up, Squirty took off. I went ahead alone and found Squirty, then went back to where Debbie was waiting with the camera. Debbie tried to come back to Squirty by walking closely behind me, but she didn't fool the wary bear for a second; Squirty took off huffing for the third time. This time, Debbie stayed behind for good, and I followed Squirty up into the ice-damaged area, where she found a suitable place to bed down, but before she did that she wanted to liberate the kibble I had in my bag. I had to fight her off and get it out myself, as I knew she wouldn't bother with the zippers. I left her monitoring the wind blowing up the hill, and returned to find Debbie.

By November 1, Squirty had gained even more weight and girth, and I realized that she might stay up all winter if I kept giving her treats. So I stopped feeding her on the third and found her at a new den site on the fifth, a very elaborate maternal den with a fully excavated chamber and an entrance under a poplar tree that was growing out of a large old blowdown. She had dug the chamber in dry red soil and had dragged bedding material from about sixteen feet away. It was a well-chosen location—

with relatively little slope, well-drained soil, and an old brush pile and stone wall nearby. She checked me for food and played with me for a while, then went back to raking leaves.

Within a week, she had over 250 square feet of leaves dragged into her den. Since digging the den, she had been staying right there, going inside at night and resting on top during the day. When she was all the way inside, her signal could only be heard from one side and was very weak. By monitoring it from a distance, I could tell whether she was in her den or not without disturbing her. Alert and patient, she waited for the oncoming bad weather.

On December 5, she was in her den when I came upon it, but she crawled out to greet me. When I first attempted to measure her girth, she made the "eh, eh, eh" sound to tell me to stop. I tried to remove a burdock from her fur, but she set her ears back as a warning, then held my arm in her mouth as a message to stop. I was eventually able to measure her girth at thirty-nine and a half inches, considerably smaller than her fall peak of forty-three. I gave her four cookies and about six ounces of water. She took the soda bottle to her den and left it there; something to chew on over the winter.

There were two inches of snow on the ground as I walked in to check on her five days before Christmas. I stopped about twenty-five feet from the den to take pictures and was about to leave when I heard a moan of recognition coming from the den. Squirty slowly emerged, leaving a short trail of freshly laid tracks behind her. After getting the "eh, eh, eh" on my first attempt, I taped her at thirty-nine inches, then gave her a treat of three cookies and about eight ounces of water, but she didn't finish the water. After a few more minutes of checking my breath, my camera, and my person, Squirty carefully placed her feet exactly in the tracks she had made emerging from the den, backing in carefully. As I left, she watched me from the entrance with her head resting softly on one of her paws.

My plan was to leave her alone for the rest of the winter, but on January 24, worried about the amount of rain we were having, I went to check on her. I approached the den to listen from thirty yards away but couldn't hear anything. I moved to within fifteen yards and still couldn't hear anything. Finally, I sneaked up to where I could see that the den entrance was sealed off with ice and snow. At a distance of about eight feet, I listened and heard the faint high-pitched squall of a recently born cub. I left quickly so as not to disturb anything.

CHAPTER 21

Squirty Has Cubs

HIKING IN ON March 19, I spooked three ravens off the ground within sight of Squirty's den and was immediately concerned that something might have happened to the cubs. As I hurried over, I could see by the tracks in the snow and ice that she had already been outside the den quite a bit. I also noticed that she had broken off a hardwood sapling, which I thought might be some form of marking, or perhaps just done out of boredom. I called to her, and she crawled out to greet me. She was ravenous, so I gave her a small treat and went to look in the den for the cubs. When I turned on my video light and shined it inside and still didn't see any cubs, I started getting more concerned. But then, when I stuck my head a foot and a half down into the den, I finally saw two cubs hiding in a small recess in the back. They were small, weighing about three and a half pounds each, and were hiding their heads and presenting just their backs to me without making a sound. I was so relieved to find them safe, I decided that was enough for the day.

Returning the next day, I brought two video cameras, one to film the cubs and one on a tripod to film Squirty and me. I also brought about three pounds of kibble to keep Squirty out of the den while I filmed the cubs. Squirty came out of the den quite quickly when I arrived, so I had barely time to set up the first camera to film her coming out to greet me. She met me by the den, I dropped the bag of kibble, and she grabbed it in her mouth and started backing back inside. Realizing my plans would be dashed if she ate the dog food in the den, I tried to grab the bag back, spilling the kibble on the snow. That hadn't been my plan, but it worked; she began to eat. Improvising, I used the torn bag to pour water in for her to drink. She then let me past, and I proceeded to film the two cubs in the den.

The cubs were playing with two toys. One was a piece of deer antler that I had given Squirty a few days before; she had picked it up in her mouth and backed down into the den with it. The other toy was a peeled piece of the green hardwood that Squirty had fabricated from a broken sapling outside the den. My videotaping went well for more than ten minutes, when the cubs suddenly had a squalling little fight over the toys. I backed out fast, knowing full well what was about to happen, and Squirty leaped between me and the den. Although I had nothing to do with the cubs' fight, I knew where their mother would place the blame. That was it for filming cubs in the den. She went inside, and I continued to stay and film from outside the den for a few more minutes until she erupted from it in an aggressive stance. I stood up to leave, and she responded with an abrupt false charge, and when I turned my head and started to step away, she attacked, grabbing my pants and a little bit of my calf in the process, and pulled me backward for a step. As fast as the attack had begun, though, it was over after that one step. She didn't follow up but continued to eat the kibble instead.

I shut down my cameras, then tried to approach her again before leaving. She casually reached out with her paw and flexed, then clinched her claws in the snow. Enough said. I left. It had been a memorable encounter, made a bit harder to forget by the nasty bruise on my leg that lasted for a week or so.

I didn't come back for three days, and when I did I brought another three pounds of kibble. Squirty stood up to waltz with me and tried to remove the food from my hands prematurely. This time I was ready, and she didn't get it until I wanted her to. Then, instead of trying to film her cubs, I just sat with her while she ate. She allowed me to measure her girth at thirty-seven and a half inches, which along with her body length of fifty-three inches calculated to a weight of about 187 pounds. After that, I sat on top of the den and filmed her as she finished eating and drank the water I brought. At one point she came over to me to sniff my breath and offer me her soft moans of approval.

When she had enough food, she checked the den, then turned and came for me with a drawn, squared-off face and false charge, letting me know in plain bear terms that it was time to leave. I backed off about ten yards and continued to film as she raked and dragged dry litter toward the den. She false-charged once more, and I backed off even more to about thirty yards. To tell me it really was time to leave, she fixed her eyes on me with a hard stare and began walking sternly toward me; I could tell exactly what she meant. Squirty was giving me regular lessons in bear communications, lessons that continue to serve me well as I apply them to the ongoing problem of bear-human conflict.

For the next few weeks, I visited Squirty and her cubs almost daily, each time with a two- to three-pound bag of kibble and usually with a video camera. For as long as it took her to eat the dog food, she was consistently friendly and would allow me to shoot footage of her or the cubs or both, but after she was finished eating, things would vary from day to day. Sometimes, she would tolerate my presence for as much as an hour afterward, letting me observe as she nursed her cubs and then playing with me afterward; other days, she would boot me out almost immediately. I learned to read her intention to evict me from the way her eyes would twitch just before she put on the long face that immediately preceded her move to give me the boot. But short or long, the continuity of my visits over time allowed me to observe in great detail the way she mothered and protected her cubs.

One thing I noticed right away was that she seemed to be intentionally selecting and bringing to the den sticks about two feet long and an inch in diameter as toys for her cubs. Soon the area around the den was littered with them. It was equally fascinating to see how quickly the cubs became adept at climbing; by April 6, they were out and up a tree when I arrived, even though they were barely a foot long and looked as if they weighed no more than four pounds. The cubs began to cry when I arrived, but as soon as Squirty moved to the base of their tree and moaned, they came down and took a nap. She could just as easily tree them by breaking brush as she walked away. I realized the value to Squirty in fostering her cubs' climbing, for it was their ability to tree that would allow her to go off and forage. By April 7, she had moved them forty yards from the den to a large white pine, where they could sleep fifteen or twenty feet up off the ground.

Bob Caputo of *National Geographic* magazine spent the second week of April with us, as part of his months-long process of photographing and writing a feature article on the bears and me. For the time Bob was here, Squirty established a remarkably specific set of guidelines, first eating the food I would bring and then giving us only a certain amount of time to take pictures before kicking us out with the long face and false charge. Not only was the shooting time she allowed consistent from day to day, but so was her established shooting distance of about thirty-five yards for Bob. By comparison, she had been allowing me to go right up to her and had relaxed her "go away now" messages to a simple lunge without the preceding stink-eye and huff.

In May, Neil Rettig and Kim Hayes came back to continue their video shooting for the second *National Geographic Explorer* special. Although they were treated to some very aggressive displays of Squirty's tolerance level for strangers, they were treated better than Bob Caputo. Squirty knew them from the time they had filmed "Mother Bear Man" when she was a cub. Now on their return they could film for as many as ninety minutes before being asked to leave.

A typical day would go like this: As soon as we arrived, I would give Squirty her kibble snack, which would generally take her and her cubs about twenty minutes to eat. Then would come the hour-and-a-half grace period during which she would nurse, play with her cubs, or sleep until—almost as though she had set an internal alarm clock—she would walk over to get a drink of water. When she finished drinking, she would stand momentarily, at which point I would tell Neil and Kim, "She's checking her watch."

Squrty would then walk toward the cameras and false-charge, her signal that the shoot was over. Sometimes Neil would want to shoot a little bit longer, and she would stand directly in front of the camera performing what Kim called "The Great Black Wall" act.

But what was truly fascinating was that Squirty's actions were always so deliberate. So much so that I could stand beside her and touch her while she delivered a full-blown, drawn-face, squared-off-lip, snorting false charge at the other two. And when she finished, she would look up to me with a peaceful—almost as though she was proud of her performance—look.

In spite of her performances, though, Neil and Kim got some great footage. Particularly memorable to me was the sequence of Squirty standing on her hind legs to rescue the cubs from a branch they were dangling from and lowering them to the ground carefully, a sequence that was repeated five times. We all wondered: was she trying to teach her cubs something by removing them from the branch so many times, or was she just playing with them?

After being evicted early one day, we came back the day after and filmed for the usual allotment of time. Neil started with a close shot until Squirty kicked him out right after she finished eating. While Kim and Neil retreated, I stayed with her for a while, and the cubs came down from a tree. She tried to get them to nurse, but the cubs were nervous about me being there and went back up. Squirty then crawled onto my lap, where she napped and played gently as if inviting the cubs to come down and join in. They hung off branches above us and watched instead. Squirty finished the day with the by-now-routine going for water with her cubs, then charged up over the hill and scattered Neil and Kim. I remained, but she gave me a light swat and snort, so I backed off while she held the high ground, where she then full back-rubbed the tree we had been leaning against. She waited for us to leave before returning to her cubs.

On another day, we were walking in to see Squirty when I noticed that Kim reeked of citronella. It was the biting height of blackfly season. "Kim," I said. "What's that smell? You really shouldn't have that on."

Kim prides herself on her smart mouth and replied, "It's all natural and better than that deet you use."

I just smiled and said, "We'll see."

As soon as we got there, Squirty false-charged Kim, then came over to give her a full body rub, starting at her foot and working upward. There was a bit of terror in Kim's voice as she quietly asked, "Ben, what do I do?"

I told her to just relax. "Squirty gets a sexual response from certain aromatic compounds," I said. "That's why male bears bite the red pines in the spring, releasing compounds to attract females. They smell a lot like what you've got on. You've just tapped into her response behavior, that's all."

That didn't help much. Frozen with terror, Kim averted her eyes to avoid contact with Squirty's, a self-defense tactic she had learned while filming mountain gorillas in Rwanda. Meanwhile, Squirty the masseuse was rubbing down Kim's back, and her paw worked its way under Kim's sound pack, pulling off the headphones Kim was wearing. She and Neil used them to converse while filming wildlife. Squirty leaped away when Kim's next words were broadcast out of the open headset, thereby ending that close encounter of the olfactory kind.

It would be an understatement to say that strange odors can be terribly distracting while working with bears. I think Kim now understood that "all natural" didn't necessarily mean the product was free of side effects.

On the last day of shooting, Neil had to set up close because he forgot his long tripod, a proximity that Squirty didn't like at all—she tried to drive him out immediately after eating. When that commotion settled down, I gave the little girl cub a soft stick of red licorice candy, which she got to chew on until Squirty took it away from her and ate it herself. The cubs were tired and slept, so I walked away. Squirty followed me, only to be attracted to Kim's pack, which still had a residue of citronella from the previous day. We had to wait for Squirty to finish giving it the once-over before retrieving the pack.

Neil felt a bit shorted in not being able to film more and told me he wanted to stay and see what would happen if we ignored Squirty's first warning. I cautioned against it, but it wasn't often I got volunteers for an experiment, especially one that promised to be as lively as this. Plus Neil was a big boy; he knew what he was doing. He'd been among the mountain gorillas of Rwanda, right? So when he asked again, I said, "Why not?"

So Neil stayed by his camera when Squirty false-charged, stopping about three feet away. When he didn't move, she looked up at him for a second or two, then leaped forward, swatting him lightly before he could even react and taking his leg in her mouth ever so gently. Holding his leg, she just looked up at him as if to say, "I could do a lot more, but I'm letting you off this time."

That was enough for Neil; the shoot was over.

By June, the two cubs had gotten comfortable enough with me that first the boy and then a few days later the girl got brave enough to put my finger in their mouths. After that, they sometimes played with my shoes and pants cuffs. But they remained shy and cautious. Whenever they weren't brave enough to try an approach to me, they'd position themselves between Squirty and the tree, looking like meerkats ready to bolt upward into the high branches. Often when I came to visit, I would find them together with their mother sixty feet or more up a tree; as cautious and healthy as they were, a raiding male bear would have had great difficulty doing them any harm. The safety that Squirty afforded her natural cubs by being with them all the time in these first critical months, I had only been able to achieve by enclosing my orphaned foster cubs behind protective wire. And while she was the living proof that my makeshift method worked, I had no delusions as to which was the preferable way. Seeing her here in the wild with her own offspring was an emotional and intellectual reward that I had barely allowed myself to think about in the dark and uncertain days at the beginning, and now it had come true.

Bob Caputo's return in early June provided the springboard for an unanticipated experiment. On our first shooting session, Squirty drove Bob out with a vigorous false charge right after eating her kibble. Needing more time than that, I devised a plan to see if on the next outing we might buy some additional minutes from Squirty by having Bob throw her another bag of food after the first false charge.

Before going out that next morning, I happened by chance to get a phone call from Richard Wrangham. We discussed Squirty, her cubs, and the photo shoot in progress, and then I told him, tongue in cheek, that a two-pound bag of kibble had bought us about forty-five minutes of shooting time before Squirty kicked us out. He laughed and said, "If you can buy another forty-five minutes with two more pounds of kibble, I'll be impressed."

Out on Lambert, Squirty made her move right after she finished her regular kibble. I had told Bob not to give her the new second bag until after she false-charged, thereby showing her intention for him to leave. On cue she false-charged him, and he tossed the bag halfway between himself and her—also as I had instructed—making her decide between advancing toward him or picking it up. I had told Bob I was fairly certain she would go for the food, not him, and that's just what she did, picking up the bag and taking it back to the tree. Upon finishing off the bonus bag, she got up and walked toward Bob, checking to see if she'd spilled any kibble on the first trip. Then she moved to a position eight feet in front of Bob's tripod while he continued shooting the action and she proceeded to give him a conflicted stare, with twitching eyeballs. (I had seen this stare before when she had difficulty making a decision whether to kick somebody out or not.) After about a minute, she turned back, and for the next forty-five minutes by my watch, she slept and relaxed with the cubs at the base of the tree. Not until a loud airplane went over did she wake up. She stood up and took several steps toward us, stared for several minutes, gulped, made the long face, snorted, then turned to her cubs and with a quiet "shush" she treed them. That was our signal to leave.

The next day, she false-charged Bob from a distance, then went up to him with conflicted eyes and requested her bribe. She didn't try to chase him out again, and we left while she was sleeping.

The temperature was in the nineties and Squirty was up in the tree with her cubs when Bob and I arrived two days later. I set up a remote flash close to Squirty while she finished her first bag of food. After she came to see me, she went to Bob looking for the second bag, which he tossed to her. She returned to eat it, then went back out toward Bob. First she false-charged and then flattened the flash I had set up, after which she proceeded to false-charge Bob. Either we broke her trust setting the flash up so close, or she decided she could have her food and kick him out to boot. Whatever the reason, her message was clear. We left.

About the time that Bob left, I named the cubs Snowy and Bert, and soon they repaid the favor by allowing me to walk with them for the first time. I took a short nap with the three of them, and Snowy, the female named for Snow Hill where she was conceived, came up and pulled on my jacket, then sniffed my ear. Bert, actually Lambert for the hill on which they were raised, held back. They each weighed about sixteen or eighteen pounds, and he was the smaller of the two; they were competing for the limited amount of milk that Squirty produced, and Snowy, being female, was more aggressive on the nipple. I expected that as summer foods became more available, he would grow past her in size.

On June 18, Squirty was waiting for me at the first clearing near Roy Day's turnout, with the cubs up a large pasture pine. But when I produced the food, they came right down and ate it with me only two feet away. Snowy was curious and friendly, while Bert was shy.

Afterward Squirty tried to mug my truck for more food, and I had to tell her no. As she walked off, I gave her a quart-sized plastic bottle of diluted maple syrup as a treat. She bit off the cap, then carefully carried it in her mouth without spilling to the base of the pasture pine, where she was able to lick up more than half through the small opening by reaching straight down with her tongue. When the contents got out of reach, she held the bottle at an angle to get more, and when that tactic no longer worked, she tried to bite off the constricted neck. But the only effect of that was to crimp the opening, which she then tried to open back up with her claws. The plastic was too stiff, however, so she simply poured the remaining syrup on the ground and licked up what she could. To me, this was a convincing demonstration that she understood not only the concept of a vessel but how to reopen the spout once she had crunched it.

As June slid into the heat of July, I learned that Squirty might be having a territorial squabble with another sow and cubs. Neil and Kim had come back to get more footage for the *Explorer* special, but when we went out to find her it was raining, and that ended the shooting for the day. I then went alone to where she was east and downhill from the den, near the boundary line. I heard a lot of chomping as I approached, followed by the sound of bear claws scrabbling up a tree. When I got there, a sow and two cubs ran north, away from a large pine. Assuming it was Squirty, I called out, but she didn't stop. Then I heard more chomping coming from up in the pine. It was Squirty, forty feet up. She had been in the middle of a confrontation which I had just interrupted. When Squirty realized it was me, she gulped and climbed up to one of her cubs. At that point, I left her a bag of food and departed.

I returned two hours later to find her still in the tree and the food untouched. She greeted me with chomping, then came down and ate three-quarters of the food, leaving some for the cubs—a first. She paced in a sunken trail radiating out from the tree and kept looking at another pine; I spotted Snowy way up near the top of it, so I walked down to the base of that tree to get a better look. Squirty climbed back up into the big pine with Bert and faced in the direction of the other, where Snowy was. I started to leave, getting forty yards from the tree when Squirty started gulping, climbed down in a hurry, and went to rescue Snowy, gulping all the way. Bert then started down behind her, and Squirty quickly ran back up that tree, keeping him up there. Snowy came down from her tree, and Squirty met her halfway. Bert joined them at the bottom of the big tree. With the confrontation behind them and things returning to normal, Squirty tried to get the cubs to come to nurse, but they were too busy swatting, snorting, and moaning to oblige. Bert finally came over to eat some kibble, and Squirty was in the nursing position when I left.

The next day, Squirty had moved back to her big tree and was up in it with her cubs when we arrived. All three came down to eat, then went back up in the tree. So did I, so Neil could film Squirty and me together in the tree, since she wouldn't come down. This was the first time I'd seen Squirty uncomfortable on the ground with the cubs, and I knew it had to be due to her confrontation with the other female.

When we came back a day later, we caught Squirty walking with her cubs above where I usually park my three-wheeler. They all were very hungry and ate kibble together until Bert swatted and snorted Squirty away from the last of it, a behavior that I saw two more times at this stage of his life, when he was still the smaller cub. Through his emotional outburst, he seemed to be communicating that he had a greater need for the food, and Squirty, by backing off without retaliating, seemed to honor his demand. I hand-fed Snowy so she could get some kibble. I didn't think the cubs had eaten much solid food after the encounter with the wild female and cubs.

Meanwhile, I was having a few conflicts, too. But mine were over time, not territory. I had two new cubs of my own.

CHAPTER 22

The Moose Mountain Cubs

BACK ON MARCH 14, John O'Brien, a local forester, had called to say that he had found two bear cubs on nearby Moose Mountain, where he had been managing an ice damage salvage cut. Nobody had seen the sow leave, but there were skidder tracks that nearly straddled the den, which was an earthen depression underneath a couple of dead spruce poles in a small dense stand of young spruce. The cubs were cuddled together on the spruce poles when they were found; undisturbed snow covered the bottom of the depression, indicating the cubs had been abandoned before the last snowfall on March 12. The logging had started near the den on March 11, but there was another skidder trail operating for several weeks before that on the other side of the den, and John found them on March 14 after hearing loud squawks and shrieks, vocalizations that would only be made in distress.

The cubs, a male and a female probably ten weeks old, weighed four and a half pounds each, with body lengths of seventeen and fourteen inches, respectively; their noses were red from frostbite, and their front paws, barely an inch and a half wide, were bloody from holding on to the spruce poles. Their squawks of distress when John first arrived indicated hypothermia.

Randy Cross, the Maine Department of Inland Fisheries and Wildlife expert who handles sixty-five to a hundred sows a year as a part of the department's long-term reproductive study, told me he thought they should be solid and weigh seven pounds at that body length. He said cubs out for three days wouldn't lose noticeable weight; we decided that the cubs had been abandoned for closer to ten days. We had got them in the nick of time.

Soon enough, that early scare was forgotten, though, as they took to their foster home as readily as all the other cubs had. By April 1, they were eating well and felt solid when I picked them up, but I still worried about them. Once I had realized how long they had been abandoned, I knew there was a chance that one or both of them would develop the same separation anxiety that had plagued LG. Squirty, Curls, and the Boy, who had come directly to me from their mother, had showed no such problems, but already the new little male was showing some of the same signs that LG had at this age.

Eventually we would name the girl Yoda because she would often hold her ears like the *Star Wars* character, and the male Houdini for his propensity for escape. Their lives ran on a similar course with the other cubs we raised, but they did benefit early not only from my hard-gained experience in fostering so many other cubs but also from what Squirty was teaching me as she raised her own two of the same age. I looked forward to the day I could introduce these two sets of "cousins" to each other, but even before that happened I knew I had an unprecedented opportunity: to compare my results to hers. At least to the extent that might prove possible.

In mid-April, Debbie, Phoebe, and I transferred the two orphans to the cage on the Turnpike Lot, and the next day I took them on a walk in the woods, where the two climbed their first trees. Within a week they had settled into what was by now the familiar routine. Phoebe or I would spend twenty or thirty minutes with the cubs after feeding, primarily to watch them play or respond to their needs by allowing ourselves to be climbed on, kissed on the lips or in an ear, or just generally being available for play.

But as I said, I'd learned some things, as a few examples will illustrate:

On April 27, when I walked them alone, the cubs turned ornery as dusk fell. The boy (we didn't name him Houdini until June) bit me twice for no good reason that I could tell, so I grabbed him by the scruff of the neck and held him. After a few loud squalls, his eyes rolled toward me in submission, and I let him down. He then crawled up on my legs and began playing gently, as if in remorse.

On May 5, while taking them for a walk around the pond, I chewed beech buds and let Yoda smell my breath. She got very excited and bit and chewed several of them, then kept soliciting more of my breath and jumping at my face. After that, they both started searching for more.

At the end of that same walk, I snorted like Squirty and false-charged to keep them from following me when I left, and to my great delight it worked. They were confused, but so had been Squirty's cubs when I watched her do it to them. It's a false distress signal, so it has to be done very convincingly to be effective; Squirty did it with a gulp as she moved toward them. I wished that somehow I'd been able to thank her for the tip—mom to mom, so to speak.

We kept Yoda and Houdini at the Turnpike Lot until mid-August before moving them to the big open-topped cage on Lambert. The ride over went smoothly, and it took only three or four zaps each for the two cubs to learn about the electric fence. Squirty and her cubs had been coming and going around the cage, and in no time at all the two new cubs picked up their residual scent, letting me know where it was by stiff-legged walks and urine-marking.

The other thing they did right away was to discover a hole in the fence. When I came back the next day, they were both gone. I didn't see the hole and had no idea how they had gotten out, but on the other hand I knew we hadn't given Houdini his name for nothing. I caught up to the little miscreants as they were about to cross the Appalachian Trail. They poker-faced me when I put them back in the cage, not letting on at all that they knew there was a hole; they just waited till I left them alone, then jail-broke again.

Fool me once, shame on you; fool me twice, shame on me. I found the hole the next day and repaired it while they watched and moaned their disapproval.

For the next couple of days, the new cubs and I played a bit of unintentional hide-and-seek with Squirty and her two cubs. I could tell by her tracks that Squirty had been by the cage early on the morning of August 22. When I let them out, Yoda and Houdini sniffed and slow-licked the tracks but didn't use a stiff-legged walk or mark on them, which told me they recognized her scent. Maybe they had smelled it on me. In any case, they followed her scent to the spring pond before I pulled them off it.

Three days later, in the morning after I knew Squirty had been there, I took the cubs down to the clearing. Again they acted as if they had found bear scent but knew whose it was. Yoda did full back rubs on my leg four times in the presence of it, though.

Finally, two days after that, we all met up when the cubs followed me as I went to see Squirty at the base of Snow Hill. At first, everyone went up a tree but me. (Out of solidarity, I guess I should have, too, but there are times when coming down on the side of scientific objectivity has its plusses.) Once Squirty came down and started to feed, her cubs came down, too. Yoda and Houdini came down as well and started to circle Squirty and her two at a safe distance of about twenty yards.

Although I had known it from separately measuring them, it was nonetheless fascinating to see Yoda and Houdini in comparison to Squirty's cubs. The orphans were nearly twice the size of Snowy and Bert, a differential that I knew was due to the fact that Squirty's resources were limited and mine weren't. She could only produce so much mother's milk while she waited for the late summer foods to ripen and for her cubs to learn how to eat them, while I could make up as much cub food as I wanted.

For her part, Squirty was very tolerant of the two newcomers, as if she was clearly aware that these were my cubs, not just some unaffiliated strangers. Only when Houdini came up behind her to about fifteen feet did Squirty wheel and give chase, sending him clattering up a tree. She then walked over to me completely relaxed and continued to feed. Yoda stayed clear, but Houdini came down and continued to circle, then started snorting and swatting trees out of nervousness. When he got too close, Squirty treed him again. And then went back to feeding.

I marveled at her command of the situation, since I knew that this meeting would have had a much different outcome had Yoda and Houdini come to it with a natural mother instead of with me. Between two wild females a prolonged battle would have ensued over property rights, not over how close one of the cubs got to the wrong mother. Once again, Squirty had shown me her impressive ability to deal with an unexpected situation. She knew these cubs were with me, and she figured out how to deal with it in a way that had to run counter to all her territoriality instincts.

CHAPTER 23

Squirty's Dynasty Begins

WITH YODA AND Houdini successfully reestablished in the area around the Lambert cage, my life became a bit easier since they were now closer to the main event, Squirty and her cubs. The Lambert clearing where the orphans would now spend much of their time was, in fact, part of Squirty's home range. But adult bears are unpredictable, even when you know what they're going to do. Right about then, Squirty decided to expand her range.

She and the cubs had begun traveling to the berry patches on the Hollis and Beal lots, which were a mile and a half and two miles from the clearing, respectively. So instead of saving time by having all my bears relatively near each other, my daily routine didn't change much at all. I'd start by walking the orphans near their cage and then having to drive somewhere else, usually east of Lambert in the area between Smarts Mountain and the two ponds, to locate Squirty and her cubs. Most days, I'd be content to pick up a signal so I'd know approximately where they were, but occasionally I would hike back in, following the tone to pay them a visit.

As her cubs grew, they not only traveled farther but ate more, too. By the middle of August, Snowy and Bert had been eating half of the kibble treat whenever I brought it, and by mid-September, they were trying to hog down most of it. Bert had, as I knew he would, grown bigger than his sister by now and was trying to dominate the food bags entirely. On September 10, I watched as Squirty ended that day's attempt with a resonating blow, but less than two months later she allowed the tables to turn.

By then, as the impending onset of winter had driven her to begin assessing potential den sites, Squirty had begun to fashion a good one on the southwest face of Lambert at an elevation of about 1,650 feet. The site was at the base of a large white pine, in a mess of blown-down trees surrounded by small standing spruce, yet still open to the winter sun and near the crest of the hill to limit runoff flooding in the spring. There was a small seep ten feet away for drinking water. She had broken off spruce branches and stripped birch bark for bedding material. There was even a nearby alternate: a downed tree with an upright root mass and also surrounded by small spruce. Judging from the scats, she had been at work for three days before I met her and the cubs there for the first time on November 5.

Two days later, she had raked in more bedding material and bent over several small spruces to shield the wind or hold insulating snow. I found her not far away at the base of the ledges just under the Appalachian Trail looking for acorns, a hunt that all three abandoned happily when I produced the small bag of dog food I had hauled up there with me. When the food was about half gone, Bert warned off both his sister and his much larger mother by standing over all the remaining kibble— about three pounds—and moaning whenever either of them got close to it. But this time Squirty, still obviously hungry, didn't discipline Bert the way she had in September. Instead she paced about him making gestures of strength: moving some logs, tearing others apart, and completely bending over a live striped maple that was an inch and a half in diameter, about the thickness of a baseball bat handle. Then she rubbed her entire back on the pole-sized trees on each side of the food Bert was defending. Finally, she appealed to me to intercede by standing upright, leaning on me, and giving me a message bite on the shoulder. When I answered her by spreading the food around, they fed peacefully until Bert and Snowy had a food fight. Squirty ignored them and ate what she wanted.

After seeing this same defend-and-horde behavior in so many bears,

I have concluded that an adaptive pattern has developed within the species that allows a smaller bear to get what it wants or needs with an emotional demonstration that a bigger bear will honor without fighting back. In this way a female, for instance, can ensure an adequate food supply for her cubs by vigorously warning off a much larger male who would have no trouble taking it all for himself. Pretty civilized when you think about it.

It took Squirty another month to settle on a den site.

CHAPTER 24

Confrontation and Resolution

I BEGAN MY New Millennium bear year on March 20 when I snowshoed over three feet of snow to Squirty's den on Lambert, following her radio-collar signal to find only that: a working radio collar in an empty den. The cubs had taken it off over the winter. Scats near the den had beech buds in them, and there was a bed made of spruce boughs on top of the snow, so it seemed they had been out and about for a while.

This was doubly disturbing. Coming in to check on them just a few days before, I had tracked a sow and cubs in the snow toward the Lambert trailhead, but when it started getting late and I picked up Squirty's signal coming from the area of her den, I had abandoned the track and gone home on the now mistaken assumption that I had been on the trail of the wrong bears.

Now with her useless collar in my hand, I could at least still see what was left of Squirty's departing tracks, so I followed them up and over the ridgeline. But traveling on snowshoes was terrible in the deep slushy snow. Once I was over the top of the ridge, not only had her tracks completely melted away, but I was exhausted from the difficult going anyway. I wondered if the tracks I had seen a few days earlier, which were long gone by now, had been Squirty's or not. If they were from the other sow and cubs that I knew were in this general area, it could be a real problem.

Now it was even more critical that I find her. For nine straight days starting on the twentieth, Phoebe and I searched all of Squirty's usual haunts on Lambert for fresh sign with no luck and a growing sense of unease. A week into the search Phoebe found a baby-sitting tree with fresh claw marks and a well-defined bed at the base of it, on the yellow-blazed boundary line near the Appalachian Trail about a mile from Squirty's den.

When I hiked in on May 29 to check it out for myself, I found that it was only seventy-five yards away from a spot Squirty had thought about using for a den in the fall of 1998. Near it I found another large pasture pine with beds used the previous season by a sow and cubs. But they weren't the beds of Squirty, Snowy, and Bert, because I had been with them. I hadn't realized how close the other sow's maternal area had been to Squirty's—within a half mile. There was a fresh scat, but I didn't know who had left it, Squirty or her competitor. At that point, I had to take over the search myself, even though Phoebe had helped raise Squirty. Squirty was—and still is—a one-human bear.

The realization that the other sow and cubs were so close was frightening. Squirty's basic range without any competition was five square miles. Without a collar, she would be tough enough to find in an area that big, but with the very real chance that she might be driven even farther away by an older dominant sow, I had to face the possibility that I could lose contact with Squirty altogether. Spurred on by that unhappy thought—and by the fact that I was finding very fresh sign where bears had been foraging for bark beetle larvae—I redoubled my efforts to find her and her cubs.

The very next day I did, and what a relief it was. Cruising the Norris lot, I found freshly disturbed leaves where a bear had fed on leftover acorns, so I started calling. Within minutes I saw dark movement back in the trees uphill from me; it was Squirty and her cubs filing down to say hello. She had run away on my noisy approach but had then waited to see who it was that spooked her.

They were all very friendly, especially Squirty, who let me put on a new collar and measure her without any fuss. She had lost a lot of weight, taping only thirty-four inches at the girth. The cubs looked as if they now weighed about forty pounds each. Bert wanted immediately to play with his mother's new collar, but she disciplined him off it with a single message bite. Undaunted, he decided to slow-lick and rub his head on my hat instead. Then, when he got no message bite from me, he lay back and held the hat with his paws while he played with it. All in all, a very satisfactory reunion.

The next day, Squirty and the cubs were still where I had found them on the Norris lot. They had raked in leaves to make a bed at the base of a large pine near a small stream. Squirty let out a hungry moan when I arrived, anticipating the two three-pound bags of kibble she knew I'd have with me. While she and her cubs ate, I noticed that she had fresh gashes on each cheek; they could only have come from fighting, almost certainly with the other sow. Bert spent quite a bit of time playing with my boots and, when I made it easier for him by lying down, the rest of me. Both cubs now had nice new canine teeth.

While the cubs played, Squirty did her "feats of strength" routine with a two-inch sapling near the bed tree, muscling it over and bite-marking it in the process. I hadn't yet figured out the function of this move, but I had found saplings marked like this near other bed sites. After that, she came over to me and had me empty my pockets for her so she could check out everything I had carried in with me.

For the rest of April and into May, I visited the three bears every other day or so. With the wind in my favor, I was able one time to sneak in quietly without being noticed right away. Snowy and Bert were playing by running up a leaning log, then jumping onto a young beech tree. First one would do this, causing the beech to swing over, then the second cub would jump on the other, swinging the tree wildly in the other direction and knocking both of them off it to the ground. They played this game three times.

For her part, Squirty was ever alert and on patrol. I didn't find any more fight wounds until mid-May, when a pair of new gashes appeared on her back by the shoulders. But I could tell from her watchful demeanor and the stiff-legged sets of warning tracks, which she had laid down to stake out her claim, that the conflict was still very much on. Perhaps Squirty's recently attempted move over to Cole Hill with her cubs had precipitated a new boundary dispute.

That she was alert to every sound in the area was confirmed by Bill Nichols during the first week of the May turkey-hunting season when his squealing call brought not a strutting gobbler to his concealed position but a full-sized mama bear and her two half-grown cubs.

"Hi, Curls," he said when she got to within ten yards, sending the two surprised cubs running off but not their outraged mother. Maybe she just didn't like being mistaken for her sister, or maybe she really didn't like being talked to by something that looked like a tree, but she stood her ground and aggressively chomped and huffed at the camouflage-clad apparition before turning and slowly moving away.

The competing sow and her cubs weren't the only other bears around, of course. Wild bears came and went, Curls was somewhere in the area, and then there were Yoda and Houdini, now out on a large tract of land beyond Reservoir Pond.

At least that was where I thought Houdini was. What I didn't know yet was that he had been driven off by Yoda's first male suitor of the breeding season and, being emotionally challenged like most young males, had traveled thirty miles in three days. Immature and naive, Houdini lacked the benefit of a natural mother's home range and protection and was therefore thrust into the dangers of dispersal prematurely. Attracted by the smells of other bears and readily available food, he was soon drawn into a hotbed of misguided home feeding—both of birds and bears—in Eastman, a large development of expensive vacation and retirement homes in Grantham. Getting a report of a collared bear, I drove down and retrieved him in a carrying box in the back of my truck, then returned him home, only to have him run off again, this time to Canaan.

The Canaan episode was a classic. Following a scent plume that included aging meat loaf, old bread, and other sundries emanating from an unprotected bag of garbage on the back porch of a Blaine Road resident named Barry Chase, Houdini came out of the woods practically on a dead run, making a beeline for the mother lode. Unfortunately, Barry was out in the backyard washing his car at the time, about halfway between Houdini and the porch and pretty much on a dead line with both. Thinking the attacking bear was coming for him, Barry turned in a panic and ran toward the house.

"Next thing I know," he told me when I got there later, "this black streak goes right by me like I'm standing still. Beats me to the porch by a mile, picks the garbage up on the fly, and keeps right on goin' across the lawn and back to the woods."

I tracked Houdini down and took him back to his old haunts around camp. In the morning, I let him out of the cage, and he headed directly toward Enfield, where I had to go retrieve him the very next day. That's when I jailed him in the cage on Lambert.

On the last day in May, I found that a bear with a four-and-a-half-inch track had tried to break into the cage while Houdini was in it. It could only have been Curls, a frustratingly close encounter since none of us had seen her in three years.

While Houdini was in there and possibly getting visited by Curls at night, his sister Yoda also came to visit but wasn't as welcome as she had been as a cub. Now an adult, she was beginning to impinge on Squirty's territory around the clearing. I was there visiting just at dark on the evening of June 2 when Yoda appeared. Squirty false-charged her scent twice while the cubs went up a tree, moaning, chomping, and huffing. Then Squirty chased Yoda all the way to the top of a tree while making a resonating, chesty, "Huh, huh, huh, huh!" that drove home the message "You don't belong here!" with an authority hard to miss.

Now that it was June, I knew that the dispersal of Snowy and Bert was imminent. They were old enough and ready. I planned to put a radio collar on Snowy so I could monitor the kin relationship between mother and daughter, but Bert I would leave uncollared. Radio-tracking is time-consuming and expensive; I could keep track of him instead with remote cameras to see how long he stayed in or near his mother's home range. Since I didn't know exactly how the family breakup would play out, I really wanted to be on hand to see how it was done. Would Squirty do it herself, or would the arrival of a large mating male be the instigator? Would there be some sort of preliminary signs that I would be able to discern? One way or another, I knew, it would happen soon.

Too soon, as it turned out. I got a signal tone on Squirty from the Highwalls pasture on June 9, and when I went in to see her, she was alone. There were Snowy and Bert tracks in the soft mud, but no sign of the two cubs. A large set of male sunken tracks at the clearing, along with his scat mark by the lower apple trees, told me the story. The cubs were gone. Either they had left on their own as soon as he arrived, or the large breeding male had driven them out.

Two days later, he began trying to do the same thing to me. And so began the most intense and exciting bear encounter I've had yet. It lasted seven days.

On June 11, I found Squirty in the open hardwoods of a particularly rugged piece of land behind Jasper Day's camp. When I first arrived, she ran from me, but then she stopped, came back, and began to eat her kibble. That's when I heard the sound of another large animal moving just out of sight in the nearby underbrush. As soon as I heard his rapid, agitated huffing, I knew Squirty had a boyfriend. And a big one, from the sound of it.

At first he wouldn't let me see him. Staying about forty-five yards away behind a comfortable amount of cover, he continued to complain by huffing and chomping. In earnest. First he loudly false-charged, then took down a dozen hardwood saplings for added effect. Which it certainly had on me; now I knew he was even bigger than I first imagined. I decided I didn't need to see him, at least not while I was between him and what he wanted. So, hoping to be a distant observer rather than an up-close participant, I moved thirty yards to my left. He moved the same way, so I moved farther out of the way. Finally, he cut back toward Squirty and circled behind her and to her right, continuing until he made a full circle around both of us. While he did that, I started getting glimpses of him, and the more I saw of him, the bigger he got.

Meanwhile, Squirty calmly finished her kibble and moved to the base of a large pine nearer to me. The big male bear came with her; he was even closer now, and complaining more. It then became clear that Squirty hadn't yet established a relationship with him, for she started defensively snorting, huffing, and chomping back at him.

He really was big. What I couldn't accurately judge from the ghostlike glimpses I kept getting in the thick green vegetation, he clarified when he swatted the ground so hard it sent Squirty up a large pine tree; to me, it reverberated from the unseen giant like a pile driver. I was genuinely intimidated. Then he did it again. Now I was genuinely frightened. I had no idea what he would do next.

But it wasn't all threat and intimidation. Squirty was definitely treating him like a stranger, but intermingled in her defensive posturing she would emit an alluring soft "Maw, maw." And between his fits of power, he would reciprocate with a soft moan of his own, one that I had often heard from Houdini.

Now it really was time for me to leave, but I had left my pack and telemetry antenna uncomfortably close to where the big guy was holding court. Finally, though, I caught the shape of him moving back down a small ravine to lie down at the base of another large pine. That was my chance. I quickly grabbed my gear and left.

But halfway back to my truck, I turned to see Squirty following me. I sped up. Thrilled as I was to have witnessed the emerging courtship between her and her mate, I wasn't convinced that luring Squirty away from him was the best idea I'd recently had. Then, when I got to the clearing, I could hear another male bear moving in the bushes. It seemed like a real good time to hop in my truck and leave the three of them to sort this out among themselves.

The next day, I went in on Roy Day's road below the cage. As she often did when I was out looking for her, Squirty cut my scent trail from behind and came up to say hello—with her mate right behind her. This made returning to the truck for my camera a little difficult, but I really wanted to record whatever might happen.

Telling myself that now was a good time to start applying some of my hard-earned knowledge of bear behavior, I decided to walk right toward them. My heart was thumping, but the big guy quickly got out of the way, complaining the whole time. Squirty then followed me—and he followed her—back to the truck. He was careful to stay in cover, but he always positioned himself to be as close to her as possible without being seen. I tried to bring him out by placing some food for Squirty out in the center of the opening in the trees. Instead he circled around to sit on the bank above her. I had hoped to get some clear pictures of him, but it was obvious that he wasn't going to cooperate. Tomorrow, I thought. Maybe tomorrow.

I arrived at the clearing at midday and parked my truck where I normally do, then turned on the telemetry gear. Squirty's signal was so clear, I knew she was close. She was. I closed the door and turned to find her right there looking at me. My first words were "Where's your boyfriend?" She didn't have to answer. Down over the bank and about twenty feet away, I heard his grunts. Each day, he was following her closer and growing less wary of me. Which only made me more wary of him. Now I watched as he moved through the trees below me until he came to an opening, where he suddenly lunged into the open, coming directly at me chomping and huffing, at last openly displaying his huge adult head, his near perfect black coat, his broad muscular shoulders, and a massive body that even in its springtime leanness had to weigh every bit of four hundred pounds. As quick as it came, the false charge stopped, and he went back over the bank. He had just let me know that he wasn't hiding in the bushes anymore.

While Squirty ate her treat, the big male stayed down over the bank but kept popping up like a jack-in-the-box to see what was going on. That was okay—I liked him down there. But when Squirty finished and climbed into the back of my brand-new pickup truck to check out a piece of moose hide I had put there, it was too much for the big guy. Up he came, out into the open again and on my level now.

I was standing about ten feet from the back of the truck, and he went to the other side and stood up to look into the bed at Squirty. She then backed him off with the same reverberating "Huh, huh, huh, huh!" vocalization that she had used to drive Yoda away, but this time with much less intensity. Clearly, she was communicating to the male that she was not yet ovulating and that he should stand back. He did.

Bears are stimulated ovulators, which means that although a female may be in her period of estrus, which in New Hampshire runs for about five weeks starting the first of June, she needs to find a mate that stimulates her sufficiently to trigger actual ovulation. This big male obviously fit the bill for Squirty. I knew he would pursue her, staying close and trying to get even more so as her ovulation neared. Squirty, doing her part, wouldn't let him get close enough to mate until she was ready.

Squirty jumped out of the back of the truck with the moose hide in her mouth, ran by me up the trail, and sat down with it. The big male tried to get between the truck and me to follow her, but decided that was too close. He respectfully swung a wide arc around me to position himself behind Squirty. It then became a peaceful picture with Squirty sitting in the grass and this frustrated but patient monster lying down behind her, the two of them about forty feet from me.

But there's always a calm before a storm. Squirty decided to show off her relationship with me by walking over and nuzzling her head into my arms, a little demonstration that didn't go over too well with the big guy. He then came at me in an exaggerated, offensive strut—snorting with his head held down and drool hanging off his lower lip. Halfway to me he veered off and charged into the brush, plowing down dozens of saplings to enhance his show of strength and displeasure. Squirty then ran over and met him in the bushes, which seemed to calm things down. A few minutes later, Squirty came back to me, stood on her hind legs to brush noses with me. Only fifteen feet away, the big guy's head stared at us out of the bushes, but he held back. Squirty was saying good-bye to me for the day and ran off over the knoll. The big male made a wide arc around me and followed her off into the forest.

A day later, June 14, Squirty's signal was coming from the Snow Hill breeding area when I arrived at the Lambert clearing. Without giving it much thought, I drove my truck as far as I could up the Smith Mountain Road before parking and setting out on foot with my video camera to find Squirty and her mate. He had respected me, and I had respected him the day before, so I didn't see any reason why I shouldn't visit them again today. After about a twenty-minute hike following the signal, I caught up with them on a thick spruce knoll on the west side of the hill. When I was close, I called to Squirty. I stood on a small plateau in the middle of a steep, wooded slope. There was a fair-sized boulder behind me and enough of a clearing that I thought I could get some video if I stayed here and let them come to me.

It worked. Squirty came when I called and appeared from the thick underbrush just ten yards above me on the slope. She hesitated and looked back before jogging down to me, letting me know the big male was still with her. I hadn't doubted it for a minute. I gave her treat to her, and she sat at my feet and proceeded to eat it one piece of kibble at a time, which was perfectly normal; but considering what was about to ensue, I wasn't fully prepared for how long it would take her to finish the treat.

Then the male approached. I could hear his heavy footsteps before he appeared out of the underbrush, reminding me how huge he was. I hoped he would stay where he was, keeping his distance as before, but today he casually made his way down the slope toward me. He didn't stop. At about twenty feet away, he started chomping and huffing. At fifteen he urinated, then broke into the head-down-and-drool strut he had shown me the day before. Then, only ten feet from me, he lunged onto a pole-sized log, moving the heavy tree trunk as if it were balsa. This was way closer than I wanted him.

But aside from his defensive posturing, this large, dominant animal still wasn't showing any truly aggressive tendencies; his ears weren't back, he wasn't making the roaring moan, and he didn't have ugly written all over his face. Between his fits of long face, squared-off lip, chomping, and huffing, he looked perfectly relaxed, and throughout everything he did he kept his ears in the Mickey Mouse position. It was a reassuring sign in a less-than-reassuring situation. His boldness suggested that

Squirty was about to ovulate and he wasn't taking any chances at losing his place at the front of the line.

Meanwhile Squirty, comfortable with the fact her mate's complaints weren't about her and that the situation was under control, sat peacefully at my feet snagging one piece of kibble at a time with her tongue.

I could see from the movement in the male's eyes that some kind of thought process was taking place, and it was pretty clear that I was included in those thoughts. If I took my eyes and video camera—which I kept rolling the entire time—off him to film Squirty at my feet, he would immediately rush at me with a false charge. I tried this a half dozen times with the same result. As I had long ago learned with lesser bears, my eyes were my best defense. Even this huge male wouldn't hold eye contact with me for very long before looking away. All this was happening at less than twelve feet of separation.

Fifteen minutes into this stalemate, he tried to move next to Squirty, making the "gulp, grunt" vocalization as he approached her; I recognized it as the same one she had often used to call up her cubs. But she still wasn't ready for him and held him off with a soft "Huh, huh, huh." He was a gentleman and backed up, then sat down just five feet away from me. This was *way* too close. Now I was just one lunge away from becoming an inert part of the forest, and very conscious of that fact. Had I been wearing a heart monitor, I would probably have broken it.

Finally, he climbed back over the log and lay down where he had been before. Wisdom being the better part of valor, and delighted at the luxury of a full twelve feet of distance between me and the big guy, I decided that I had intruded on their bliss enough for one day. Now would be a good time to leave.

As I had been standing there, a number of thoughts had been streaming through my mind. Did this bear see me for what I was or as another bear? That one was easy: he saw me as a human. If he thought I was competing with him for the right to mate with Squirty, I would have been gone long before now. So I was an outside annoyance. But did he have any reason to harm me? No, I didn't think so. If I were to just walk away, he should be relieved, right? I thought so, but apparently I wasn't thinking as clearly as he was. Which I was about to discover.

With him comfortably at ease, I made a move slowly to my left between two spruce trees and the boulder behind me. Those two steps telegraphed my intention, and the big guy rose to his feet, locked his eyes on me, and moved quickly to block my exit. I slid back behind Squirty. She pinned her ears and rose on her feet and lunged at the big bear with a forceful "Huh, huh, huh, huh, huh!" that stopped him in his tracks. His eyes still glared at me as he sat down, and now he wasn't averting them. To say I was thankful that Squirty had such leverage in the situation was an understatement even to myself. She had just saved me from a potential mauling. Or worse.

Again, the big male climbed back behind the log and relaxed. While it still wasn't clear to me why the big bear didn't want me to leave, I later put it together that he obviously had an image of me walking off with Squirty following. This close to her ovulation, he wasn't going to let that happen.

A bit disbelieving of what had taken place, I decided to try it again. This time, I stepped to my right, and again he locked me in a stare and instantly erased the space between us. But again Squirty interceded, and again he stepped back.

A feeling of helplessness came over me. While I was safe standing behind Squirty, I was no longer in control of the outcome of the situation. I was under arrest. I had been collared by a bear. And there wasn't anything I could do about it.

So I kept my camera rolling, documenting the entire encounter even with the outcome still in doubt. The only scenario I could imagine that would let me go unscathed was if Squirty would move quickly away when she finished her kibble, leaving the big guy to decide whether he wanted to make trouble for me or go after her. My bet was that he would go with her.

Miraculously, that's just what she did. And just what he did, too, but not before stopping to let me know with a hard stare that he preferred that I not follow them. That was okay by me. The feeling was more than mutual.

I think I would have stayed away completely after that, the way I had two years ago, except I had to feed Houdini, who was still in the cage on Lambert. So the next day, I drove my truck right up to the cage to keep it handy in case the big thug was around. Happily he wasn't, but not long after I finished feeding and visiting with Houdini, Squirty appeared in the clearing. That was my cue. I slowly faded over toward my truck while looking out for her mate. Squirty decided to come to the truck with me. I looked around nervously, but she seemed to be alone.

"Where's the big guy?" I asked.

He was nowhere to be seen. Squirty grabbed a bag of kibble from the back of my truck and went in the bushes to eat it. I got a little braver and sneaked over to look up the trail down which she had come.

There, about fifty yards back, looking relaxed and unconcerned, was the big guy, lying down. In a bad movie he would have been smoking a cigarette. I was no longer an issue.

CHAPTER 25

Bears in the Backyard

W ITH GROWING BLACK bear populations and an ever-increasing sprawl of human development, conflicts are inevitable and increasing. The question is: will we learn to live with this magnificent animal?

I can't answer my own question, but what I do know is that the bear has become a serious student of human behavior. With intelligence comparable to that of the great apes, the black bear routinely distinguishes between threatening and nonthreatening human behavior. The same bear that so peacefully drains your bird feeder while you watch through your sliding-glass doors also successfully evades human predators during the hunting season.

Now it's up to us. And we can go a long way in that direction by answering two simple questions: Why do some bears become "nuisance bears"? Why do some communities have more problems than others?

Over the years I've tried numerous methods to deal with bears that were causing problems for people; most of these methods have resulted in marginal to poor results. I fired a gun in the air when LB and LG got close to my buildings; they just sat there. Then I remembered: Bears don't watch TV—the reports were just noises to them. Taking it to the next level, actually shooting them with apples or plastic bullets, didn't solve any problems and proved lethal for LG. Trapping and relocating can sometimes be successful, but this method is expensive and works only on wild animals. It wasn't much use at all on my rehabilitated bears. Electricity was the one thing that both wild and rehab bears feared. Electric fences are very effective at keeping bears out (or in, if that's the case). Still, mine was a ratcheted, piecemeal approach, and as I thought about the problem, I slowly realized that most of the traditional solutions that weren't working were anthropocentric; we understood what they were supposed to convey, but the bears didn't. It was time to approach the problem from the bear's point of view. And that's when things started to fall into place.

For starters, it's all about the food.

There is nothing that will motivate a bear better than food, but the problem is that very little work has been done experimenting on developing effective ways to use it. It seems that all the creative thinking stopped when these words—*food conditioned* and *habituated*—started being used to describe problem bears. Nobody wanted to push bear control efforts in the direction of the problem itself. But when bears are already food conditioned or habituated, how can you do any further harm to manipulate their behavior using food?

In the fall of 1999, I helped Conservation Officer Tom Dakai with a situation involving a woman who had been feeding bears in her residential yard for several years. She had as many as eight to ten bears coming to her feeding station, which could be seen from a busy town road. But to get to the feeding station, the bears had to cross through other people's yards. Some of these folks were terrified of bears and concerned for their children. Because they regularly crossed the road to get to the feeder, at least one bear got hit by a car. For weeks prior to the hunting season, sightseers and bear hunters parked along the road to view the bears. Then when the season opened, somebody with a license to do it (I won't use the word *hunter* since most real hunters wouldn't want to be put in the same category as someone who would do this) shot the biggest bear within sight of the feeders. The situation had gotten pretty bad until Tom finally got the woman to stop feeding the bears. But the neighbors worried that they would be terrorized in their houses and yards by bears suddenly cut off from food. I suggested a plan using the same food the bears had been fed, only delivered to them deep in the woods and in good cover. We fed the bears that way until the acorn drop occurred in October, when we stopped altogether. The bears were weaned successfully, with no further problems.

I have found food to be a quick and easy way to defuse difficult situations like this. Given a choice, bears will always take food at a more secure location. One of the big reasons for an increase of bear activity in residential areas is a seasonal shortage of natural foods in the nearby woods. Establishing select feeding sites can be effective in such situations, but it's important to have a specific plan, a limited feeding program, and a definite end. There is a science to this, and an understanding of bear behavior and natural food habits are important. Proper sites are secure: remote, in good cover, and not readily accessible to hunters. But if it's done correctly, bears will communicate the whereabouts of relocated food sites in order to share them, making it cost effective to maintain the needed bait sites.

But that's a temporary solution. The only real cure to residential bear problems is for people to clean up food or garbage that may attract bears. Be responsible if you choose to put out a feeder. Understand that there is no such thing as selectively feeding wildlife; your feeders will ultimately attract any animal in the area. Even though you may only be trying to attract chickadees, you might come home one night to find the biggest bear in the forest standing on your deck. If you—or your neighbors—don't want him back, take away the food.

But as I've learned over and over, that's easier said than done.

One woman phoned me after having a bear on her deck for the first time. I asked her if she was feeding birds on the deck. She said she was, and that she liked to feed the birds. She asked me a number of general questions about bears and then asked whether she should have concerns for the safety of her children if the bear came back. I assured her that most of the bears that come to feeders are well fed and are not likely to be dangerous and that her kids would be safe with normal parenting practices, but I didn't recommend tying a child to a tree when the bear did show up again. She continued to worry about her children and pressed me to tell her what to do. So I finally said, "You know, you could stop feeding the birds."

That was a novel concept; it hadn't even occurred to her.

Another time, a man called whose father was in his eighties and had a weak heart. The family feared the bear they had attracted to their bird feeder might aggravate the old man's condition. What could they do? they asked. I made the obvious suggestion: Don't feed the birds. But they chose to continue feeding anyway. One wouldn't think the choice would be that difficult.

In the summer of 1999, I followed the movements of a young male bear who had become a specialist at raiding bird feeders. He happened to be missing half of his right ear, so he was easy to identify. We have a pretty good e-mail list in Lyme, and through it I requested reports on bear activity in town. With the help of those reports, photos, videos, and personal sightings, I was able to determine that in a four-by-twelve-mile swath through town he had located and demolished bird feeders at thirty-three homes. Most people who feed birds have between one and five pounds of seed out at a time; at 160 calories to the ounce, that little guy had a pretty good strategy. I thought to myself if all of these people showed up at the same cocktail party and started talking about bears at their bird feeders, they would think the town was overrun with them.

When a bear walks into your yard, its motive is simple: It wants food and will go about finding it in pretty much the same way it would in the forest. Squirty, for instance, when she smells ants in a log, will bite and claw the log into splinters to get at them. But bears don't have our standards of etiquette; a locked porch with a bag of birdseed on it will be treated like a big stump full of ants. A stone wall where chipmunks have stored the corn they took from you might one night get strewn around as if a bulldozer went over it. The clapboards on your house that you didn't know had insects behind them might suddenly get shredded. Remember, nothing good ever happens when people with food invite bears to approach their houses.

I met a woman in Pennsylvania who bragged to me about how much she and everybody in her neighborhood liked their bears. She showed me the pole her bird feeder was on; this pole had been bent so many times, it was serpentine. Yet when we reached the door of her house, she said, "Now I've got a problem. The bear came a foot from this door, and that's too close."

That's our fickle nature in a nutshell. We invite the bear into our yards, intentionally or unintentionally, and then if it breaks one of our rules we complain. Or sometimes worse—we shoot the bear. I repeat: Nothing good ever comes from attracting bears onto your property with food. If a bear gets your bird feeder, stop feeding birds until winter. Or if you must feed, put an electric fence around your feeders. These fences are very effective at keeping bears away from almost anything. Bears do not like electricity.

But if simply holding back could solve bear-human conflicts over the free meals, there wouldn't be the large and growing problem we have today. The difficulty is that because bears are so highly evolved, they're all individuals. Just like us, they have highly variable personalities and personal histories. Thus it isn't always a seasonal shortage of wild forage that drives many of the local bears to approach people and their settlements; sometimes it's a social problem that affects just one of them. Houdini's tragic life story is an unfortunately good example.

Of the twenty-six bears we've raised, Houdini was one of only two that developed a taste for bird feeders; the other was Bartlett, who was orphaned at seven months old when his mother was shot attempting to enter a home. Bartlett's brother, Lieutenant, didn't have a problem, and Houdini's sister Yoda wasn't a problem either—until the spring of her third year when she suddenly started seeking human food. In Yoda's case I suspected there was a specific reason, which we eventually discovered. But first let's concentrate on Houdini.

When the Big Male (he's been capitalized in my mind ever since our confrontation) bumped Snowy and Bert into the beginning of dispersal, they still stayed in the protection of Squirty's home range and territory. Snowy now enjoys life occupancy and represents the beginning of Squirty's mother-to-daughter territorial dynasty, while Bert, who is still tolerated in his mother's home range, enjoys the chance to develop and gain experience in black bear social relations before being jettisoned into the full dispersal that every male eventually faces. With all of the food and support I could provide, I couldn't provide this kind of sanctuary for any of my yearling cubs. On top of that, I couldn't know the nature and extent of the black bear social fabric on the land where I would place them. Yoda and Houdini would just have to adapt, just as all my other bears, Squirty included, had been required to do before them, but I didn't foresee any more trouble for them than for the others. I was wrong. Houdini had been sent up to the big leagues with two strikes already against him. His first was that he never got over the psychological effects of his early abandonment and starvation. And the other was that we released him with his sister, Yoda, with whom he had an extra-strong bond, the way orphans often do.

The trouble began right away. At eighteen months, her first breeding season, Yoda attracted a wild male who attacked Houdini on May 14, driving him into full dispersal before he was ready. Young, immature, large for his age, and emotionally damaged, Houdini then headed out on a three-day journey along the Mascoma River south through Canaan, Enfield, and finally into the Eastman development in Grantham some thirty miles away. I got the not-unexpected phone call from Kip Adams, the bear project leader for New Hampshire Fish and Game. He said Houdini was hanging around a house that fed wildlife and as a result had routine visits from black bears. Houdini had read the "it's safe to feed here" signals left by the other bears and thus got his introduction to the fact that good meals were available at human homes.

I wasn't anxious for him to go this route, so I drove down, talked to the people, and located Houdini, who was taking a nap in the woods nearby. He followed me to the truck, where I sedated him for transportation back to Lyme. First I returned him to Yoda on May 17, only to have him evicted again; and again he headed south. I picked him up in Canaan where he had gotten into an odoriferous garbage can full of food. I returned him to camp on May 20, where he lasted a couple of days before heading south a third time. I followed him as he moved through wetlands on the east side of Moose Mountain until he ran head-long into the town of Enfield and Mascoma Lake. Discovering the best-hidden route he could, he made it through most of the town unnoticed by following an abandoned railway that had been converted to a footpath. This led him to the large lake, which he was unwilling to cross. There he found clusters of shorefront camps, where he secured a bag of shelled sunflower seeds (a real delicacy) and tipped over a grill. On May 22 the Enfield police arrived and tried using cracker shells on him with no success. Again I retrieved him, and since I now had the cage on Lambert secured, I put him in lockup.

The cage on Lambert was a godsend in my effort to break this string of setbacks. Unfortunately, the cage was in Squirty's territory. Things went well for several weeks, although I noticed several bite marks in the door and suspected that Squirty—or possibly Snowy or Bert—was trying to break in to get Houdini's food. The last day Squirty was with the Big Male, she tried to climb in the cage but was repelled by the electric fence; again I thought she was after his food.

Several days later, on June 26, Houdini was terribly anxious and started leaping on me and attempting to message-bite when I brought him his food. By this time, he was a good five-and–a-half feet tall when he stood and weighed 165 pounds. I had a little handheld shock zapper that would back him off as soon as he saw me take it out, but this time I didn't have it with me. He actually punctured my hand with a canine before I reached the door. Something was clearly up, but I didn't have a clue until I arrived the next day.

As I approached the cage, I heard the sound of pine boards breaking. I ran up the hill to the cage to see Houdini (at least I thought it was him) ripping three-inch chunks of wood out of the back of the shelter. I ran to the door of the cage to calm him down, and there stood Squirty. Houdini was so far up the large pine in the cage, I could barely make him out. I asked Squirty what she was doing in there. She didn't answer; instead she quietly lay down to finish off Houdini's food. It wasn't until the following day, when I discovered she had ripped a three-by-five-inch piece of skin off Houdini's ankle (ouch!), that I figured out what she was really up to. Squirty was letting him know it was time for him leave her territory.

He licked his wound to keep the flies off and to promote healing for a few more days in the cage until he heard me talking at the clearing. I guess he didn't realize I was talking to Squirty, since he broke out of the cage and came down to greet me. You could see "Oops!" written all over his face as he slammed on the brakes. Too late. Squirty's reaction was immediate: her ears went back, she ran right at him, and they were off. I thought it would be a short chase, so I grabbed my telemetry gear and ran after them. But within five minutes their signals disappeared. That meant they were on the back side of the hill, and I wasn't going to catch up on foot.

I got in my truck and drove toward Reservoir Pond until I picked up the signal, then parked and hiked three-quarters of a mile toward the signal until I found Squirty. She greeted me calmly—then sauntered over to the base of a large white pine, where she had Houdini at bay. She embossed her warning to him at the base of the tree by repeating a stiff-legged walk until she had carved a very distinct path of sunken footprints. They had run a mile and a half before she finally treed him. I left after Squirty demonstrated that she might like to keep him up there awhile by making a bed and going to sleep near the base of the tree.

That was enough for Houdini. The next morning, I met him on his way south again, and then I followed him daily as he traveled. He moved slower this time, and I kept hoping he would find an area in the big woods. On day four I met him in a clear-cut on Finn Casperson's large timberland property; as always, Houdini was happy to see me. While we visited, he fed on sarsaparilla berries and ants, until a gust of wind came carrying the smell of a wild bear. Houdini raised his head and sniffed. Complete terror came across his face, his eyes bulged and twitched rapidly before he snorted and in a burst of speed disappeared into the thick green vegetation.

It was becoming clear to me that territorial bears already occupied all of the places where I would have liked to see Houdini set up residence. I continued to monitor his movements south to Enfield, a town fragmented with roads and human development. It seems as though the higher the density of human population, the less territorial are the bears and the greater the amount of human food available to a driven wanderer like Houdini. His radio collar identified him whenever he was seen, ensuring a report on every bird feeder or garbage incident he got involved in. I called most of the people to find that almost all of them had other bears in their yards before Houdini. Most of the people regarded him as a small bear, even though he weighed about 165 pounds, because he still had a baby face.

More than likely, Houdini was finding these human food sources by following the trails of other bears. I say that not just because other bears had been seen at most of the houses, but because of his success. He was going from one bird feeder to the next as soon as he hit town, and finding an amazing amount of food. And in the process turning himself into an unwitting fountain of data. I kept in regular contact with Kip Adams as we shared the valuable insights he provided on an almost daily basis as to why a bear comes into contact with and becomes reliant on human foods. But I really didn't like that. I was nervous about Houdini's adventures because most of the bears that associate too closely with humans come to a bad end. Kip was more optimistic, and very understanding. "He's not acting any different than any other bear in that situation," he said.

In August, I picked Houdini up again and put him in the lockup on Lambert. By this time, Squirty was busy fattening up for the winter and didn't come by the clearing very often. Snowy and Bert would keep him company from time to time, as was evident by the well-worn trails around the cage. On August 28, one of his visitors, a two-hundred-pound male (I caught him on one of my cameras), got Houdini so excited that he chewed through the pine boards on the back of the shelter and followed him off into the woods.

But this bear was a friend. Houdini followed him north instead of fleeing to the south the way he had done all the other times. This break-out coincided with the opening of the hunting season—more specifically, the baiting season, in which New Hampshire hunters are allowed to put out large, pungent baits to attract bears within range of their guns or bows. Soon Houdini showed up at one. (I knew the hunters and spoke with them annually about not shooting radio-collared bears, and as a return courtesy I let them know if one of my bears was in the area. It's a system that's worked quite well.) With the aid of telemetry, I knew Houdini stayed in the area for almost three weeks, but he was only seen once and photographed with a remote camera once. There was also an abundance of beechnuts in the area.

Then it happened: his friend was shot and killed. Houdini fled. I got a report on him on September 18 in Alexandria, twenty-five miles away. This was not the first time something like this had taken place. Two years earlier, Teddy had made an abrupt departure from a beech stand he was feeding in, leaving the area just hours after a hunter shot a larger male bear. I suspect friendship or mentoring may be common among male bears, and between males and females without cubs. With my remote cameras, I've more than once filmed small males following larger ones, and subadult females with older males outside the breeding period.

I picked Houdini up in Alexandria and returned him to the cage on Lambert. Things were different this time as Squirty was already fat for the winter and was looking for a den. In early October, Snowy ripped off the door to the cage and released Houdini; they were still together when I arrived the next day. Houdini stayed inside Squirty's home range with Snowy and Bert until it was time to den in early January. After a week-long search, he crawled under a blowdown and partly excavated a den.

That winter was longer than normal so I woke him once to see how he was doing, to check out his den, and to give him a treat of leftover Christmas cookies. I woke him from a sound sleep, and he convulsed with shivers as he crawled out to greet me. Wildlife physiologists believe those very exaggerated muscular shivers, along with their ability to recycle urea to form protein, are how bears maintain their strength through their long winter sleep.

Because of the unusually deep snow, it was almost the first of May before Houdini could leave the area of his den. I found several beds he had made on top of the snow out of spruce boughs and birch bark. As the snows receded, he traveled over the top of and onto the western face of Winslow Hill, which faced our camp. For several days I tracked his progress as he fed on beech buds and occasional pockets of beechnuts where the sun had melted the snow between the boulders below the rugged ledge face.

I had just made a deal to deliver this book, and Jack Macrae had driven up on April 19 from New York to start working on it. Several times prior to coming up, he'd hinted that he would like to see a bear, but we were at the sloppy height of spring mud season and I wasn't sure Jack was up for a mile or two hike to track down one of the bears. I took Jack out to the Turnpike camp to see the bear cage, and while we were there Frank Cutting, who lives on the road at the base of the ledge, stopped by. He had been cooking steaks on his grill two nights before and then last night, twenty-four hours later, he had Houdini in his yard wondering if Frank might be doing it again. Jack and I had to drive by Frank's place on the way home. As we passed, I scanned the woods and said, "Hey, look! There's a bear coming down the hill!"

I stopped the truck and we jumped out; it was Houdini. He was now huge. Not only was his baby face replaced by a very adult visage, but he had grown considerably over the winter. I told Jack not to move and to fix his eyes on the bear while I went over to get reacquainted with Houdini, which we accomplished with a quick wrestle followed by Houdini putting his claws on my shoulders and checking my breath. He really was a big boy now. I then asked Jack to get Houdini some corn from the truck, then to drive to camp, where I'd dropped off a road-killed deer the previous morning. Houdini and I walked. Once the bear spotted the deer, he grabbed it and effortlessly dragged it up the ledge, picking his way carefully and with some apparent forethought, since the hill was steep and the deer heavy.

With plenty of food he would stay nearby, I thought; besides, it was way too early to get into the cage on Lambert Ridge, where the snow was still piled high at that elevation. I also thought he would do fine once some natural food was available. Maybe the bad days were behind us, even though his appearance at the Cutting's cookout was troubling. Meanwhile, Jack was wondering how I had pulled that bear out of my hat.

But after four days of seeming contentment around camp, Houdini was suddenly heading south at a quick pace. I suspected a conflict but didn't have the details. On the second day, he was on someone's deck eating sunflower seeds in Enfield. I spoke to the shaken owner; he hadn't at all liked the adult look of Houdini's no longer cherublike features. I told him it wasn't wise to feed birds on his deck, then gave him a quick summary of my findings as to the social communication of food sources by wild black bears. He agreed to stop feeding birds until winter. In the Kilham Bear School, he got a rare A.

By the third day, Houdini had traveled nearly thirty miles back to Eastman. This was trouble and I knew it, but I needed a few days to get the cage on Lambert ready for him.

I didn't get them. Houdini finally went after seed on the wrong person's deck and was shot three times by a 9-millimeter semiautomatic pistol. Conservation Officer Greg Jellison told me that the man had heard a noise and thought he had an intruder. When I got the collar back from Greg, the buckle was stretched way out of shape. I asked him what condition Houdini had been in, as I had seen him just four days before he was shot. Greg said there was a bear bite at his throat that just missed his jugular, and he had another bite on his forearm. So again Houdini had traveled south under duress. Knowing him as well as I did, I knew Houdini's preference was to be in the woods, not near humans and their houses, but the circumstances of his life kept leaving him little choice.

Ten days later, the man who had reported Houdini on his deck at his bird feeder in Enfield called. "I cleaned up the feeders like you said," he told me. "But this morning there was a large fresh bear scat on the deck." I told him Houdini couldn't get the blame for that one, unless it was his ghost.

It really was hard suddenly losing Houdini like that, just when he was reaching his maturity and would soon be able to stand up to the wild bears that kept driving him away. With LB, the Boy, and now Houdini all being shot, it wasn't much consolation to Debbie, Phoebe, and me to reflect on the statistics that predicted we should be losing even more of our bears to people with guns, either hunters or frightened property owners, and that a disproportionate number of those would be males. Statistics don't mean much laid against an individual with whom you've spent so much shared time, enjoying each other's company. And compilers of mortality tables haven't held their subjects in their arms, fed them from infancy, let them suckle on their ears, and wrestled safely with them even when they've grown up and become stronger than you are. Nobody ever mothered a dot on a graph. Or cried when it got erased.

As I said, it was hard. Phoebe even said that's it, we're not taking in any more boy bears. She half meant it, too. But we wouldn't be doing this if we were too emotional to recover from setbacks. As I write this in the late summer of 2001, Phoebe's got her hands full. She's helping Yoda establish a disputed territory, and she's also working with two new orphans we got just this year, Snuffy and Stumpy, the latter named because of a hind leg lost to a speeding car. They're both little boys.

The reason Phoebe is still so involved with two-and-a-half-year-old Yoda is an even more specific version of what led to Houdini's troubles: absence of a natural mother's territorial protection. The story of her troubles, though shorter and happier than Houdini's, reveals perhaps even more.

It is very difficult to know what the social structure of an area is before placing a female cub. Only one thing is sure: where she gets set down will be her home for the rest of her life. We had placed Yoda and Houdini in a large wilderness area three miles east of Lambert Ridge, far enough away so there wouldn't be a conflict with Squirty. Despite Houdini's troubles, Yoda seemed to have the run of the area. She did make an attempt to return to Lambert in the fall of her second year but was sent packing by Squirty. Through all of her second year she stayed out of trouble despite twenty or so camps and homes along the shore of nearby Reservoir Pond. She also remained free of any scars that would have indicated she had been fighting. When she came out of the den in her third year, she fed on leftover beechnuts and emerging growth. Then, in early May, she received the first fighting scar on her face.

In June, she traveled with a mate for a couple of weeks, and that's when the trouble really erupted. She started tearing screens on a remote unoccupied building that had been used as a summer-camp dining hall. Then she got attracted by the smell to a thousand or so empty beer cans waiting to be recycled behind an occupied house and was clever enough to find a cooler with eight cold Millers and a few nonalcoholic O'Doul's. She drank all the Millers, didn't touch the O'Doul's.

My initial response was to apply adverse conditioning, which included an electric fence around the camp's cook shack, black powder blanks, cracker shells, trapping on site, and releasing. Of all those, only the electric fence was effective.

It really bothered me that this had become an acute problem with Yoda; it had appeared out of nowhere. To me, something seemed so terribly wrong that Yoda was screaming for help. I talked with Phoebe, and she agreed to go find her every day, bring her a small offering of food, and walk with her to see what was going on.

Within a week the problem was apparent: the resident clan of related females was forcing Yoda out of all the good feeding areas. Phoebe witnessed more encounters with other females in her first two weeks with Yoda than I had in three years with Squirty. Yoda's primary battles were with a wild subadult female who was smaller than Yoda but dominated her because she had her mother's backing. But now Yoda had Phoebe, and as the weeks went by, with her accompanying ace, Yoda would pursue and engage her enemies. I don't think Phoebe, as gentle a soul as ever walked the planet, felt like much of an enforcer, but in the social hierarchy of the black bear, where every gesture counts and disputes are more often won by body language than by tooth and claw, that's what she was. And a pretty intimidating one at that. In her neck of the woods Yoda was reestablished as a force to be reckoned with.

An interesting feature of this episode was that Yoda didn't become a target until she was ready to breed, a behavior that may have a general application. Looking back, I realized that the wild bears have shown altruistic qualities toward all of our cubs until the maturing cubs represent a real threat to the wild bears' breeding territories.

But even troubled bears like Houdini and handicapped ones like Yoda don't become nuisances without human assistance. There are plenty of well-meaning people who even after being visited by bears continue to put unsealed food in their garbage, continue to feed birds throughout the summer, and many who intentionally feed bears at their homes.

Some bears are incidental and opportunistic feeders of human foods. Most of our homes are built in the valleys on the richer soils near wetlands, and many are right in or abutted by forest. These same areas are where the bears' natural spring and summer vegetative foods grow: jack-in-the-pulpit and the wild lettuces. Most human foods, especially sunflower seeds, have twice the calories per gram of beechnuts or acorns. Under the right conditions, almost any bear can be seduced to experiment with them.

Some bears become experts at extracting food from human habitats. They haven't necessarily lost their fear of humans as much as they have become skilled at observing our body language, a natural extension of the way they study each other. These same bears, seemingly untroubled by nearby people, are no more likely to be shot by hunters than any other bear. I once stood with a group of people watching a bear feeding from a bird feeder sixty feet away; people were talking, some had binoculars, and the bear couldn't have cared less. But when I stared directly at him and took one step in his direction, he took off.

All of which leads me to the most difficult aspect of human-bear interaction: one-on-one confrontation.

One day, while I was with Gene Thorburn, Hanover's animal control officer, we got a call that there was a bear in someone's chicken coop. Gene told me this was the same place where a fisher had gotten in the year before and killed all of the chickens. It was a little ominous to pull into the dooryard to find the landowner walking away from the chicken house with a shotgun across his arms. "Did you shoot him?" we inquired.

"No, it was just a young bear in there eating the chickens' grain," he replied. "Besides, I like bears."

The young male bear was one I knew. He had already earned a pair of yellow ear tags with the number 383 on them after being captured just off South Main Street. He was relocated fifty miles away, only to return to the same porch seven days later. I located his winter den in a ravine between a motel and a large retirement community very close to town. He continued raiding bird feeders in Hanover using river and stream banks for cover. He never took a bird feeder or beehive that he couldn't access directly from vegetative cover. Number 383 had dodged a bullet that day in the chicken coop, but he had become what I call a "specialist," a bear that lives primarily on human-supplied food.

Young bears are not like raccoons, which live their lives in one backyard. Bears travel and share their bad habits with many people as they go. I was envious of the people who started Number 383 on his life of crime. They were able to feed him, enjoy him, take pictures, but not take any responsibility for the outcome. Almost every one of the cubs I've raised has worn either an ear tag or a radio collar. My work is scrutinized, and I shoulder the responsibility of all of my cubs' actions. Although there have been isolated incidents, none of my bears, not even Houdini, have turned out anything like Number 383.

On the last day of March, about eight at night, I got a phone call from the Hanover police: a bear was on West Wheelock Street, near the cemetery, hanging around a dumpster. Concerned that he might get mixed up with some Dartmouth students, they wanted to know if I could persuade the bear to move on. I suspected the bear was Number 383 since he was the most active problem bear in Hanover at the time. At this point, Number 383 had experienced most of the conventional means of getting him to leave, so I decided it was time that I became the dominant bear.

Debbie and I met the officers on a back street near the dumpster. The bear appeared from between two buildings, stood in the headlights of the cruiser for a moment, then turned toward the cemetery to walk away. It was quite an image: only the soles of his feet reflected any light, so all we could see were his feet as he disappeared into the night.

I grabbed the little pocket flashlight from the door of my truck and proceeded to walk after him. Following just the sound of his footsteps in the leaves, I closed to about twenty feet from him before he let out a snort and took off with a burst of speed. He ran and treed on the back side of large white pine. As he peered from behind the trunk, I shined the weak beam of the flashlight in his eyes and delivered to him my rendition of the guttural "Huh, huh, huh, huh, huh!"—trying to put some emphasis into it to let him know that this was my territory and he should leave. He bailed out of the tree and for the second time, snorted and ran off into the darkness.

I knew he wouldn't be back that night, but I didn't expect him to leave town. A few days later, a man phoned to tell me that Number 383 had been at his feeder in Lyme. A week later, I received several calls from Orford, several weeks later from Wentworth, then Warren, and, finally in the fall, from Piermont. Number 383 not only had left but had gone far away and kept going.

I spoke with numerous people, who called to relate stories of Number 383's whereabouts and antics on his push northward. He was gaining quite a reputation on his campaign stops. He acquired more familiar names, such as "Tags" and "Buster." He would "tube" a bird feeder by popping its top and drinking it like a beer. As a vote getter, I think he could have won an election in there somewhere. But not everyone would have voted for him. There were a few folks on the way who were terrified, concerned for the safety of their cats, dogs, and children. And he still had that affinity for grain and chicken coops. I didn't hear from him again after he got to Piermont and didn't know whether he got elected or not until a year or two later. He didn't. His name had been taken off the ballot and put on a bullet when he got caught coming out of a horse barn.

The technique I used on Number 383 was a combination of the specific vocalizations I had learned over the years and a message-sending technique I learned from Squirty when I started watching her closely to see how she handled both her cubs and the various intruders who came by, me included. It's simple enough. When she wanted me to leave, Squirty would lock her eyes on me, then walk in my direction in a purposeful manner. It all made sense: when she locked on with her eyes, she defined the target; when she walked toward me, she demonstrated her intent; and with her purposeful or stiff walk, she transmitted her mood. My friend Mark Ellingwood, a senior biologist with New Hampshire Fish and Game, found out how effective it is when I took him in to see Squirty. She was downhill from us at the base of her baby-sitting tree when we arrived. Mark stayed back about forty yards, and I went down to see Squirty. She gave me a quick greeting, then went right around me toward Mark. He quickly got her message and said, "Ben, I think we should leave." I got between Squirty and Mark, and we left her alone.

Bears are signalers. They are going to let you know their every move in advance. If, of course, you can recognize their signals. I'll try to explain these in more detail, but let me offer this advice first. If you encounter a grown bear in the wild, it's going to send your pulse up and your mind reeling. It's only natural that you won't be calm. So instead of trying to remember and classify the bear's body language and vocalizations, just pay attention to the general tone of the animal. Try to assess the bear's mood *between* its bursts of display. Does it have a pleasant face, or does it appear scared? Have I done something to provoke it, or is it just looking at me? You may never have seen a bear in your life, but you've got some deep instincts that will allow you to judge the attitude of the animal looking back at you. Keep your wits intact and trust them.

In 1872, Charles Darwin wrote *The Expressions of the Emotions in Man and Animals,* and at that time he recognized that man and animals shared general expressions of emotion. More recent research, such as that described in *Animal Vocal Communication: A New Approach* by Donald Owings and Eugene Morton, shows how vocal behavior in birds and mammals is related to their physiology. Most animal vocalizations are motivational in nature and are generated through their larynx, which is tied through their central nervous system to their emotional state. This means—and here's the part that you'll want to remember in the bear woods—that most birds and mammals are honest with their vocalizations. If they growl or make harsh sounds, they really are angry; if they make soft sounds, they're trying to appease. It's true with us, too; we can lie with words, but for the most part the tone of our voice will reflect our emotional state. For a bird or mammal to deceive or bluff with sound, it has to generate that sound in a manner that won't reveal its true emotional state. So even when the bear in front of you is chomping its teeth together, snorting, huffing, swatting, or even false-charging, none of these actions reflect the bear's emotional state. They're all mechanically generated sounds. They come from the head, not from the heart. So stay calm, hold your ground, and try to judge the heart.

I know this won't seem like the standard advice you've heard before. Because most people are afraid of bears, we're bombarded by sensational films, books, and stories all with one theme: Bear Attacks! It's hard to walk past a newsstand or the wildlife shelf of a bookstore without seeing that exact phrase with that punctuation. In reality bear attacks are exceedingly rare when compared to almost any other cause of human death or injury. And black bear attacks are virtually nonexistent.

Nevertheless, if you live in or travel to bear country, you ought to be knowledgeable of bear behavior. I'm speaking about black bears because that's where my experience lies. Although some of what I say applies to grizzlies as well, much of it does not; grizzlies are larger and much more aggressive animals that can and do kill people every year. This much is comparable: even when bears are being fed, or feeding from bird feeders, or panhandling from tourists, they are still bears so they will treat you like another bear. The problem is that bears are very physical with each other. Even though they may look and act like a big dog, a sudden miscommunication like trying to pet one may result in a sudden and unavoidable swat or bite. Bears, unlike dogs, take offense at being petted. Bears play by bear rules and know nothing of ours. Close contact between uninformed people and bears is a script for disaster. So the answer is straightforward: don't get close.

While walking in bear habitat, be aware of bear sign and what it looks like: are there fresh-looking scats, logs broken open for ants, broken-down fruit-bearing vegetation? If you see any of those signs and don't want to see the bear that left them, let it know you're there by walking off-trail to break sticks, the primary first alarm that most bears listen for.

If you do see a bear at a distance, enjoy watching it and either back off or wait for it to leave. Do not approach it. Bears do have a strong sense of personal space—a distance that varies from bear to bear from which they won't back down. If you end up inside that defensive perimeter, which may be anywhere from ten to fifty feet wide, you are likely to experience a combination of highly intimidating behaviors, including: the squared-off lip or long face; jaw popping; huffing; swatting; and false-charging. Some experts regard these as fear- or stress-related. I prefer to think of them as defensive or motivational displays separate from the bear's mood, which may be fearful or stressed. Or it may not be.

My experience tells me to observe the bear's mood before it squares off its lip. That's the animal you're dealing with. I put on a demonstration for Steve Weber, now the wildlife division chief at New Hampshire Fish and Game, when he came up to help me tag some of the bear cubs in 1996. Little Girl 2 was too big for me to grab, and we had her cornered on a post in her cage. I put a heavy glove on one hand and held an ice cream cone that I got from a visitor in the other. I offered LG2 a lick from the cone, and she obliged; then I approached her with the gloved hand. Her lip squared off and she chomped. I offered the cone again, and again she licked it. I went back and forth four times, and her demeanor changed four times. Finally, I touched her with my gloved hand, and she swatted it. These actions demonstrate that everything that follows the squared-off lips is a defensive or motivational display. Remember how I could pat Squirty on the head when she was false-charging the National Geographic crew? Her message was clear that she wanted them to leave, but she wasn't angry. There was no stress involved in her decisions; the film crew had simply exceeded its allotted time, and she wanted them to leave.

When I observed Squirty and her mate together for the first time, they each squared their lips, popped their jaws, huffed, swatted, and false-charged each other; at the same time, Squirty seductively "mewed," and he responded with an appeasement sound of his own. Those honest vocalizations told me what was really going on.

I've concluded from long experience that you can't judge the nature of an individual encounter between a bear and a human on the basis of whether the bear is displaying one behavior or another. For a bear may use the same displays in different intensities for different contexts.

Having fixed interpretations of any individual bear behavior can be dangerous not only to a person encountering a bear but also to the bear itself. It's the escalation of fear that leads to bad decisions. There have been a number of bear attacks that I've read about that could have been avoided if the situation hadn't been misread. Some victims have dropped to the ground into protective positions because they thought the bear was about to attack. That, unfortunately, is a self-fulfilling prophecy; they were attacked. Bears, like dogs and many other animals, will enforce their dominance when an adversary displays weakness. I found that when I filmed the Big Male with Squirty at too close a distance, he would rush me every time I dropped eye contact with him. He was testing my resolve.

It's my experience that black bears take eye contact very seriously as a position of strength. If my eyes are on them, they will usually avert their stare. If their eyes hold on me, it's a sign they intend to motivate me. If they then walk toward me, I better leave. When I was up close with Squirty and her young cubs, I could tell when she was about ready to throw me out because her eyes would twitch before her lip squared off. Then she would snort and lunge at me.

So what do you do if somehow you get too close to a bear? Stop moving and use your eyes. Keep them directly on the bear. Use them to study the bear so you can determine its attitude toward you. By keeping your eyes glued to it, you'll also be letting the bear know that you're strong; by not moving toward it, you'll be letting the bear know that you're not trying to motivate it. If you feel compelled to back up, do it when the bear is relaxed, and keep your eyes on the bear. But chances are the bear will move away first.

Well, it's easy to read all this in a book. I recognize that for most people, trying to understand a large meat-eating animal's mood or emotional state in a close encounter is just not going to happen. I also realize that expecting people to have a laundry list of preconditioned responses to certain bear behaviors can be confusing and dangerous. Believe me, I really do know. As they say, I've been there and done that.

So let's leave it at this.

Read as much as you possibly can about these fascinating creatures that I've come to know and love. Look for them in their woods, and try to keep them out of your backyard. And if you are ever lucky enough to see one at close range, try to keep this simple message in your head:

Hold your ground, stay calm, maintain eye contact, and let the situation resolve itself. It will. Your experience will be extremely intimidating and exhilarating, but what you'll get in exchange will be the adrenaline rush of a lifetime.

And I do mean that. Of a lifetime.

CHAPTER 26

What Is It About a Bear?

THINKING BACK OVER the thousands of hours I've spent with Squirty and all the others, what stands out is that I always spent time with an individual. Not a companion like a loyal dog always quick to please, but a headstrong individual with whom I had to continuously negotiate in order to maintain a relationship. An animal that not only would communicate its fears and desires directly to me but would manipulate me to abide by its own rules to satisfy them. An animal that could recognize loyalty when I offered it, and would for me alone reciprocate by lowering this much-feared and hard-hunted species's best defense—distrust of humans. In short, I've known all my bears, and all my bears have known me.

But this fine-tuned awareness of people wasn't just directed at me, the one who had stepped in as their mother and raised them. Squirty, who of all my bears has seen the most people, still recognizes and treats them as individuals. I'm the only one with her complete trust; the rest she accepts according to how long—and how well—she's known them. Remember how she treated the two different National Geographic crews? Neil Rettig and Kim Hayes, who knew her as a cub, got more time with her than Bob Caputo, who was a newcomer. She didn't tolerate any of them for very long, yet I could pat her on the head while she was false-charging to drive them out; her focus was singular.

What is it about a bear? Why are we so attracted to them even when they scare us so? Is it because they are so fearsome and inscrutable, or because they remind us of ourselves? I think it's the latter. And I'd like for you to agree with me.

I want to start by pointing out to you some details of the highly social group of individuals I've introduced you to in this book. Together we have met individuals who share resources and security, who form hierarchies, who have structured kinship relationships. As the cubs developed, I've tried to show you evidence of their social play, ritualistic mechanisms to meet strangers and decide if they're to be friends or not, social communication of food sources, social learning mechanisms, and even social security (sorry, but I had to call it that). I hope you've seen an animal that's been remorseful, empathetic, fearful, selfish, altruistic, joyful, and deceitful; and that you've noted its mechanisms for solving disputes and demonstrating need.

I've tried not to generalize when writing about the bears we've met together; instead I've made a real effort to describe what we've seen in specific detail and in terms recognized by others in the behavioral sciences. But whether you're a practicing primatologist or just someone curious about me or my bears, I have to warn you in advance: While I stand by the accuracy of my observations, analysis of their meaning is based on the published scientific record (skimpy on bears, staggering on chimps); principles of evolutionary theory; logic; reason; and a few assumptions—a brew that hasn't always led to being right. Only time will eventually sort that out. In the meantime, you can decide for yourself.

The earliest form of communication between me and my cubs has always been physical: their intentional use of bites, paws, or body to illustrate or emphasize a point, sometimes painfully but most of the time carefully restrained. When LB or LG first used the slow-bite on me, for instance, I didn't know what, if anything, it meant. Clearly, it was a message of dissatisfaction, but it wasn't at all like the sudden defensive reaction of a dog snapping out of fear or pain. A bear's bite was by contrast always measured, and even when it hurt it never broke the skin. But knowing that something is meant to be a message doesn't help decode it; until I figured out what was actually irritating the bear, it was still just a bite.

And figuring it out wasn't always easy. Some bites I never did decode, while others became clear only after much repetition. A good example was the way I was met with a full body rubdown and forceful bite on each forearm whenever I intervened on Squirty, Curls, or the Boy while there was a wild bear in the vicinity. Once I realized that the wild bear was the common factor, and that this response never occurred in any other situation, the explanation fell into place. My bears felt obligated to come to me whenever I showed up, but quickly made an effort to cover my scent with their own, so as not to scare away their friend. Then, to show their displeasure at me for disrupting the situation, they would bite me on the forearms. It really made perfect sense. In fact, with a few behavioral substitutions, I suspect many parents of teenagers will recognize some similarities here. (From what I've heard of a few untamed kids, the bite on the arm might even translate directly, but the full-body rubdown would be fairly unexpected.)

Early as their physical messages appeared toward me, among themselves verbal communication came even earlier, starting, as I learned by listening in on Squirty's newborns still deep beneath the snow in their winter den, from birth. All the primary vocalizations—and they are many and varied—appear to be instinctive rather than learned, since they were consistent in both sets of my motherless cubs and, to the extent that I was around to hear them, with Squirty's natural cubs, too. It makes sense. The need for two individual bears, unknown to each other and meeting in the woods, to communicate basic intentions and moods to one another is critical. Intelligent animals living in a large social unit (chimpanzees and wolves, for instance) have much less need for generally recognized vocalizations and could learn them within the group. But even humans—who have developed complex language learned within the group—still use innate body language and verbal intensities to communicate emotion and mood.

This isn't to say that bears aren't complex and nuanced in their vocalizations, as I hope I've been able to help you hear in your minds as we've taken this literary walk in the woods with my bears. I've identified a number of basic forms, each of which can carry levels of intensity and commitment, so maybe it's time I put them all together into a little phrase book. But I'll have to warn you that many of these are variations of moans and sound very similar to an untrained ear, and are equally hard to describe:

The sound of contentment: A rhythmic, droning chuckle, coming from somewhere inside like the purring of a cat but much louder and deeper, made whenever a cub is happy or content. Always made when nursing but often well past that age at other happy times.

The pigeon coo: Pretty much the same sound as the bird's. Made while falling asleep or during times of quiet joy.

The "Baa WoOow, Baa WoOow": A cub distress call.

The undulating roar: Made at times of extreme emotional distress.

The moan of recognition: A series of moans made when the cubs would recognize me.

The soft appeasement moan: Made in the company of another adult bear indicating recognition, acceptance, and bonding.

The hungry moan: A series of moans made when the cubs were telling me they were hungry.

The undulating moan: Made at times of severe nervousness.

The irritated moan: A series of variable-length moans that sound irritated to the human ear, always made when the cub was not happy about something.

The roar: Just that, indicating severe anger. Made every time I provoked a cub to do something against its will.

The "gulp": Made at times of severe nervousness.

The "Eh-eh": Made when wrestling to limit biting or to signify enough.

The "Mew-mew": Made when seeking company that should be nearby.

The "gulp-grunt": Used by females to call cubs. Also used by males to solicit females during courtship.

The guttural "Huh, huh, huh, huh, huh": Means "No" or "Get out!" or "You are trespassing!" depending on the context of the confrontation. Also used at other times to tell another bear to back off, the way Squirty did when the big male got too close to us both.

The balance of the sounds I've heard bears make aren't vocalizations. They are mechanically produced sounds such as teeth-clacking, huffing, and swatting used as defensive and motivational displays.

While this is nowhere near an exhaustive list, it does capture some of the range and expressiveness of these vocalizations that fit nicely into the classifications described in the book *Animal Vocal Communication: A New Approach*, by Donald Owings and Eugene Morton. They recognize that "avian and mammalian vocalizations reflect differences in motivation, the same individual producing a range of vocal frequencies and even combining different signals into compound vocalizations." Owings and Morton go on to say that increases in rate and loudness function like our own exclamation marks to emphasize urgency. No wonder I could understand the cubs when they spoke to me as if I were another bear; as humans, we use vocal intonations in pretty much the same way.

But it is with their noses that bears leave us and most other species on the planet far behind in ways to communicate with each other. To say that a bear is olfactory is like saying a fish tends to swim. The labyrinth of their scent-defined world is so rich and complex, and their physiological adaptation to it so advanced, that I doubt we will ever truly comprehend it. If you've got nothing else from spending some time with my bears, I hope that you will at least come away with the sense that they live in a world whose shifting boundaries are completely different from our own, and that those perimeters are defined largely by scent.

For starters, that difference can be seen when we realize that bears and other olfactory-oriented animals make statements just by walking around and leaving a trail of airborne scent. Let's think for a moment about the implications of just that. Why in the work of evolution does that scent trail even exist? And since it not only does but also seems to have been strongly selected, how is it beneficial to the bear?

I think the answer is that airborne scent has evolved as a direct form of communication that allows one bear to know when another is close enough to encounter, even if by the social standards of us visually oriented creatures that distance would signify separation, not proximity. For a bear in the forest, airborne scent information may get to another bear a mile away, but for these large omnivores who need so much personal space just to feed themselves, a mile might be too close, depending on who that other bear is.

But a bear's nose is so finely tuned that even at that distance chances are good that the receiving bear will be able to identify the other one. It has taken me thousands of hours to become convinced, but I now know that the information carried in the scent would contain the specific identity of the other bear if they knew each other, or if not, then certainly the gender and probably the maturity level—juvenile, subadult, or adult—of the stranger. It's likely that much more information is delivered this way, as I've also noticed that bears can somehow "aerosol" their scent: sometimes I have to stick my nose deep in Squirty's fur to smell her sweet, mild caramel-like odor, and other times the bear scent I smell in the air is so strong that it will almost knock me over. The other indicator of complexity is the wide range of chemicals that showed up on the mass spectrograph when Jim Worman, a visiting chemistry professor at Dartmouth College, ran samples of LB's and LG's scents. It's possible that scent could also carry information about kinship and other social messages yet to be discovered.

We receive equivalent information visually: how another person is dressed, what jewelry they may be wearing (a cheap watch? diamond earrings? a nose ring?), or even their apparent mood. All are signals relevant to the need to differentiate our individual identities in a dense population. Bears, on the other hand, don't need to dress for success or be too concerned with body piercing. (The decorative kind, at least. Although, as we've seen, I suspect they sometimes enhance their personal identities by rolling in selected smells.) With population densities in the vicinity of one bear per two square miles, it is more important to get out a simpler message: Hey, I exist. I'm over here.

That message is transmitted by scent, and it comes in several varieties. When scent travels in the air, I call it "live" since it's a physical extension of the bear itself, a continuous stream of aromatic molecules streaming from the bear's living body. But for all its initial strength and direct connection, live scent doesn't linger long. Drifting with the wind, evaporating in the sun, it has a life that can be measured in terms of hours.

The second variety of message left by a bear when it travels is the scent that gets transferred to twigs, branches, leaves, and grasses when they come into contact with the bear's hair. The information is the same as in live scent, only now it's in the past tense, lasting for a couple of days. In the ursine world, this is the daily news. The cubs would work these situations very intently, sniffing to locate every twig and branch that was touched by the passing bear, huffing to enhance the scent, and slow-licking to identify it. They would continue until they were satisfied; often taking five to ten minutes or more. Although I have seen the cubs track this type of scent for considerable distances, the process was too slow to actually catch up with the bear that left it. But apparently that wasn't the point; I have observed cubs locate mark trees, bed sites, and feeding areas many times in this manner.

The next variety of scents includes those left on purpose: marks on bear trees; marks on other trees; urine marks; scat marks; walking over saplings; arching the back to mark overhanging branches; stiff-legged walk; bite marks; and genital drag marks. Each of them, even the stiff-legged walk, is an olfactory message purposely left.

These intentional methods give the bears a wide range of variables when they mark a trail as they explore a new area, emphasize a trail by walking over saplings so their mate will know where they are, or simply to return to a food source easily once they have left it. When I visited Squirty after she had first gone off on her own, I usually gave her a treat of kibble when I caught up with her, and usually she ate it all before we did anything else together. Twice, however, she ate some of it right away but wanted to show me around before she finished, so she marked with urine beside the food, then walked over saplings for the first hundred yards as she led me away, thus leaving herself a scent-blazed trail right back to the kibble.

The primary bear tree in New Hampshire is a red pine, popular among bears not only for the location of a preferred tree but for its chemical composition. Red pines possess more aromatic chemicals than any other tree in New Hampshire. The trees are usually scattered and define different travel corridors. Male bears bite the trees several weeks prior to the breeding season. The height of the scar indicates the approximate height of the bear, as the scar is made by a bite that concludes a full back-rub display.

Without the foreknowledge that bears use scent for everything they do, it might be easy to incorrectly characterize these important trees as visual markers. They're far more than that. In 1998 I set up a remote video camera along one of the trails passing through a corridor of red pines and filmed nine adult males and two adult female bears from June 1 to July 7. What I've learned was that sows respond to the odor released from the evaporating sap where the male bear bit the tree. This remarkable form of tool use is not reserved for just the red pine, either. Male bears will bite other trees as well, including oak, ash, spruce, hemlock, balsam, or whichever tree makes the best attractant when they move into a female's core range. This strategy is used not only to attract females, but to mark, advertise, and regulate feeding areas. Remember the story of Kim and the citronella bug repellent? It had the same properties as some of the odors coming out of a bite tree. That's how I knew she was in for an up-close encounter when Squirty got a whiff of it on her.

The red pine bear tree can also be employed for claiming usage of an area. Bears will routinely mark over another's scent, but the act of marking by itself doesn't establish territorial dominance. The scent mark only does that when one bear physically establishes domination over another. None of my cubs were ever afraid of male bear scent until they had an adverse encounter with a specific bear. After that, they always showed fear upon smelling its scent.

The other sign I usually associate with these sites is sunken footprints. These, as you'll remember, are the result of one bear responding to the unfamiliar scent of another by scuffing the ground with its feet. LB and LG recognized each other's scent and did not respond with the stiff-legged walk, and all the other cubs have done the same. Bears tend to walk in their own tracks, so the more activity at one of these sights, the more pronounced the sunken footprints; another message of bear activity.

But it isn't all olfactory, all the time. In the fall of 1998, I interrupted Squirty attempting to dig out a den under the root mass of a tree that had been down for several years. When I was ready to leave, she decided to follow me, but before leaving she marked the spot with urine and did a stiff-legged walk, impressing a path of sunken footprints in the wet leaves. She then went back to check her urine mark, realigned with the path of sunken footprints, and made them more prominent by going over them a second time. She may have been making the site easier to find on her return, or more likely marking it as hers in case another bear came along. In any case she was clearly concerned about the depth of the footprints as a visual mark.

But if bears have such a complex and varied system of communication among themselves, the obvious question is: why? If they're so solitary for so much of their lives, what is the value of being able to transfer such a wealth of information back and forth between one another? Why did all those messaging systems—olfactory, vocal, visual, and physical—develop in a nonsocial animal?

The answer is that they didn't develop in a nonsocial animal. They developed in a *very* social animal. Black bears aren't any more solitary than we are. I'll come right out and say it: Black bears are a fully developed social species successfully occupying the same time and place as humans, evolving not behind us but beside us. They are, in fact, altruistic. But because they each require so much territory, they direct this reciprocal altruism toward unrelated fellow bears that they will never even meet, something that our closer relatives, the supposedly more highly evolved great apes, do not do—their cooperation is only within troops of recognizable members. The black bear's solution to the problem of species survival hasn't placed it below us on the evolutionary ladder; it has placed it on a different ladder, climbing beside us, so to speak.

So, having said that, let me try to prove it to you. We've already done the fieldwork together, spending all those hours observing and interacting with the cubs and the other bears in the New Hampshire woods. Now let's try to put it together into a system that makes sense. Just like the cubs did themselves, we'll start with play.

Social Play

"The study of social play provides an opportunity to pursue the suggestion by Niko Tinbergen (1972) and others (Schaller & Lowther 1969) that we may learn as much or more about human social behavior by studying social carnivores as by studying nonhuman primates." In their 1998 book *Animal Play*, from which this quote is taken, Marc Bekoff and John Byers point out both the difficulties and potential value of trying to study animal play. For starters, it is hard to define, even though most of us can recognize it when we see it, and then there's the problem of gathering the data to begin with, since the observer has to be with young animals every day in order to see it happen. Well, I was with my cubs almost every day, and I certainly did see it happen. So, to the extent you've been with me, did you. Let's try to analyze what we saw.

When Squirty, Curls, and the Boy awoke from their yearling hibernation, I had a CBS camera crew with me that kept me from spending the amount of time with the cubs that I otherwise would have. For more than a week, I had no opportunity to play with them. Squirty and Curls were standoffish toward me, and the Boy, while emitting the irritated moan one day, slow-bit his canine tooth into the back of my hand. Something was obviously amiss between us, so on the first chance I could manage I took them for a walk. But even that was abnormal and strained. Reluctant even to start out, the cubs moved slowly along behind me, feeding on beechnuts for a while before following me up the hill toward a bear tree. Halfway up the hill, they sat down, so I joined them. Then they decided to play. First Squirty launched herself at Curls, then the Boy launched himself at me, and a twenty-minute roughhouse session ensued. Afterward I took a half hour nap entwined in an ursine mass. Everything was back to normal.

If I hadn't fully grasped it before that day, the bonding function of play was now indelibly made clear to me. Without it, my relationship with the cubs had slowly eroded; with just one session of it, all was restored.

The most common form of bears' social play is wrestling, which includes biting, tackling, and chasing. It began with my cubs when they were eight weeks old, and continued into adulthood. As far as I know, it never really stops (although the purpose becomes more defined) even when they are big enough to really hurt each other. But like so many of their potentially harmful interactions, this one has evolved into ritual, complete with a safety valve: Although I didn't pick up on its meaning until I was well into my second set of cubs, I now know they use the "Eh-eh" vocalization to limit bite pressures from their opponent as they wrestle. Squirty, as an adult, first used it on me as a "that's enough" signal when I tried to pull burdocks out of her fur, but by then I knew what it meant. So I used it right back at her ("That's really enough!") when she upped the ante to a discipline-bite when I kept pulling the burdocks anyway.

But just entering into play is high-risk among animals fully equipped with the means to kill. As Bekoff and Byers write: "Given the possible risks that are attendant on mistaking play for another form of activity, it is hardly surprising that animals should have evolved clear and unambiguous signals to solicit and maintain play." To illustrate their contention, the authors point out the "play bow" used by coyotes and other canids including the domestic dog to signal that the intent of an upcoming action is to play, not the aggression that it would be without the signal.

While bears don't play bow, they will "head-wag" prior to a charge and attack, signaling the intent is play. The head is held low and swung back and forth fairly quickly as they start to charge, then launch themselves onto their sibling. Or—and this is how I learned to recognize it—me.

Another signal of intent used by LB prior to launching himself on me was the double take with his eyes. But because I also saw him use the same sign of intent before climbing a tree after red maple flowers, I can't be fully sure the sign was meant to signal play; it certainly seemed to signal his intent, since it wasn't unusual for the cubs to use many of their signals with different meanings depending on what they were doing at the time. As with one of our own languages, the hardest parts to learn are the idioms.

Remember the sumo-wrestler dance that LB and LG used to do so frequently, first facing off and mouth wrestling, then quickly going up onto their hind legs until one ultimately pushed the other over? The instinctive, stereotyped, and ritualistic characteristics of this form of play suggest its importance to cubs' later, adult lives. An indication that all bears practice it in their infancy was that Teddy, the single orphan cub raised without siblings or age-mates, performed this same sumo contest with an imaginary opponent, a spruce sapling. This dance is, I believe, a mechanism that allows unknown bears to assess each other on initial contact, judging their ability to become friends or not. Because they all do it as cubs, all bears, including strangers, recognize the signals leading up to the event.

Remember Teddy? He's the one who had a number of other imaginary friends, including the special piece of wood that he treated as his love interest, and the stuffed teddy bear that he carried with him from bed site to bed site after he was released into the wild.

It was the repeated observations of so much ritualized play that first indicated to me that bears are far more social than previously believed. This became even more revealing when I realized that with bears, unlike most social carnivores, there is no direct paternal investment in raising the cubs. In keeping with the ways of the black bear, the only time I saw the father of Squirty's cubs was during that seven-day mating period in June. After he fathered the cubs, the biggest contribution that he made to their upbringing was indirect; by going away, he didn't compete with them and their mother for resources.

Because bears have such a relatively solitary lifestyle, I wondered if the social nature of their play might not leave open the door for them to be social in other ways later, perhaps in the sharing of food, security, or even—a litmus test of higher-order species—altruism toward others.

Learning and Teaching

Play, especially socially directed play, leads naturally enough to learning. Remember when LB and LG demonstrated that they could identify foods or nonfoods simply by holding them in their mouths, and that I gradually discovered that this was a specially adapted form of "Kilham organ" testing? This suggested to me that they had some sort of genetic library of chemicals that signaled to them yes or no. The concept of this library was pretty neat, but then I concluded that there had to be a mechanism for information to get into the library in the first place. How that could happen remained a mystery until I spent time with Squirty, Curls, and the Boy. Prior to that, even though LB and LG would converge on me every time I got on my hands and knees, I dismissed it as either coming to see what I had found or wanting to play or to suckle. With the set of three cubs, I finally put it all together when I noticed that they were audibly sniffing when they did the same thing. Aha! They were soliciting information. Until then, I had wondered how they could tell one green plant from another if all they were doing was watching me.

To test my idea, I took the three cubs to the log landing, where I got down on my hands and knees to forage on red clover, a species I knew was food but which they hadn't yet eaten. As soon as I began browsing on the clover, the cubs converged on me. When I offered them my breath, they all stuck their noses in my mouth to identify what I was eating, then immediately started searching, finding, and eating the plant themselves. Ever since then, I've noticed that all my cubs observe each other while foraging; when one cub makes a discovery, another will come over, solicit its breath, then search for the same food.

This method of learning goes one step further, for not only do the cubs learn what to eat, they also get assurance that it isn't poisonous. One day while taking a distinguished and knowledgeable gentleman on a walk with the cubs, I happened to mention that the cubs would not eat any mushrooms. To demonstrate, I grabbed the next mushroom I came to, and my guest exclaimed: "Don't offer them that! You'll poison them! It's a deadly amanita!"

"Just watch," I said.

All three cubs came up to see what I had, and when I gave it to them they clawed it up and put small pieces in their mouths for identification. Then Squirty put her head up to my mouth and solicited my breath. I offered it to her, showing that none of the mushroom had been in my mouth, and she just straightened up and walked off.

In a 1987 study published in the journal *Physiology and Nature* by Bennett Galef Jr., J. Russell Mason, George Preti, and N. Jay Bean, the researchers found a similar behavior in rats, a very social species. The researchers found that the rats communicated with their breath not only what was good to eat but what was safe to eat as well. The researchers then learned that even after they trained the rats not to eat a certain food, usually by putting lithium chloride in it to make the rats sick, the rats would eat the food again if they smelled it on the breath of another rat.

The next step up the developmental ladder from learning is teaching, since the act of teaching is an act directed at another individual. As you might expect, behaviorists have studied animal teaching at some length. In 1992, Tim Caro and Marc Hauser, in an article titled "Is There Teaching in Non-Human Animals?" identified several types of teaching that they expected might be used by nonhumans. "Opportunity" teaching—providing opportunities to learn (essentially what I did for my cubs)—is considered the simplest form. "Coaching"—shaping behavior through reinforcement (what the cubs did to me to be sure I understood their way)—is somewhere in the middle. And "demonstration" teaching, or showing how something is done, they considered the most complex form.

Bears use demonstrations all the time. I did it with my orphans when I selected the clover and showed them they could eat it by putting it in my own mouth, something I have seen Squirty do with her own cubs. This can be deemed not only an olfactory demonstration but an olfactory imitation as well, because the learning response is immediate: The cubs select and eat that food right then. And continue to eat it for the rest of their lives

Other examples of bear demonstrations may not be so obvious until you know what you're looking for. Ian Sterling witnessed the following scene, which he describes in his 1988 book *Polar Bears*: "The intense interest shown by one cub was really quite comical. Its mother was a master of the aquatic stalk. She would flatten herself into a water channel in the ice and then painstakingly push herself towards the seal. Meanwhile, her cub stalked along a few feet behind her, in plain view, watching its mother intently. Needless to say, the seals went down their holes long before they were in any danger."

Sterling saw this only as a funny incident where the inexperienced cub got in the way of its own next meal. In fairness to him, the intention to teach in this anecdote might be questioned with the argument that the mother might have been just trying to catch a seal. But it was clear to me that she certainly knew the effect that walking in plain sight would have on the hunt or she wouldn't have been down in the water channel. That she knew exactly where her cub was is beyond question, at least to me; a mother bear always knows where her cubs are, especially in times of high stress and intensity. So it seems likely that the only reason she was in the water channel was to demonstrate to the cub the proper way to stalk a seal, since she had to know that with the cub walking in plain sight right behind her, they weren't going to catch that particular seal.

For the *National Geographic Explorer* special, "Realm of the Great White Bear," a similar scene was filmed. Only this time, the film crew had killed and cut open a seal to draw in a sow polar bear and her cub. The approach of the bears was then filmed, and a close-up in the running film reveals an olfactory response from the mother to the scent of the seal. She can smell blood and fat, completely different odors than would be emitted from a live seal and odors that she knows intimately. She now knows that there is a dead seal on the ice, not one that needs stalking, a differentiation elementary to the bear but critical to our understanding of what we see happening in the film. For then, in spite of her knowledge that the seal is already dead and is there for the taking, she performs the aquatic stalk anyway as her cub plods along on the ice beside her, clearly an attempt at demonstration teaching. The producers of the film missed the importance of this act.

Christopher Boesch, in his 1991 article in the journal *Animal Behavior*, "Teaching Among Wild Chimpanzees," reports on a wild chimpanzee mother who stepped in when her daughter was having trouble learning to crack nuts with a stone hammer, and then demonstrated the technique with slow and exaggerated motions. The daughter retrieved the hammer and painstakingly imitated her mother and succeeded in cracking the nuts. Citing this and other examples, Anne E. Russon writes in her chapter "Exploiting the Expertise of Others" in *Machiavellian Intelligence II* that demonstration teaching exists only in the great apes and for only the most demanding skills like cracking nuts with stones. I'm tempted to say "Nuts!" but I don't want to seem flippant or to belittle the painstaking work and difficulty of coming to conclusions that characterize the work of any of us in this field. I will say that I think she would benefit from casting a wider observational net, especially if it fell on the far side of the bears.

But it's not easy to see the behavioral similarities between bears and the other more widely studied species. The relationship between mother bear and cub is far more isolated—and harder to observe—than the same bond between animals growing up in a group situation. For a mother chimp in a close-knit troop, demonstration teaching may, as Russon has observed, be unusual, but that may be because of the richness of the environment for opportunity teaching, not because the technique itself is so rare. For a mother bear spending eighteen months alone with her cubs, demonstration teaching is not only a logical adaptation but one that she appears to apply regularly.

Deception

If an animal is smart enough to learn and to teach, the next question as we work our way up the hierarchy of intelligence is: Can it use deception? Not to be confused with natural camouflage or instinctive blending into the surrounding terrain, what behaviorists are looking for here is a planned deception applied in a specific situation.

The psychologists Richard Byrne and Andrew Whiten offer a straightforward definition of deception: "Acts from the normal repertoire of the agent, deployed such that another individual is likely to misinterpret what the acts signify, to the advantage of the agent." In his chapter in *Machiavellian Intelligence II*, Marc Hauser describes a further refinement, intentional deception: "Thus, in order for an individual to intentionally deceive another, it must have the capacity to represent its own beliefs, to understand that by engaging in some action it can alter someone else's beliefs, and as a result of such actions, that individual will be misled into believing something that is not true (i.e. that it deviates from some notion of reality)."

While I can recall a number of examples where I believe the cubs' actions rose to the level of intentional deception, there are a few that really stand out. One seems unequivocal. Remember the two times LB lay down in my path and pretended to sleep, trying to prevent me from leaving when he wanted to stay near his mate? LB knew that I had always waited for him in the past when he took real naps while we were out on walks. This time, when it was to his advantage to stay, he attempted to deceive me based on his prediction of what I would do.

Another example, perhaps more open to interpretation but still convincing to me, involves marking trees. When a bear does a full back rub on a tree, its last act in this stereotyped display is to rotate its head and bite the tree; the height of the bite therefore indicates the height of the individual leaving the mark. Curls, Squirty, and the Boy came across a food-marking bite tree at the blueberry patch, and since they were seven months old it was obvious that at their height they weren't going to leave much of a statement as to their stature. Curls took the initiative and started climbing the sapling hornbeam. As she climbed higher, the sapling began to bend until finally, at a height of five and a half feet, the height of an average adult female bear, she held on with her teeth as the tree bowed under her weight, leaving a mark at that more respectable elevation. Now her mark was high on the tree, and the scent of all three cubs would leave a deceptive message that perhaps an adult sow and cubs were using the blueberry patch. Had Curls tried to increase the status of the cubs by anticipating that another bear might misread the new bite mark she had left? I think so.

A final example involves Squirty and her second set of cubs. These cubs were smaller on the first of May when I initially saw them than were Snowy and Bert at the same age. I hadn't had the opportunity to spend as much time with them as I did filming the first set. Whether or not that was the reason, Squirty was quite aggressive at protecting her cubs from me, and for a long time she wouldn't let me near them. But of course they were always at hand when I came for a visit, almost certainly up a nearby tree. I have been around sows and cubs often enough to know that it's not unusual for a sow to periodically look up at her cubs; it's a fairly distinctive behavior and not usually seen by bears without cubs, except very occasionally when they're looking to see how much food might be up there. In that early spring, there wasn't much food to be found in the trees, so I keyed in on Squirty's eyes in trying to catch a glimpse of her cubs. But she fooled me. For the next several weeks, Squirty would routinely sit under the wrong tree and look up at cubs that weren't there. I could usually spot them some distance away.

Self-awareness and Theory of Mind

The definition of "theory of mind" is the ability to read the desires, beliefs, and intentions of others—that is, recognizing that an animal other than oneself has a mind. It's generally recognized (but hotly debated) that only humans have such an ability while animals simply react to the actions of others and lack the ability to read minds, which isn't to be taken in the pop-science sense. "Reading a mind" here means performing actions based on an assessment of how another mind is reacting to them. It means that the animal performing an action knows that the one reacting to it has a mind with which to react.

So as you read the following account, you will have to be the judge. Or, a better analogy, the jury, since like a judge I'll have to issue this instruction: To be fair, you must also disregard any references I've made previously to remorse, empathy, or deceit.

Let's now look at my most dramatic example: my encounter with Squirty's large mate. As unnerving as the encounter was for me—and I presume for the big guy—I did have an unprecedented opportunity to be part of the action. I will spare you (and myself, thankfully) repeating the details and just discuss the significant points.

The initial significant action was Squirty's reaction to the Big Male when he first came on the scene: She responded to his snorts, chomps, huffs, and swats with ones of her own. Next, she followed me on several occasions, leaving the big bear behind. Then on the day before she ovulated, she made two gestures of affection toward me in his immediate presence. When he got too close to her with his advances, she would back him off with a gentle "Huh, huh, huh." (Remember, this is the vocalization that has negative meaning based on context and intensity. In that context she was saying, "Not yet." In her conflicts with an intruding female, she used a greater intensity that would translate to "Get out and stay out.")

When I met the two of them again on Snow Hill, the day she was about to ovulate, Squirty did not respond to Big Male's snorts, chomps, huffs, and false charges, indicating that she was comfortable with the fact they were aimed at me. With Squirty at my feet, Big Male made his first advance on her with a seductive "gulp-grunt," which she spurned with a gentle "Huh, huh, huh." His response was a gentlemanly retreat behind the log ten feet away. He and Squirty were head-to-head, making him about four feet from me. It was at that point I decided to leave them alone for the day, but when I tried to retreat to my left, Big Male got out of his bed, locked eyes on me, and advanced, blocking my exit. Before he could reach me, though, Squirty made a very aggressive lunge, with her ears back and a strong "Huh, huh, huh, huh, huh!"—backing him down before he could get to me. Once he settled behind the log, I tried to leave to my right, and the whole performance repeated itself.

Obvious questions arise. Why didn't he want me to leave? Because with her this close to ovulating, he didn't want to take the chance that Squirty might follow me. How did he know that Squirty might follow me? Did she signal her intent to follow me? Or did he predict it through a thought process of his own? Was he projecting her actions based on past experience? Was he reading her mind? You decide.

The next question: Was Squirty protecting me from harm by him or was she saying to him, "No, not yet"? My experience tells me that bears have an uncanny ability to read body language. As I said, she wasn't responding to his snorts, chomps, huffs, and false charges, demonstrating she was comfortable that they were displays aimed at me and not her. When he responded to my attempts to leave by locking his eyes on me and advancing, he was telegraphing his target and intention: me. This was no seductive "gulp-grunt" aimed at her. I think she knew exactly what was going on. If so, it was a remarkably altruistic act.

If not, it was much appreciated anyway. I'm not sure you would be reading this book if she hadn't done it.

Cooperation

In dry years when the early woodland crops of beaked hazelnuts and beechnuts fail, the bears in this part of New Hampshire turn with astonishing consensus to the irrigated cornfields of the Connecticut River valley, a feeding activity that's virtually nonexistent in normal years with good early mast crops in the more secure forest. Such a drought year was 1995. With permission from George, Rendell, and Pat Tullar, I spent a considerable amount of time trudging through their three hundred acres of corn along the river in Lyme and Orford. Before I even got to the cornfields, my sources had told me of six bears that had been shot there by hunters. The first day I was in the corn, I heard several bears go out ahead of me, two small ones that I could discern from their tracks and a sow with three cubs that ran in front of Karen Tullar and Lynn Cook as they were jogging on the road nearby. I found several other fresh large tracks in the corn, indicating a minimum of fourteen to fifteen bears using those cornfields.

I followed the bears' main access trail, which was worn down to the dirt, back across two paved roads, and up onto wooded Orford Ridge, where it split into a network of trails. I found where these trails crossed the Orfordville Road three miles away, and received reports of corn scats on Smarts Mountain some eight miles away. That didn't surprise me: radio-collared bears have been reported traveling fifty miles to corn. The movement of strangers along this network of trails surely wouldn't go unnoticed, and the scats deposited along the way left messages of what food was available as well as its location.

In 1997, another dry year, I flew with Lyme pilot Andy Lumley along a twenty-five-mile stretch of Connecticut River valley cornfields, where I found and photographed evidence of bears in only 7 of the more than 125 fields of corn. These marked trails and actual congregations suggested that the bears not only were advertising the location of these food sources but were somehow benefiting by sharing them. Remember when LB and LG left me on the hill and walked right over perfectly good acorns on the ground to eat them where the wild bears had? I was beginning to see a deeply ingrained pattern.

It's a pattern not limited to black bears. There is plenty of evidence that all bears like to feed where other bears do. Accounts are commonplace of bears gathering at salmon streams, dumps, and, as I saw for myself, cornfields. In his 1996 book *Polar Bears: Living with the White Bear*, Nikita Ovsyanikov describes a congregation of fifty to seventy polar bears feeding on 104 walrus carcasses that were killed when a lost pilot, flying low in the fog over a walrus rookery, caused a stampede of 20,000 animals. It took two days for observers to get to the site, and by then there were already eight bears working the carcasses. The next day there were three more, and by the sixth day when Ovsyanikov arrived there were twenty-five. By day twenty-one, there were fifty-six polar bears feeding on the carcasses.

Even with the simplest explanation, that each of these bears directly smelled the rotting carcasses in the wind, the speed at which this congregation formed is a remarkable event. Ovsyanikov writes: "It is true that polar bears hunt alone. I never saw them cooperate to kill a walrus, and if the polar bear's main prey is the ringed seal—a prey much smaller than the hunter—then there is no evolutionary need for the polar bear to develop cooperative hunting skills. What I soon discovered, however, was that they do cooperate in consuming prey."

Because polar bears, unlike wolves or other true predators, don't have specialized teeth (a polar bear is actually a carnivorous omnivore),

Ovsyanikov concludes that the more bears involved in opening a walrus carcass, the better. He documents routinely seeing four bears feeding from the same walrus carcass, sometimes eight, and once fourteen bears feeding side by side. "In fact," he goes on to say, "when eating from the same carcass, the polar bears were more tolerant of each other than highly social wolf packs."

All of the biologists who have observed large congregations of bears have reported social hierarchy and resultant behavior, which they've extensively analyzed. Observers have calculated complexities of rank and file in the way these aggregated bruins allocate preferred locations, time allowed, and other subtleties of social position jockeyed for, gained, and lost. Almost any week of the year you can find yet another videotape of the Alaskan browns doing exactly that in front of the Park Service–escorted photographers during the salmon run on the McNeil River. Some of those dominant grizzlies have gotten more airtime than Kanzi the chimp.

But with all that is known about these gatherings of bears—and even of some of the individuals within them—what remains almost completely unstudied is how the bears know how to find a group-sized excess of food in the first place. In the scientific literature that I have been able to find, there are no references to actual cooperation among bears in finding food. Yet they seem to do it all the time, wherever they are found, from polar bears on carcasses to black bears on beechnuts. Ovsyanikov, in a statement that applies to all bears, puts it clearly: "Polar bears are known to have the most sensitive noses in the animal kingdom, although the way they might communicate through odors has not been adequately studied."

Well, Nikita Ovsyanikov, I think you're right. But I'm trying.

A friend and former houndsman, Ed Green from Fairlee, Vermont, told the following story to me one day in my gun shop. He was called out when a bear had killed some sheep in a pasture in Haverhill, New Hampshire. Ed, with his hounds, started the dogs on the bear in the sheep pasture, then ran, treed, and killed a male bear. Ed was sure that they had gotten the right bear, since his dogs had tracked it from the scene of the crime, but the farmer wanted to be certain, so they opened up its stomach, where they found sheep remains. Nonetheless, being a cautious Yankee of the old school, the farmer brought his remaining sheep into the barn. The very next night, another bear broke into the barn and killed some more sheep. That bear was run and killed as well. Ed's conclusion to me was: "You know, I think those bears follow each other around."

But being a bit of a Yankee of the old school himself, Ed wasn't finished telling stories. The next one he told me was about picking up a bear track in the snow where it crossed the road on Warren Heights. He said it was a single track and that he and Ed LeCroix took it with the hounds. About a half mile into the woods, Green said to LeCroix, "You know, Ed, this is an awful sloppy track. I think we're following two bears."

"There couldn't be," responded LeCroix. "If there are, they're walking step for step in the same tracks." But about a mile and a half out, the tracks split apart and went off in two different directions. Ed told me he thought there was twenty-four hours' difference in the age of the tracks.

If this were true—and there's no reason to doubt his expert opinion— this apparent tracking to a food supply still might not signify actual cooperation between the two separate bears. But it certainly demonstrates not only the relative ease with which one bear can follow the sign of another, but the very specific step-for-step way that it often chooses to.

While there still isn't enough clear evidence to prove that formal cooperation exists in bears, it does appear that the required mechanisms to develop intentional recruitment toward excess food are present. In the 1994 book that he coedited with T. R. Halliday, *Behavior and Evolution*, P. J. B. Slater writes: "[Robert] Trivers (1971) was the first to argue that altruistic relationships could arise between unrelated animals, through a process he referred to as 'reciprocal altruism'. That is much the same as cooperation between animals, but with a time lag so that, instead of gaining an immediate benefit, one benefits on one occasion, the other on another. There are various prerequisites before such a system will arise."

Those prerequisites, as Slater lays them out, include the requirement that the animals be in a stable group and each live long enough to both learn and display some altruism; that the animals know each other as individuals and be able to detect "cheating" (accepting a benefit without returning one); and that the cost of performing an altruistic act must be low compared to its benefit. "The species, which most obviously meets these requirements," continues Slater, "is our own. Indeed, a high proportion of human social interactions are based on reciprocal altruism. But, as far as other species are concerned, convincing examples have been rather rarely described." Citing examples of vampire bats sharing blood that only one has obtained, then reversing roles later, and of sub-dominant male baboons taking turns distracting the alpha male so the other can mate with one of its females, Slater goes on to say: "Despite these examples, there is no doubt that instances of reciprocal altruism are rare. One reason for this is that animals in social groups are usually related to each other and, without long-term study or good knowledge of relatedness, the effects of kinship are hard to exclude."

What Slater is really saying is that instances of *observed* reciprocal altruism are rare, but that may be because it's difficult for researchers to differentiate it from kinship altruism, the scientific term for "blood's thicker than water." And in troops of primates and prides of lions, where so much research money gets spent, he's probably right.

He would do well to turn some attention to bears. They can live up to forty years. They recognize individuals among themselves (and among humans, too, as Bob Caputo found out). Their primary altruistic act, marking with scent, is virtually cost-free in comparison to the bene-fit of finding food. And they don't band together in family units, so the beneficiary of the altruism is not only rarely kin but rarely even seen. A bear's reciprocity isn't one-on-one like Slater's examples of bats and baboons; the time lags are so great and the individuals so scattered that it's rendered without the possibility of an individual keeping score. But that's not necessary. What is required for reciprocal altruism to be a benefit to the long-term health of a species is that it stay in balance for the breeding population as a whole. But if that's the case with bears, how did it come about?

Compared with other large omnivores, bears are unusual in that the males are not part of the family unit, which disperses at eighteen months; the male therefore spends the preponderance of his life sepa-rated from kin, and the females spend only that initial year and a half with each set of cubs, whom they may or may not ever see again. By July of 1997, my own family breakup had taken place with Curls, Squirty, and the Boy. Squirty and Curls, once inseparable, now fought and divided the land into two distinct territories. The Boy, excluded from both, tried to keep using the area around the cage, which was the only area of over-lap in the female territories, but would occasionally leave the area alto-gether after what I suspected were conflicts with larger males coming in to check on Squirty and Curls. On July 27, a two-acre patch of raspberries ripened well within Curls's newly established territory; the bushes were loaded and all in the full sun. For the previous four days while Curls had been feeding on jack-in-the-pulpit nearby, I had gotten no signal on the Boy. But when I arrived to check Curls's signal at the new berry patch, they were both in there feeding together. Until that time I hadn't recorded the Boy within a half mile of that patch, although Curls had made periodic trips into his area. I wish I'd been there to see how they had come back together, but it is certainly conceivable that Curls recruited the Boy to help eat a surplus of food that would soon disappear.

But even if that event was altruism, it was still between known kin. Just recently when I was trying to get a dropped telemetry collar back on Squirty, something interesting happened to indicate that the practice extends beyond family. On the days that I could get out there, I would meet Squirty at the Lambert clearing at a specific time to give her a small bag of corn which she had to take directly out of my hand, a way to maintain my relationship with her without attracting other bears by leaving the food on the ground.

I hadn't seen Snowy for about a month, but she knew my schedule, too. So I was pleased but not surprised when she showed up on August 20, 2001; I handed her a small bag of corn. She grabbed the bag in her mouth and ran down over the bank to the base of a large white pine. Soon Squirty arrived but wasn't acting as though I should try to put her collar on; she was snorting and swatting the ground as she sniffed the air coming from Snowy's direction. I took another look and learned why: Snowy had brought a friend with her, a four- or five-year-old male who weighed about 175 pounds. He was sitting patiently about ten feet from her as she ate her corn. With about a third of it left, she picked it up, carried it a little way, and shared it with him.

Two evenings later, only Snowy showed up. This time, I poured her corn on the ground, forcing her to eat it near me. When she was almost done, she came over and looked in the back of the truck for another bag, then looked expectantly at me, so I poured a little more on the ground. She left and came back in about five minutes with another male bear, this new one smaller than she was. He came within twenty feet of me but wouldn't come up over the bank despite Snowy's repeated efforts encouraging him to do so. After I left, my remote camera filmed them feeding together. These were two wonderful examples of friendship and favors granted outside the family unit.

But the basic system remains in force: Female bears defend the feeding territories where they raise their cubs, and male bears travel to find food where they can, working their way through a deep-woods maze of already claimed female territories and other areas temporarily occupied by larger males. In his 1987 monograph *Effects of Food Supply and Kinship on Social Behavior, Movements, and Population Growth of Black Bears of Northeastern Minnesota*, Lynn Rogers describes this system of males traveling and living on the periphery of female territories in some detail. He told me of one male who left his breeding territory in the early summer, traveled 176 miles to feed for the summer, then returned to feed on the fall mast, hibernate, and breed in the spring. It's a harsh system on the subadult guys, but the fact that they and the dominant males roam to find new food could be beneficial to females and cubs in times of local shortages. In fact, this strategy may have evolved because a sow's mobility is so constrained by her cubs' limited ability to travel. One has to wonder what Snowy was getting in return for her altruistic acts.

At the same time, these dominant male bears are at the top of the hierarchy; it would make more individual sense if they stayed home and used their power to eat all the food they wanted. Why don't they? One plausible evolutionary answer is that the larger males who choose to avoid possible injury by not fighting with the territorially aggressive females have over time lived longer lives and bred that predisposed gene into the species. But there would still have to be a mechanism to foster the short-term continuation of that long-term benefit. Another, perhaps more likely, model is that females hold the prospect of mating over the males. The male who cheats by competing with a sow and her cubs would be less likely to have the chance to mate.

What would happen if the large hungry male decided to cheat by going after the sow's limited food supply? For the sake of argument, let's say that the sow weighs 120 pounds and the male weighs 350. What kind of response from her would be required to get him to change his mind about eating her food? The one you and I have seen in both cubs and adults: a highly emotional and very aggressive one. Remember how early it showed itself, when LG as a cub would defend a food supply and LB would honor it by leaving her alone and not striking back?

But the bears' food-allocation system is far more complex than just a one-on-one negotiation. Most of it is about sharing, the cost-benefit ratio of which is very low in bears: All that's required to participate is to lay down a scent trail. But if the slight enhancement of a scent trail were all there was to the system, it wouldn't be very remarkable; every animal leaves a scent trail recognizable to its own. But with bears it's just the beginning—the entry fee, if you will—to a more complicated system of food optimization, one that's not readily apparent without careful observation and analysis, of which a lot more needs to be done.

Before we go on, let me address why I think the details of this system have been missed in previous studies. The primary reason, I suspect, is that because bears have always been considered secretive and dangerous, most of the studies on them have been based on telemetry. While indispensable even to me, telemetry has its limitations. It cannot supplant the kind of firsthand observation offered by Lynn Rogers's methods with habituated bears and mine with free-ranging orphan cubs. Much of the success in studying behavior in the great apes was derived from methods developed or inspired from Jane Goodall's work with habituated food-conditioned apes at Gombe, methods that met with so much resistance and outright dismissal when she first began to report what she was learning. More intensive research along the path that she blazed will be needed before the secrets of the wonderfully complex bear can be similarly unlocked. Together in this book we've only scratched the surface, but let's try to see what we've uncovered so far.

The first thing we have observed is that every one of my bears has shown a tremendous and ongoing interest in the activities of other bears. On top of that, there's been no general effort to conceal marks as they went to food, quite the opposite usually. In their environment of annual and seasonal shortages of food supplies, why haven't bears evolved to do just the opposite—hide their paths to the foods they do find, even in times of plenty? Let's consider that.

It is fairly clear that if an animal only has enough food to survive in its home range, the motivation would be strong to defend that supply. But what happens if that same animal has a surplus of food—let's say enough to feed eight animals—in its home range and, say, four animals that had no food in their home ranges arrive to eat? The most reasonable thing for the prosperous one to do would be to share rather than fight, because to fight would mean to risk injury. To risk injury when there is plenty of food wouldn't make sense in terms of evolution. So they all share. But next year the tables might be reversed, or at least altered. All the same players could act out switched roles without any need to remember, without keeping score; they would each just act according to their Darwinian self-interests. In that way, reciprocity might develop over time because the frequent changes in the food supply from one home range to another would trigger the need to share so often that natural selection of those who left scent trails to food over those who didn't would have enough iterations to come into play.

However it evolved, the necessity of locating and sharing concentrated food sources remains critical for all bears. Because the cost of a system like this is so low, and the benefit so high, according to Trivers, the reciprocation involved might not be apparent. Although it has not been documented, recruitment of other bears by intentional marking to excess food supplies would also be of very low cost to individual bears. The environmental conditions of the northern climates that produce the severe shortages and surpluses, it seems to me, set the stage for a system of defending and sharing food supplies. This adaptation could help explain how bears are able to thrive in some of the harsher environments of the world.

As an illustration I'll use beechnuts, which would be in abundance in a bear-clawed beech stand, and which in a given year might have as many as ten bears working it, coming in, as we've seen, at different hours of the day or night depending on their individual status. If there was no other available food and only half of the stands in this part of New Hampshire have nuts due, say, to a scattered late frost, these bears may have arrived from thirty miles away. The nuts are highly valued as they might be the only available food right now, they're concentrated with more than enough for all the bears, and they aren't prone to decay. The only limitation is how much fall feeding time is left to the bears in order to put on enough fat to hibernate and survive the winter. But special navigational skills and knowledge of local terrain are required to locate this critical food source. Sows with cubs might not be mobile or subadults not experienced enough to know it even exists. Collaboration by using extensive systems of scent trails could contribute to fostering access for many bears to this sparsely available but critically needed food.

But finding food and knowing how to share it are two different things. In their daily food fights LB and LG demonstrated the basic mechanisms for just such a control-and-defend system. As you remember, the cubs were fed from a beam with their bowls cemented down about four feet apart. I didn't realize it at the time, but this setup was the perfect and repeatable test for the two main ingredients of a possible black bear judicial system. Demonstrated at that early age were the concepts of fairness (the cubs would constantly switch bowls to be sure that one wasn't getting more than the other) and punishment (the fight that broke out when one tried to take more than the other). The same type of fight broke out when LG was unfair and put her paw over my ear so LB couldn't suckle or when LB cheated by sneaking through the cage and barricading LG from getting in the cub door. Snowy and Bert fought over nipples as they nursed on Squirty. As I've discovered the hard way in my six-year relationship with her, Squirty has a number of rules that whenever I break them result in a quick and explosive behavioral adjustment.

In the section "Reciprocal Altruism in Human Evolution" in his book *Social Evolution*, Robert Trivers writes:

> Moralistic Aggression. Once our strong positive emotions have evolved to motivate altruistic behavior, the altruist is in a vulnerable position, because cheaters will be selected for that which takes advantage of these positive emotions. This, in turn, sets up a selection pressure for a protective mechanism. I believe that a sense of fairness has evolved in human beings as the standard against which to measure the behavior of other people, so as to guard against cheating in reciprocal relationships. In turn, this sense of fairness is coupled with moralistic aggressiveness when cheating tendencies are discovered in a friend. A common feature of this aggression is that it often seems out of proportion to the offense that is committed. Friends are even killed over apparently trivial disputes. But since small inequities repeated many times over a lifetime may exact a heavy toll in inclusive fitness, selection may favor a strong show of aggression when the cheating tendency is discovered.

Trivers goes on to say, "This sense of justice involves two components: individuals share a common standard or sense of fairness, and infractions of this standard are associated with strong emotional reactions and aggressive impulses."

As horrific as each of my cubs' fights over food was, starting with an emotional eruption of roars, open-mouthed lunges, biting, and pushing, it was at the same time apparently genetically choreographed; directed toward the head, neck, and shoulders, all areas where only limited damage could be inflicted, the moves were the same every time. Once the fight was over, it was over; there were no residual flare-ups. The fight was practiced every single day for the first year of the cubs' lives, and then without warning, and coincidentally about the time they grew their adult canines, they developed a vocalization that put an end to their practice. Among adult bears, similar fights could occur between two males fighting over a female in estrus, two bears over a prime fishing position, and just as telling, they would not occur when there was enough of any commodity to go around. These fights between adult bears have produced some pretty nasty-looking flesh wounds, but they are usually directed toward intimidation, not serious harm; they typically do not eviscerate or try to kill one another. Because my cubs practiced this behavior, and it was instinctive (they certainly didn't learn it from me!), it seems to meet Trivers's definition of a sense of justice: sharing a common standard and addressing infractions of it with emotional responses and aggressive impulses.

There was no such fuss, by comparison, with my pet dogs Scotty and Peewee when they were fed their supper. They always ate from their own bowls, and they never fought over food. Scotty would try to bait Peewee when they each were given a goody. Peewee would eat hers, and Scotty would take his and drop it in the center of the floor, then back off three feet and wait for Peewee to make a try for it. When she did, he would growl and keep her from taking it. The game would go on for hours, but with no explosive emotional response.

The great primatologist Frans de Waal, in his 1996 book *Good Natured: The Origins of Right and Wrong in Humans and Other Animals*, writes:

> Early human evolution, before the advent of agriculture, must have been marked by a gradual loosening of the hierarchy. Food sharing was a milestone in this development: it both marked the reduced significance of social dominance and provided a launching pad for further leveling. It is therefore relevant for us to understand its origin. In a straightforward rank order, in which dominants take food from subordinates, the flow of food is

unidirectional. In a sharing system, food flows in all directions, including downward. The result is the relatively equitable distribution of resources that our sense of justice and fairness requires.

Reality may not always match the ideal, but the ideal would never even have arisen without this heritage of give and take.

Reciprocal altruism or cooperation in bears, if it exists, would be nowhere near as complex as it is in human society. But the simplicity of the bears' system may offer new insights into the origins of our own development. It seems likely that the heritage of give and take that de Waal describes arose in us from environmental conditions of shortages and surplus that parallel the circumstances of food sharing in bears. It may turn out that Carolus Linnaeus's linear classification of nature may be somewhat misleading as it doesn't take into account the effects of this sort of convergent evolution, where dissimilar species become more alike due to overlapping selection pressures as they occupy the same time and place.

Who knows? I like to think it's been our mutual sharing of so many of the same problems of survival that has allowed bears and us to end up so closely related, if not so much in DNA then certainly in the many ways we react to the world around us, and to each other.

With that in mind, I would like to leave you with one more story, a well-documented historical account from Warren, New Hampshire, a small town not far from my home here in Lyme: In June of 1873, a small girl, age three, wandered off into the woods. Neighbors searched for her for four days before beginning to lose hope. When they finally found her she was unharmed but hungry, sleeping under a large pine tree with bear tracks all around her. She said that a big black dog had found her and slept with her every night to keep her warm.

Epilogue

By snowmobile and snowshoes I slowly worked my way uphill through the deep snow to Squirty's den. The Appalachian Trail was packed down by the climbers and hikers who had come and gone through the winter, and as long as I stayed on the trail my snowshoes worked well, keeping me comfortably on top of about three feet of snow. But covering the last quarter mile down the back side of Lambert was another story: the den was under a rock ledge on an icy, steep incline. I tried to sidestep with the snowshoes, but my boots kept slipping out of the bindings. I had to go the last hundred yards to the den without snowshoes, muscling through waist-deep snow. Dogged by an unpleasant vision of not being able to get up the hill to get back out and being forced to take the two-mile hike out the other side of the mountain, I pushed on anyway.

It took some hunting, but eventually I found the den. It was completely snowed in, but fortunately Squirty had marked the location by destroying a sapling in front of the entrance. Leaning over in the waist-deep drifts, I placed my ear to a small opening in the snow and rock. Coming from deep inside were the barely audible sounds of chuckling cubs.

Acknowledgments

I would like to thank all of those who helped read and comment on my manuscript for their encouragement along the way: My wife, Debbie, who has read every rendition since the beginning and, by holding a real job, has been my primary source of funds. My sister, Phoebe, for her help and interest in working with the bears. Ed Gray for his encouragement and efforts to keep this project going. Sy Montgomery for her writing tips and enthusiasm. Donella Meadows and Noel Perrin for support and encouragement. Charles Wysocki and Richard Estes for their time and expertise relating to sensory organs. James Worman for helping me with the chemisty of bears. Jamie Paksima for connecting me with the right literary agency. Jonathan Diamond and Jennifer Unter for being the right agents. Jack Macrae for his interest in the story. Katy Hope and the rest of the people at Henry Holt for their efforts. Marc and Lilan Hauser for their critical comment and encouragement. George B. Schaller for his advice and availability over the years. Richard Wrangham and Richard Estes for their enthusiastic support. Robert Caputo, Amy Wray, Neil Rettig, Kim Hayes, and everybody at the National Geographic Society who has helped tell this story.

Very special thanks to the members of the New Hampshire Fish and

Game Department for the support, consultation, and equipment loans. Donald Normandeau and Jim Paine, Sr., without whose support and confidence this project would never have taken place. Forrest "Frosty" Hammond whose idea it was for me to raise the first set of cubs. Lynn Rogers for his support and for letting the world know that it was possible to work closely with bears. Steve Stringham for his interest, advice, and unheralded and early efforts to work closely with bears. The Vermont Fish and Wildlife Department for their support, donation of cage materials, and equipment loans. Joyce Knights, Jerome Robinson, Sid Lea, and Mary Daubenspeck for much appreciated advice. Thanks also to the people who helped with cages and the like: Ken Uline; my brother Josh Kilham; Roy Day; Tony Ryan; Shannon, Bob, and Sandy Green.

And, finally, a special thanks to all the landowners over whose land I've wandered following these bears.

Index

About the Authors

BENJAMIN KILHAM is a woodsman and naturalist who over the past twenty-five years has discovered and then field-tested a new, exciting wildlife biology.

ED GRAY is a naturalist writer and the founder of *Gray's Sporting Journal*. They both live in Lyme, New Hampshire.